Bruno Paul

William Owen Harrod

Bruno Paul

The Life and Work
of a Pragmatic Modernist

Edition Axel Menges

720.8
P32h

Printing and binding: Daehan Printing and Publishing Co., Ltd., Sungnam, Korea

Editorial supervision: Nora Krehl-von Mühlendahl
Design: Axel Menges
Layout: Helga Danz

Contents

Acknowledgements

This work would not have been possible without the kind and gracious assistance of Julia Graf and Susanne Droste, Bruno Paul's daughters. The generosity with which they shared their memories of his life proved invaluable.

Of all the archivists who assisted me in my work, I am most indebted to Dietmar Schenk of the Universität der Künste in Berlin, the curator of the largest surviving collection of Paul's papers. I am also grateful for the patient assistance of Helmut Bauer and Christian Hell of the Münchner Stadtmuseum; Ursula Hummel of the Monacensia Literaturarchiv und Bibliothek in Munich; Gudrun Libnow of the Germanisches Nationalmuseum in Nuremberg, the curator of Paul's postwar correspondence; William Peniston of the Newark Museum; Michaela Rammert-Götz, curator of the Vereinigte Werkstätten archives in Munich; Rita Wolters of the Werkbundarchiv in Berlin; and Alfred Ziffer of Munich, who organized the 1992 exhibition »Bruno Paul: Deutsche Raumkunst und Architektur zwischen Jugendstil und Moderne«.

The following individuals provided me with information concerning Paul's residential commissions, or kindly invited me into their homes: Georg Heinrichs of Berlin-Zehlendorf, owner of Haus Auerbach; Mimi Furst of New York, the daughter of Edmund Traub of Prague; Ronald Gerns of Bögner, Hensel, Gerns & Schreier of Frankfurt, the owners of the first Haus Herxheimer; Jana Krchova of the Delegation to the Czech Republic of the Commission of the European Communities in Prague; Dr. Knut Kühn-Leitz of Wetzlar, owner of Haus Friedwart; and R. Rathai of Wiesbaden, owner of the second Haus Herxheimer.

I am thankful to Hansjoachim Fröhlich, Bürgermeister of Wiesenburg; Heiner Haschke of the Karasek-Museum in Seifhennersdorf; Annette Hellmuth of the Deutsche Werkstätten Hellerau GmbH; the staff of the Kreisarchiv Soest; Maria Makela of the Maryland Institute, College of Art; Rebecca Milner of the Victoria and Albert Museum, London; the staff of the Nellinistift in Frankfurt/Main; the staff of the Sächsisches Hauptstaatsarchiv Dresden; the staff of the Staatliche Graphische Sammlung München; the staff of the Staatsarchiv München; and Jörg Wisemann of the Gerling Konzern in Cologne.

I am profoundly grateful to Julia Harrod and Betsy Harrod for their unfailing editorial assistance. Finally I would like to thank the members of my dissertation committee at the University of Texas at Austin: Anthony Alofsin, Richard Cleary, David Crew, Peter Jelavich, and Danilo Udovicki-Selb, all of whom offered insight and encouragement essential to the completion of my work. I am sincerely thankful to the chairman of my committee, Christopher Long, to whose tireless support, generous advice and unimpeachable scholarship this work is a tribute.

Introduction

At the dawn of the twentieth century, Bruno Paul (1874–1968) stood like a colossus astride the landscape of an emerging Modernism. As an illustrator, architect, and educator, his influence was unequalled. The most important German designer of his generation, his work was ubiquitous in the technical and professional publications of his day. Paul was master of a formal vocabulary that was simple, practical, and elegant: a pragmatic Modernism suited to the needs and aspirations of the middle classes. Popular acceptance of this pragmatic Modernism in Europe and America prepared the way for the triumph of the avant-garde, and ultimately for the canonization of Modernism as the characteristic style of the twentieth century. For this alone Paul deserves to be remembered, but he was more than a pathfinder for the work of a younger generation. Throughout his life he promoted a vision of modernity that remains as relevant today as when it was first conceived.

For five decades, Paul's reputation was unparalleled among progressive German artists. As a young man he was a member of the Munich avant-garde responsible for the creation of the Jugendstil, the first modern movement in Central Europe. As a designer of furniture and interiors, he achieved a commercial success unmatched by his contemporaries Richard Riemerschmid and Peter Behrens, with whom he joined in the founding of the Werkbund in 1907. In light of his professional accomplishments, he was the most important German architect of his generation, standing with Henri van de Velde and Josef Hoffmann as a figure of international significance. Yet he made his greatest contributions as an educator. Ludwig Mies van der Rohe, Adolf Meyer, and Kem Weber were among his students, and their work developed from the practices of his atelier. As director of the Vereinigte Staatsschulen für freie und angewandte Kunst in Berlin, he presided over an institution that rivaled the Bauhaus as a center of progressive teaching. Indeed, Walter Gropius conceived his own program of educational reforms in response to Paul's example.

Despite the renown he enjoyed at the height of his career, Paul's name is largely absent from the standard histories of the modern movement. He is remembered as a pioneer, but not as an active participant in the development of the Functionalist aesthetic that began to characterize progressive design in the 1920s. His exclusion from the Modernist canon originated in the restrictive interpretation of Modernism adopted by its early proponents, following the selection of participants for the 1927 exhibition of experimental housing at the Weißenhofsiedlung in Stuttgart. When Mies planned the Weißenhofsiedlung, he did not invite his former teacher to contribute, notwithstanding Paul's contemporary work designing prefabricated modern housing for the Deutsche Werkstätten. The architects that he did consider – from van de Velde, Behrens, and Berlage to Gropius, Bruno Taut, and Le Corbusier – became the central figures in a narrowly focused Modernist historiography. Mies made his choices to support a polemical Modernism that he termed a »battleground of the spirit«.[1] Paul himself could not and would not identify himself as a begetter of such a movement. Yet his work demonstrated a close and reciprocal relationship with the practice, if not the ideology, of the Functionalist avant-garde.

Though Paul was committed to advancing the cause of modern design, by the 1920s his work was profoundly unlike that of his younger colleagues. As a designer, he promoted rational detailing and exquisite workmanship. While he embraced the stylistic vocabulary of the avant-garde, he preferred proven solutions to technical challenges; he explored new technologies, but never celebrated technology for its own sake. He regarded industrial production as a tool available to the craftsman, useful only if employed with skill and understanding. Paul's Modernism was essentially pragmatic: comfortable, practical, and efficient. It was a Modernism applicable to daily life.

Paul created and disseminated a modern aesthetic capable of challenging the dominance of the historical styles. He facilitated the transformation of Modernism from the purview of a radical avant-garde and a narrow circle of patrons into the vocabulary of mainstream design. He first achieved this end in 1908, when he embraced a simple, practical classicism that he adapted to suit the demands of standardized production. Nikolaus Pevsner credited Paul's work prior to the First World War with changing popular tastes throughout Germany, thereby encouraging the widespread acceptance and appreciation of contemporary design.[2] Paul achieved an even broader success in the 1920s, winning international recognition for his designs. His work, popularized by such ecumenical publications as *House and Garden* and the international journal *Vogue*,[3] introduced British and American readers to progressive German design long before Mies or Gropius were widely known outside of professional circles. It was Paul who prepared the way for the German émigrés who fled their homeland following the Nazi accession of 1933 and the collapse of the Weimar Republic.

Paul's work prefigured the triumph of the International Style, but it remained distinct. His designs during the final years of the Weimar Republic represented a critique of Functionalism, particularly of the poor detailing and impermanent materials that often accompanied cool, functional abstraction. His critique was progressive rather than reactionary, and it embodied his ethos of reform. He did not renounce the aesthetic of the modern movement, but advocated the continued relevance of the »timeless German building arts«.[4] In so doing, he promoted a reconciliation of the ambitions of the avant-garde with the lessons of professional experience, practices that he pointedly deemed timeless rather than traditional.

Paul's critique is largely absent from the standard histories of the modern movement, which thus ignore the very existence of a pragmatic counterpoint to the work of his younger colleagues. The historians of Modernism emphasized the role of an avant-garde to which Paul, at the height of his professional career, no longer belonged. Moreover, Paul restricted his criticism of contemporary design to the context of his work, rather than to the composition of the polemical statements of principle that are the primary documentary source for the modern movement. Throughout his life, Paul was a prolific designer but a reluctant promoter of his own reputation. Even after he had progressed from innovative and experimental youth into creative and professional maturity, he remained among the most frequently published architects and designers in Germany – albeit rarely as an author.[5] Paul was a leading member of the Werkbund and of the Prussian academy of arts, and he served as an advisor to the German government. He was director of the school that was likely the most important center of progressive artistic education in Central Europe. There was not a single prominent Modernist in Germany whom he did not know, personally or professionally, and there were few with whom he had not collaborated. He was, in fact, so close to the center of the modern movement that any consideration of its history that excludes him is, from its very conception, inherently flawed.

The early proponents of the modern movement praised it for its opposition to the reactionary Historicism of the nineteenth century. »Architecture as a continuation of the traditions of building«, Hannes Meyer wrote in 1928, »is a resignation to architectural history«.[6] But by the 1920s little remained of the much-maligned practices of the nineteenth century. In Germany, the International Style arose in opposition to Expressionism, which was an easy mark, and to the pragmatic professionalism that Paul espoused, which was not. Understanding his position is essential to understanding the development of both canonical modern design and the alternatives that emerged concurrently. Many of these alternatives have been largely forgotten.

Paul himself inadvertently contributed to his omission. He wrote little about his work, and was indifferent to personal fame. His home and office in Berlin were bombed during the Second World War, and his private papers, his possessions, and his records of fifty years of professional practice were dispersed or destroyed. He was unable to recover them, and left no accounting of what was lost. Banished from public life by the Nazis in 1933, he faded into obscurity.

Yet much of Paul's legacy has survived. Many of his most important buildings are intact and some are still in the hands of their original owners. Examples of his furniture have been collected in museums throughout Germany. His early illustrations for the satirical journal *Simplicissimus* are still extant, and his postwar papers are preserved in Nuremberg. Letters and photographs survive among the collected papers of his former colleagues, the Munich avant-garde of the first decade of the twentieth century. The Vereinigte Staatsschulen für freie und angewandte Kunst in Berlin, now the Universtät der Künste, maintains the records of Paul's administration between 1907 and 1933, including his personal correspondence and several unpublished essays. The archives of the Vereinigte Werkstätten für Kunst im Handwerk and the Deutsche Werkstätten, the firms that produced most of his furniture, have also survived. Disparate records of individual commissions are preserved in public and private collections. These resources, and the recollections of those who knew him personally, permit a detailed reconstruction of the history of Paul's life.

Paul's story is a significant element of the history of twentieth-century design, and, to a certain extent, it is a familiar one. It is the history of the development of Modernism in Central Europe, and its coalescence from the influences of Jugendstil, Elementarism, Classicism, Expressionism, and Functionalism. Paul played a significant role in this coalescence, and he deserves a place of honor in the history of the modern movement. However, his biography also encompasses a less familiar, but no less significant, aspect of the history of modern design. It is the story of a pragmatic Modernism that occupied a middle ground between avant-garde experimentation and conservative professional practice. In the end, it was this pragmatic Modernism that won the patronage of the middle classes, and established progressive design as an accepted alternative, and eventually as a preferred alternative, to the period styles.

1. The making of a pragmatic Modernist: 1874–1896

Like many in the first generation of European Modernists, Bruno Paul was deeply concerned with reestablishing a harmonious relationship between the fine and applied arts in an age of increasingly impersonal, automated production. As a child, he witnessed firsthand the displacement of traditional craftsmanship by the process of mechanization, as well as the disintegration of the social order that had prevailed prior to industrialization. Later, as a student painter, he was confronted with the increasing irrelevance of mannered, academic art to the contemporary world, and the absence of an effective system for training designers to meet the burgeoning needs of industry. As a young man, Paul confronted many of the theoretical issues that had inspired the artistic and social reform movements of the second half of the nineteenth century. In response, he embraced a profoundly personal modernity.

Seifhennersdorf

Bruno Paul was born on 19 January 1874 in the house his grandfather had built in the Saxon village of Seifhennersdorf, a predominantly rural community on the border between Germany and the Austro-Hungarian province of Bohemia. He was the last of seven children of Gustav Eduard Paul, an ironmonger, and Johanne Juliane Auguste Jentsch.[7] He was given the name Bruno in memory of an elder brother, Robert Bruno, who had died in infancy. Unlike the four brothers and two sisters who preceded him into the world, he never received a second Christian name. He was simply baptized »Bruno« in the Protestant parish church of the village fourteen days after his birth.[8] The two weeks that he spent un-christened may simply be a consequence of a harsh winter, yet his parents' confidence that he was not at risk of dying an unbaptized infant was a prescient recognition of the extraordinary constitution that would sustain him through ninety-four years of vigorous life.

According to Paul's own account of the origins of his family, his ancestors were among the Protestant families expelled from the Austrian Salzkammergut by the Roman Catholic archbishop of Salzburg in 1731.[9] Weavers by trade, the exiled family settled in the Oberlausitz region of Saxony, where they were able to reestablish themselves under the policies of religious tolerance promulgated by the government of the Saxon king Augustus the Strong. Their successful rehabilitation in Seifhennersdorf, a center of the weaving trade, accorded with the fundamental character of the Evangelical Lutheran Church in the eighteenth century. The church encouraged the diligence, self-discipline, and civic responsibility of its adherents. Paul learned these qualities, the core of the Protestant ethic, from his baptism. Yet his personal faith would also reflect the lessons of his own family history through a commitment to remain steadfast in the face of adversity, and a belief in the sanctity of honest labor.

Paul's grandfather, Johann Gotthelf Paul, established himself as a member of the small commercial class in Seifhennersdorf that was indirectly dependent upon the success of the local weaving industry. He ran a tavern near the outskirts of the town at Warnsdorfer Straße 15, serving local farmers on the first floor of the house that he shared with his wife Christiane. Later, he opened a general store (Krämerei) in a larger house at Warnsdorfer Straße 4.[10] Paul's father Gustav Eduard Paul was born on 1 February 1836 in this same house, a substantial village home built above the little river Mandau that divided the town and provided power to the weaving mills that clustered on its banks. The house was typical of the Oberlausitz, composed of simple, practical details that would exert a lasting influence on Paul's domestic architecture. »The wide, white-painted windows set beneath the long ridge of a thatch roof framed by mighty poplars and linden trees stood closer to my youthful ideal«, he later recalled of the houses of Seifhennersdorf, »than the factory windows set in their whitewashed walls beneath black tar roofs.«[11]

Very little is known about the life of Paul's father, Gustav Eduard Paul, although he has been identified as a master carpenter (Zimmermeister),[12] and a building contractor (Bauunternehmer).[13] His granddaughter described him as a joiner or cabinetmaker (Tischler), while church records in Seifhennersdorf refer to him as an ironmonger (Material- und Eisenwarenhändler).[14] According to local tradition, Gustav Paul assumed control of his father's general store in 1860 before achieving economic success selling tools and domestic ironwork. All of the accounts of his career share one important detail: in a town that was dominated by the weaving industry, he was an independent businessman, a dealer in building materials and, by most accounts, a craftsman in his own right.

1. Seifhennersdorf. The center of the village is dominated by the parish church where Paul was baptized on 2 February 1874.
2. Warnsdorfer Straße 4, Seifhennersdorf, circa 1920. In the center of the photo is the house where Bruno Paul was born in 1874.
3. Bruno Paul as a student, circa 1886.

Gustav Paul was a tradesman in the age when the traditional crafts were being challenged by the advance of industrialization. He undoubtedly exerted a profound influence on the development of his youngest son's own understanding of the role of craftsmanship in an industrializing society. Gustav was an ambitious man, however, and did not intend that his children should follow his own modest example. His wife Johanne Juliane Auguste belonged to the Jentsch family, among the most prominent members of the community and the proprietors of a weaving mill that dominated the center of the town.[15] One of the largest structures in the community, it was clearly visible from the Pauls' home on Warnsdorfer Straße. In marrying into the Jentsch family Gustav Paul made a propitious union, and he was determined that his children should pursue respectable careers. He wanted his sons to become schoolteachers or clergymen, professions that epitomized culture and sophistication in a rural community.[16]

Bruno spent an uneventful boyhood on Warnsdorfer Straße, and in later life remembered the simple pleasures of a rural childhood. One of his most cherished memories was of a pet raven, captured in the fields surrounding Seifhennersdorf. Although the bird was never truly domesticated, it spent enough time with its young master to mimic the sound of his voice. Paul's youthful laughter, prompted by the ceaseless conflict between a pet dog and a neighborhood cat, formed the basis of the raven's limited vocal repertory. Although Paul often kept dogs in later life, the laughing raven was apparently his fondest boyhood companion.[17]

Paul passed much of his youth, as he later recalled, in the yard of his father's business. There, asphalt-impregnated roofing paper provided him with his first experiences in the art of building. Together with other village boys he would gather scraps of this material, and bits of lath discarded by his father, to build teepees (Indianerzelte) and huts for their childhood games. Yet for Paul these early constructions represented more than a childish pastime. He studied, experimented, and learned through the collaborative efforts of his mind and hands the properties and characteristics of the simple materials available to him. »In the early days of my youth«, he wrote, »my clothes were inevitably stained with tar.«[18] Even as a boy, Paul began to develop the rigor that would serve as the basis of his professional success.

Bruno Paul never spoke of his earliest formal education, but he evidently attended a local village school (Volksschule) to receive the primary education mandated by the Saxon government.[19] Even as a schoolchild, the full weight of his father's ambitions fell upon his shoulders. His brother Reinhard, eigthteen years older, had followed his father into the family business, becoming an ironmonger in the neighboring village of Warnsdorf. His brother Otto, fourteen years older, was an agent for the Bruns cigarette company in Eisenach. Two other brothers had died as children, leaving only Bruno to pursue a learned profession.

Dresden

When Paul was twelve years old his parents sent him to Dresden to continue his schooling. Dresden, already known in the nineteenth century as the Florence of the Elbe, was an ideal location for a provincial youth to be immersed in European culture.[20] Paul's family enrolled him in the Kreuzschule, a municipal secondary school (städtisches Gymnasium) with a long tradition of religious instruction.[21] The Kreuzschule was a prestigious and venerable institution, founded as a seminary in the thirteenth century and Protestant since the reformation. Paul's acceptance at the Kreuzschule was a first step towards the realization of his father's ambitions, and an introduction to an educated, respectable life as a clergyman.

The earliest known photographic portrait of Paul, taken in Seifhennersdorf while he was a student at the Kreuzschule, depicts the child of a successful, middle-class family. Even as a boy, he seems to have been fastidious in his dress and personal appearance, a proclivity he would maintain throughout his life.[22] Although he proudly held the uniform cap of the Kreuzschule in his portrait, he was not an exemplary student. He apparently did not apply himself, and he never completed the obligatory nine years of study at the Gymnasium. He left the Kreuzschule after only four years.

Though Paul proved unsuited to the ministry, he was still bound to honor his father's ambition. After leaving the Kreuzschule, he enrolled at the teacher training college (Königliches Lehrerseminar) in the Dresden suburb of Friedrichstadt.[23] The Lehrerseminar was essentially a vocational school, and offered neither the cultural enrichment nor the prestige of a Gymnasium education. By enrolling, Paul embarked on a course of study that led only to the lower echelons of the civil service, yet still fulfilled his father's expectations. In Friedrichstadt, he resigned himself to becoming a teacher, and to providing compulsory primary education on behalf of the Saxon government in a school much like the one that he himself had attended as a child. He never completed his studies in Friedrichstadt, however, proving as unsuited to pedagogy as he had been to ministry. He left the Lehrerseminar in 1892.

During the time he was a student in Friedrichstadt, Paul evidently reached the momentous decision to pursue a career in the arts. He apparently worked in an architectural office in Dresden for a year following his departure from the Lehrerseminar, earning his first regular salary as a draftsman.[24] His earliest published biography stated that he was a student at the Dresden Kunstgewerbeschule (school of applied arts) during this same period.[25] If he was simultaneously working in an architectural office, he may well have received his initial training in the evening classes intended for the education of working apprentices.[26] As an assistant in a professional design bureau seeking to refine his technical skills, Paul was a model candidate for evening instruction as a draftsman. The modesty of such an introduction to the applied arts may explain why he seldom discussed his attendance at the Dresden Kunstgewerbeschule in later life. Yet it is certainly appropriate in the context of his career that he should have begun his work as an artist with the straightforward, practical instruction offered in the evening classes at the school of applied arts.

Notwithstanding the benefits of employment, Paul was not content to be an office draftsman: he wanted to be a painter. In the last quarter of the nineteenth century, the most successful German painters had attained wealth, influence and social prominence. Talented artists enjoyed a degree of freedom unparalleled in German society, and even a draftsman of humble birth could hope to be included among the painter-princes (»Malerfürsten«), the circle of prominent German artists that included Fritz August von Kaulbach, Franz von Lenbach, and Franz Stuck.[27] Paul hoped to join this intellectual and cultural elite. In so doing he could respect his father's wishes that he pursue a learned career, while engaging with his own hands in the creative process.

In 1893, Paul enrolled as a student at the Königliche Akademie der Bildenden Künste (Saxon royal academy of arts) to become a painter. In order to be accepted at the academy, he would have had to either present a portfolio of work demonstrating his abilities as an artist, or provide a letter personally commending him to one of the academic professors. He left no indication that he entered the academy on the strength of a letter of recommendation. Moreover, his experience during 1892 was fairly typical of prospective academy students at the end of the nineteenth century. Several of the painter-princes began their training in the schools of applied arts before gaining admittance to one of the royal academies.[28] Paul seems to have followed their example, and enrolled in the school of the Saxon academy on the strength of his innate ability, and the determination that accompanied his decision to pursue a career of his own selection.

When Bruno Paul was admitted as a student, the academy in Dresden was at the height of its prestige, and in the process of relocating to the palatial Akademie- und Ausstellungsgebäude

4. Kunstakademie und Kunstausstellungsgebäude Dresden, circa 1920. The academy building on the Brühl Terrace (left foreground) was designed by Constantin Lipsius and completed in 1894.
5. Drawing from life, undated.
6. Marienplatz, Munich, circa 1895. The city center, as it appeared upon Paul's arrival from Dresden.

(academy and exhibition building) on the Brühl Terrace above the Elbe. The academy building, a temple of art crowned by a faceted dome and gilt bronze statue of fame, was an elaborately ornamented pastiche of historical architectural forms designed by Constantin Lipsius. A popular building and well-known in Dresden, it was a source of considerable pride.[29] It was also a perfect symbol for the academy and its school. At the end of the nineteenth century, the German royal academies were philosophically and methodologically aligned with an inherently conservative interpretation of the fine arts. »The teaching methods were largely those of the eighteenth and early nineteenth centuries. The centre-piece of the instruction given was still the drawing from plaster-casts for the beginners and from the living model posing à l'antique for the advanced students«, Nikolaus Pevsner later wrote.[30] Such a refined and mannered approach to artistic education provided a counterpoint to the emphasis of the schools of applied arts on the education of tradesmen working in the minor arts. The belief in common principles applicable to all forms of artistic expression was a radical notion in 1892, and contrary to the conservative policies of the Saxon academy. Paul did not have long to absorb its ideology, however, since he departed within a year of his enrollment, without recording the names of his professors or the focus of his study.[31] Once he decided to become an artist, he pursued his objective with a determination wholly lacking in his earlier schooling. By the winter of 1893, Paul's ambitions turned his attention from Dresden to Munich, a city whose reputation as a center of the arts then rivaled that of Paris.

Munich

In 1894, more painters and sculptors lived and worked in Munich than in any other German city.[32] This was the era of the radiant Munich immortalized by Thomas Mann in his 1902 novel *Gladius Dei; Schwere Stunde*, the city of dreams (*Traumstadt*) of Peter Paul Althaus, the *Schwabylon* of the satirist Roda Roda. The preeminence of Munich as a center of the arts was sufficiently respected in Central Europe to allow the city's large population of resident artists to enjoy an unusually high standard of living. The opportunities available in Munich provided a powerful attraction to the twenty-year-old Bruno Paul, and to innumerable other aspiring artists. In his fragmentary memoirs, Paul recalled his years in the city. »In the last three decades before 1900«, he wrote, »artistic and intellectual tensions found a point of focus in traditional, old-Bavarian Munich.« He praised the conditions of peace and self-sufficiency prevailing in the city at the end of the nineteenth century and conducive to supporting a vibrant and diverse community of artists. In Munich, he noted, »the historical styles slowly faded. At the same time, the emerging artistic trends towards realism, contemporaneity and abstraction found opportunity and support.«[33] It was these developing trends that drew Paul to Munich, and that made the city the center of Germany's artis-

tic avant-garde. Schwabing, the artists' quarter of Munich, was the German Montmartre, and at the edge of Schwabing stood the Königliche Akademie der bildenden Künste (royal academy of fine arts), the most prestigious school of art in the nation. Each year more than five hundred students came to the academy from Europe, Asia and the Americas to learn the techniques of the »Münchener Malerei«, the Munich painting admired throughout the world.

Paul enrolled as a student at the Königliche Akademie der Bildenden Künste in 1894. The nineteenth-century matriculation book of the academy has survived, and his name appears among the students registered in the spring of that year. He was identified as student number 1246, Bruno Paul of Seifhennersdorf in the kingdom of Saxony, son of a Protestant merchant. His age was listed as twenty years, and he was referred to as a student painter, assigned to the atelier of Paul Höcker. This brief record, noted by hand in the registrar's old-fashioned script, marked the end of Paul's provincial childhood.

Paul's professor at the academy, Paul Höcker (1854–1910), was himself a young and progressive artist, one of the one hundred and seven original members of the Verein bildender Künstler Münchens »Sezession« (the Munich secession) founded in 1892.[34] His work as a painter demonstrated the realism, contemporaneity, and abstraction that Paul equated with an emerging modernity. When he enrolled in Höcker's atelier and subsequently joined the secession,[35] Paul entered the circle of Munich's avant-garde. On the cusp of the twentieth century, Höcker and his fellow secessionists led a movement committed to the reconciliation of modern art and modern life.

The Munich secession to which Paul belonged was the first such organization of progressive artists in Central Europe, and was allied with the separatist artistic movements in France that had nurtured the development of modern European painting.[36] Its establishment was motivated by a growing dissatisfaction by the more progressive members of the Münchener Künstlergenossenschaft (association of Munich artists) with the policies governing the exhibitions staged by the association. Many of the early members of the secession were inspired to join by practical considerations, the prospect of better opportunities to display and sell their works promised by the secession's policy of smaller and more selective exhibitions. Nevertheless the executive committee of the secession advocated elite and artistically pure (reinkünstlerische) exhibitions rather than the populist policies of the Künstlergenossenschaft. The ideal of artistic purity was, inevitably, associated with emerging trends in creative expression.

Höcker's work exemplified the prevailing character of the secession. Initially he had specialized in traditional genre paintings and in portraits. During the years when Paul was under his instruction at the academy, his paintings displayed the lyrical qualities of the Modernism emerging in Munich art during the last decade of the nineteenth century. The catalog of the »World's Columbian Exhibition« of 1893, in which Höcker participated, described the characteristics of his work on the eve of Paul's admission to his atelier. »The very modern note is struck by the two paintings of PAUL HOECKER, the interior of a shoemaker's workshop and the scene between the decks of the iron-clad, H.M.S. DEUTSCHLAND ... On the contrary, his large painting of ›the Nun‹ is inspired by a touch of pathos and imagination, – the grave, sweet faced novice sitting telling her beads in the convent garden alley suggests many things to any but the most unimaginative spectator.«[37] These three paintings, with their Naturalist and Symbolist tendencies, were characteristic of the secession.

Only a few drawings by Paul survive from his days as a student in Höcker's atelier: all are in private collections. They reflect the *plein-air* Naturalism that characterized the first secession exhibition of 1893, but show little direct evidence of Höcker's influence. Paul practiced drawing classical nudes at the academy under Höcker's direction, and he produced simple pencil sketches of unposed figures from daily life. But he did not illustrate the rural subjects favored by prominent Munich Naturalists. Rather, he sketched scenes from contemporary urban life, including women on a park bench, a tradesman with his pencil tucked behind his ear, and the passengers on a streetcar.

Paul's interest in drawing scenes of common daily life in Munich paralleled his political inclinations as an academy student. As a young man, he was at least peripherally involved with the socialist cause of the urban working classes. His illustrations appeared in two publications for socialist students, *Der sozialistische Student* and *Sozialistische Monatshefte*.[38] He also submitted work to the social-democratic journal *Süddeutscher Postillon*.[39] Paul later recalled his contributions to *Süddeutscher Postillon* as his first employment as an illustrator, the beginning of his career as an independent artist.[40] The journal certainly provided his introduction to social and political satire, a field to which his natural talents proved uniquely suited.

In drawing figures from modern life, Paul displayed an innate capacity for observing and identifying the essential character of his subjects. He refined his ability to suggest intrinsic qualities with a few deftly executed lines, a skill that provided the basis of his later success as a caricaturist. Stylistically, Paul's early graphic works reflected the inspiration of the Japanese woodcuts and medieval decorative design characteristic of progressive graphic art in Munich at the turn of the century. Though many Munich painters at the end of the nineteenth century remained fundamentally conservative, the city's graphic artists were far less bound to convention. Paul was drawn to the creative opportunities inherent to graphic art, though his technique developed from his academic training as a painter. His earliest graphic works were characterized by a simple palette of vivid colors, a subversion of illusionistic perspective, and an abstraction of naturalistic forms into decorative patterns – tendencies apparent in the program cover that Paul designed for a carnival party hosted by the students at the academy in 1896 entitled *Unterwelt* (underworld).

Paul's *Unterwelt* cover illustrates his alignment with the progressive faction within Munich's artistic community that created the Jugendstil. Many were Höcker's students, and regular con-

7. Königliche Akademie der bildenden Künste, Munich, circa 1890. The building where Paul studied to be a painter on Akademiestraße in Schwabing.
8. Franz von Stuck, Villa Stuck, Munich, 1896. Interior.
9. *Unterwelt*, 1896. Program cover for a carnival party.

tributors to the Munich magazine *Jugend* (youth) from which the new style received its name.[41] Yet Paul was also inspired by work undertaken outside of Höcker's atelier, specifically that of another member of the faculty, the prominent Munich artist Franz Stuck (1863–1928).[42] His *Unterwelt* cover was particularly indebted to Stuck. Superficially, it incorporated themes from Stuck's 1891 painting *Der Mörder* (the murderer), in which three furies pursued a killer fleeing his grisly crime with knife in hand. Paul's furies, on the other hand, tormented an editor grasping a pen.[43] The satiric humor of the composition, characteristic of Paul's later work, required familiarity with *Der Mörder*, which had been exhibited in Munich in 1894.[44] His *Unterwelt* cover was simultaneously an homage to Stuck's work and a parody of it. Paul condensed the striking green and orange tonality of *Der Mörder* to a sharply contrasting palette that owed more to the precedent of Japanese prints than the atmospheric presentation of Stuck's painting. Yet Paul's juxtaposition of fields of green and orange ink also suggested the spatial ambiguities of Greek vase painting or Pompeian frescoes, precedents that were of interest to Stuck in 1896 as he completed the drawings for his Munich villa on the Prinzregentenstraße. Likewise the snakes depicted on Paul's cover transformed a recurring metaphorical image from Stuck's paintings, known in Munich through the exhibition of his scandalous painting *Die Sünde* (the sin) in 1893,[45] into an abstracted, decorative form recalling the characteristic whiplash curve of the Jugendstil. Ultimately, Paul's *Unterwelt* cover demonstrated a profound understanding of Stuck's work derived from both perceptive observation and cogent analysis. Although it was a synthetic composition, the cover was nevertheless strikingly original, and embodied the rudiments of Paul's unique personal style.

Paul's early admiration of Franz Stuck is particularly significant in light of his subsequent career as an artist. Stuck, too, commenced his artistic education in the applied arts, before studying painting at the Munich academy. He began his professional career as an illustrator and, even after making his name as a painter, maintained his interest in craftsmanship and the minor arts.[46] For example, he carved the elaborate gilt frames in which he exhibited the majority of his paintings, and produced models for figurative sculptures. While Paul was a student at the academy, Stuck was designing his villa, concurrently working as architect, sculptor, decorative painter, mosaicist, and furniture designer. When completed, the Villa Stuck was a perfect Gesamtkunstwerk, a total work of art. The villa also embodied the union of the fine and applied arts that Stuck celebrated in his drawing *Kunst und Handwerk* (art and craftsmanship). In 1896, Stuck exemplified what Paul himself would later become: a proponent of a modern art that reunited multiple fields of design and craftsmanship within a single, coherent discipline. And, like Stuck, Paul would begin his career as an illustrator.

The keen and perceptive humor of Paul's *Unterwelt* cover, with its layered references, proved to have a widespread popular appeal, and was reprinted in the eighth issue of the influential journal *Jugend* during 1896.[47] *Jugend* provided Paul's introduction to the emerging field of graphic art. It was a fortuitous match; the modern graphic style of *Jugend*, which combined numerous disciplines of the applied arts, was fundamentally suited to Paul's unique talents as an artist.[48] The first defining moment in Paul's life occurred when he determined to pursue a career in the arts; the second occurred when he recognized that his future did not lie in traditional studio art, but in the new art of the Jugendstil.

In 1896, Bruno Paul was twenty-two years old. He had completed his formal education and stood on the threshold of his professional career. He had also joined the circle of progressive Munich artists committed to reshaping contemporary life through the reform of contemporary art, and he exemplified the character and experiences of the first generation of Central European Modernists. At the same time, however, he had also demonstrated a tenacious determination to find his own way in the world.

Kraft und Stoff | Bruno Paul (München) | Geist und Gemüse

2. Turn of the century in Munich and the culture of youth: 1896–1906

At the end of the nineteenth century, when Bruno Paul was a student in Munich, the cultural vitality of the Bavarian capital was unparalleled in Germany. There he joined the artistic avant-garde that had founded the Munich secession, the first such movement in Central Europe. Its establishment paralleled the emergence of modern movements in the theatre, literature, graphic arts, and popular politics, all of which drew their support from the same progressive tendencies in German society. Two new illustrated magazines, *Simplicissimus* and *Jugend*, disseminated Munich's culture of youth throughout the German empire, and launched Paul's career as an artist.

Bruno Paul as illustrator

Despite his innate abilities, Paul did not distinguish himself as a studio painter. Although he briefly operated an atelier in collaboration with his friend Rudolf Wilke,[49] this venture proved unsuccessful.[50] He soon abandoned his studio and became a regular contributor to the monthly magazine *Jugend*. Painting, even among the membership of the Munich secession, remained inherently conservative. Illustration, on the other hand, which reflected the evolving technology of photomechanical reproduction and which promised broad popular exposure, was a realm of uncharted opportunities. Paul, with the enthusiasm of youth, chose to pursue the latter career.

Founded in 1896 by the publisher Georg Hirth, *Jugend* soon established a relationship with the circle of Munich's progressive artists to which Paul belonged. Thirteen of the twenty founding members of the secession published works in *Jugend*, as did many of the »Malerfürsten«, including Franz von Lenbach and Franz Stuck.[51] The journal printed reproductions of notable contemporary works by artists as diverse as Lovis Corinth and Auguste Rodin, but it also provided opportunities for the younger artists who were responsible for the »decorative revival« of the Jugendstil.[52] *Jugend* provided a venue for artistic experimentation, encouraged by advances in printing technology that produced the strong, simple colors characteristic of the journal. Together with his Munich contemporaries Otto Eckmann, Emil Orlik, Bernhard Pankok, and Richard Riemerschmid, Paul experimented on the pages of *Jugend* with flowing curves and abstracted natural forms suggestive of the Art Nouveau of Belgium and France. Their work for the publication was representative of Munich's culture of youth during the final decade of the nineteenth century.

Paul's illustrations for *Jugend* constituted his first professional success. His contributions differed significantly from those of Eckmann, Orlik, Pankok, or Riemerschmid; they were, notwithstanding the methods of their composition, closer to the aesthetic of the graphic arts than to traditional painting.[53] His illustration *Die Frau vor dem Rad, hinter dem Rad und auf dem Rad*,[54] for example, was typical of his illustrations for the magazine. The inclusion of text and decorative borders as elements of the composition indicated his departure from the conventions of painting, as did the spare, impressionistic use of line with which he portrayed the human figure. Conversely, he depicted implements and machinery in precise if suggestive detail. As a young man, Paul regarded the artifacts of human ingenuity with analytical detachment; he did not sketch an object without understanding how it functioned and how it had been assembled. He observed human subjects with equal solicitude, but depicted them in a manner that was more empathetic than precise. Paul's emerging style of caricature was exemplified by the pair of illustrations *Kraft und Stoff* (strength and substance) and *Geist und Gemüse* (intellect and vegetables)[55], in which the soft, amorphous figures of the first illustration contrasted with the attenuated, angular figures of

the second. The visual analogy was no less effective for its simplicity, a quality ideally suited to the medium of its reproduction.

Notwithstanding his explorations of the conventions of printed art, Paul never renounced his academic training as a painter. His illustrations for *Jugend* reflected his continuing admiration for Franz Stuck. His compositions *Adam u. Eva* (Adam and Eve),[56] *Vision* (vision),[57] and *Der Sünden-fall* (the fall of man)[58] were all variations on the symbolism of Stuck's notorious *Die Sünde* (the sin). Moreover, Paul often adopted specific details from Stuck's paintings. The suggestive Lilly of Stuck's *Innocentia* (innocence) of 1889, for example, reappeared in Paul's drawing *Vision*, just as the knotted serpents of Stuck's *Medusa* of 1892 appeared as a decorative border for *Adam u. Eva*. In addition, many of Paul's captions employed the antique letter forms that Stuck preferred, such as his illustration for Victor Hardung's poem *Seelen* (souls).[59] Paul's *Seelen* was a perfect expression of the interrelationship of the Jugendstil and the broader Symbolist movement, particularly as embraced by Stuck. Yet Paul transformed the portentous biblical and mythological themes beloved of the Symbolists into a critique of contemporary society as he developed his own personal style. In so doing, he produced a series of commentaries that were both sharper and more satiric than the majority of illustrations in *Jugend*. They were, in fact, closer to the spirit of the Munich weekly *Simplicissimus*, the magazine that would make Paul's reputation as an artist.

Simplicissimus

In the spring of 1897, Paul accepted a position as an illustrator for *Simplicissimus*. Albert Langen, a Munich publisher, had established the weekly magazine the previous year in conjunction with the secession painter Thomas Theodor Heine.[60] They conceived *Simplicissimus* as an erudite literary journal, and the first issues contained songs and poems as well as prose contributions by prominent authors including the young Thomas Mann and the playwright Frank Wedekind. Although its format was similar to that of *Jugend*, *Simplicissimus* distinguished itself through its biting social and political satire. Indeed, Langen soon abandoned his original ambitions for *Simplicissimus*, and printed a magazine wholly devoted to sarcastic commentary on both the German government and popular morality.[61] This boldness prompted the Bavarian government to ban an 1898 issue of *Simplicissimus* satirizing a pilgrimage to the Holy Land undertaken by Kaiser Wilhelm II, and to condemn Heine and Wedekind to six months imprisonment in the fortress of Königstein for insulting the emperor, the crime of *lèse majesté.* Langen himself fled Munich to spend five years in Paris as a political exile. Governmental censure, however, only provoked popular support for the magazine and confirmed its reputation as the embodiment of the bold and irreverent spirit of Munich's cultural avant-garde. This spirit had already begun to manifest itself in the March of 1897, when Paul's first full-page illustration, *Entwurf zu einem Denkmal für den Deutschen Michel* (project for a monument to the average German), appeared in *Simplicissimus*.[62]

When Paul joined *Simplicissimus*, the members of the staff were retained as salaried employees. His acceptance of such a paid position was yet one step further removed from his father's ambition that he should become a clergyman or a teacher. But Gustav Paul died on 28 February 1897 at the age of sixty-one, freeing Bruno from the burden of paternal expectation. Joining the staff of *Simplicissimus* was a clear assertion of his independence, a final renunciation of his early, half-hearted efforts to enter one of the traditional learned professions.

As an employee of *Simplicissimus*, Paul published more than four hundred illustrations over nine years, in a style unlike that employed by any of the other artists on the staff. His early illustration *Entwurf zu einem Denkmal für den Deutschen Michel* demonstrated the lingering influence of Stuck and the traditions of academic art in the form of the antique altar that formed the base of the proposed monument as well as the classicizing form of his signature: BR. PAVL. However his devotion to such precedents was soon supplanted by his own emerging, idiosyncratic style, already apparent in his illustration *Vis-à-vis*, published in March 1897.[63]

Paul's graphic vocabulary was related directly to the manner in which he composed, using India ink, pencil, charcoal and watercolor. Although he utilized a variety of media, his illustrations reflected his training as a painter. As he refined his skills, Paul relied less frequently upon pencil underdrawings for his illustrations, instead composing directly with a brush. His originals were significantly larger than the printed versions in *Simplicissimus*; at an average size of 30 x 40 cm, they were painterly in scale as well as technique.[64] One of the few surviving paintings by Paul, a 1900 composition entitled *Alles eine Nummer zu groß!* (everything one size too large!), demonstrated

15. *Vis-à-vis* (Face to Face), 1897. The caption, in the dialectical German of Bavaria, reads: »Are they for real, or is this a masquerade?« »Is that a policeman, or is this a masquerade?«.

16. *Alles eine Nummer zu groß!* (Everything One Size Too Large!), 1900. Painting in the style of Franz von Lenbach, depicting Chancellor Bernhard von Bülow wearing Bismarck's gala uniform.

17. Untitled illustration for *Agricola*, 1897.

18. *Entwurf zu einem Denkmal für den deutschen Michel* (Project for a Monument to the Average German), 1897.

19. *Mißraten* (Gone Astray), 1897. »Rector: So what have you made of yourself, Mr. Baumann? – I'm a painter, Sir. – A painter! But your father was such a good, respectable man.«

20. *Sonderbarer Optimismus* (Misplaced Optimism), 1898. »Why are these modern artists always so prone to exaggeration? Nobody is as ugly as these drawings.«

his intermingling of the fine and graphic arts. The subject of the painting was closely related to his work for *Simplicissimus*: chancellor Bernhard von Bülow wearing Bismarck's gala uniform.[65] In fact, the painting appeared on the cover of the magazine in 1900.[66] Yet Paul composed his portrait of the chancellor with the confident hand and practiced eye of an accomplished academic painter. Nevertheless the work was not merely a caricature of Bülow, but a sophisticated parody of the work of Franz von Lenbach, and particularly of his well-known portraits of Bismarck, which numbered more than eighty upon the artist's death in 1904.[67] However, Paul did not parody a specific painting by Lenbach but rather his style, which was rich and luminous in the tradition of the old masters.

As in his illustrations for *Jugend*, the human subjects of Paul's illustrations for *Simplicissimus* were distorted, composed of amorphous fields of color that frequently approached pure abstraction, and were often ideally suited to mechanical reproduction. His remarkable attention to detail was manifested in his careful depiction of the military uniforms, furniture, buildings, mechanical devices, and regional costumes that endowed his caricatures with their immediacy and facile humor. The majority of the visible amendments to his originals were corrections to such technical details, or refinements to the few portraits that Paul included in his work, such as a caricature of the department store magnate Wolf Wertheim, published in the 1902 illustration *Weihnachten bei Wertheim* (Christmas at Wertheim).[68] The caption epitomized Paul's critical humor. »Why shouldn't we celebrate his birthday?« it read. »He brought our lovely Christmas business into the world.«[69] The 1898 drawing *Sonderbarer Optimismus* (misplaced optimism)[70] was also typical of Paul's work. In careful detail, he reproduced the heavy, eclectic furnishings of a middle-class German home of the last decade of the nineteenth century. Again the caption reflected his self-effacing wit. »Why are these modern artists always so prone to exaggeration?« he wrote. »Nobody is as ugly as these drawings.«[71] Paul considered himself to be one such modern artist. Yet he was well compensated for his work, and could be counted in his own right as a member of the Bavarian middle class. He was, in fact, precisely the sort of parvenu he regularly satirized. He was a reformer rather than a revolutionary, committed to change from within. He mocked the shortcomings of a culture he hoped to improve, and to which his success as an illustrator had granted admission.

Despite his prolific contributions to *Simplicissimus*, Paul found time to pursue other artistic interests. He was involved with the group of painters working in Dachau, a rural community in the marshy moorlands northwest of Munich. At the end of the nineteenth century, the quiet town was a popular destination for Munich artists seeking the inspiration of either the atmospheric local landscape or the picturesque Bavarian peasantry. The secession painter Adolf Hölzel was among those working in Dachau during the 1890s.[72] Paul was a frequent guest at Hölzel's lodgings, where he met the author and playwright Ludwig Thoma.[73] Thoma hired Hölzel and Paul to illustrate his book *Agricola*, an account of rural life published in Passau in 1897. Hölzel would provide the landscape illustrations for *Agricola*, Paul the character studies. Paul completed a series of sketches for the book in the village of Lauterbach near Dachau, composing his drawings with the keen characterization and loose manner of his work for *Simplicissimus*, rather than the lyrical style of the Dachau painters. They paralleled the origins of abstract art, a form of expression closely related to his forceful caricature. Significantly, Hölzel himself was creating purely abstract drawings by the end of the century, more than a decade earlier than Kandinsky's first nonobjective experiments.[74]

Paul's character studies for *Agricola* inspired Albert Langen to commission illustrations for several volumes in a series of modern works introduced in 1897 as the *Kleine Bibliothek Langen* (Langen's compact library). Paul provided a decorative Jugendstil cover for Heinrich Mann's *Das Wunderbare* and a cover in the style of his *Simplicissimus* vignettes for *Der wilde Jockey* by Fritz Mauthner. He also illustrated several more of Thoma's books including *Die Medaille, Komödie in einem Akt* (the medal, a comedy in one act) of 1900; *Assessor Karlchen* (Karlchen the civil servant) of 1901; and *Die Hochzeit, eine Bauerngeschichte* (the wedding, a peasant history) of 1902. Paul's cover for *Assessor Karlchen*,[75] with its bold disavowal of artistic convention and its subversive sensuality, was typical of his contemporary work. All of these books, including those by Thoma, were originally published in Munich by the Langen Verlag. Paul had introduced Thoma to Langen and the *Simplicissimus* circle or »Simpl-Kreis«, as the staff of the magazine was known, at the Café Heck on the Munich Odeonsplatz in 1897.[76] This introduction proved particularly fortuitous. When Langen began his Parisian exile in 1899, he selected Thoma, who had become a regular contributor, to edit *Simplicissimus* during his absence. Under Thoma's guidance, the magazine continued to grow in both readership and influence. Paul, who had initiated the alliance between Langen and Thoma, became a Munich celebrity, a leading member of the Simpl-Kreis.

The celebrated staff of *Simplicissimus* enjoyed a bohemian camaraderie. They shared in their social and recreational activities, and enjoyed the intimacy of an extended family. Paul traveled widely with Thoma, including a 1902 bicycle tour through Italy undertaken with the illustrators Wilke, Eduard Thöny, and Ferdinand Freiherr von Reznicek. For this group of young artists, the bicycle was a symbol of modern life and modern leisure. In fact several of these artists were employed by the Opel bicycle company[77] in 1898 to produce a popular series of advertisements promoting its products. The group also engaged in such short-lived obsessions as bicycle polo, in which Paul was an avid participant. With and without their bicycles, he and Wilke paid extended visits to Georg Hirth, the publisher of *Jugend*, in the Bavarian Alps. Paul skied in the Finsterwald with Olaf Gulbransson, and enacted vignettes from the Franco-Prussian war in a beer-cellar presentation of Thoma's *Pippinger Veteransfest*. He gathered with his colleagues to celebrate the Munich carnival, Fasching, with the enthusiastic irreverence for which *Simplicissimus* was renowned. This close-knit group embodied the spirit of the Munich avant-garde at the close of the nineteenth century. Paul commented on the life of his fellow artists in his drawing *Mißraten* (gone astray) of 1897, the caption to which read »Rector: So what have you made of yourself, Mr. Baumann? – I'm a painter, sir. – A painter! But your father was such a good, respectable man.«[78] Dismissing many of the social conventions of the waning nineteenth century, the bohemian staff of *Simplicissimus* formed their own brilliant community in Schwabing.

It was through the *Simplicissimus* circle that Paul met and courted Paula Maria Graf, the beautiful, red-haired daughter of the prominent Munich banker Friedrich Karl Graf. The young couple married in Strasbourg on 14 December 1899, far from their respective families.[79] At the time, Maria was already five months pregnant. While such a pregnancy was by no means an uncommon occurrence among Munich's young artists at the turn of the century, it would not have been expected of the daughter of a prominent financier.[80] That Paul was able to attract a member of Munich society like Maria Graf attests to the recognition he had obtained through *Simplicissimus*. He had also achieved financial security by 1901, when he, Maria, and their newborn daughter Hildegard moved into a comfortable two story semi-detached house at Gernerstraße 4 in the fashionable Munich district of Neuhausen. Paul's house, which overlooked the canal on the grand axis of Nymphenburg palace, reflected both the material success and social status that he had attained. Unlike the overwhelming majority of idealistic artists, even in turn-of-the-century Munich, the members of the Simpl-Kreis were handsomely rewarded for their efforts.

Simplicissimus and liberal politics

The year of Bruno Paul's marriage was marked by a significant international crisis that provoked an immediate response in the pages of *Simplicissimus*, offering an insight into the complex, and ostensibly contradictory, political positions of the journal and its staff. The Boer War began in October 1899 when a dispute over sovereignty between the British Colonial Office and Dutch settlers in the Transvaal escalated into armed conflict. In Germany, the plight of the Boers aroused widespread public interest as a consequence of the perceived cultural kinship between the Boers, who had emigrated from the Netherlands, and the Germans. Moreover, British military action against the Boer Republic promised to subject the whole of southern Africa to English hegemony, a triumph that would stand in stark contrast to the abject failure of German ambitions on the continent. *Simplicissimus* provided an ideal venue for the expression of ambivalent German feelings towards the conflict in the Transvaal.

Paul's drawings from the period of the Boer War were not so much pro-Boer as they were anti-English. He produced so many of these drawings during the years of conflict in Africa that he was selected to design the cover for Albert Langen's book *Der Burenkrieg* (The Boer War), a supplement to *Simplicissimus* published in 1900.[81] His drawing *Englische Zivilisation*[82] was a typical example of his commentary on the Boer War. The caption proclaimed »We can hire men for five shillings a day to carry on the greatest wars for the honor of our nation. No English gentleman would be a party to such dirty manual labor.«[83] In his drawings, Paul ruthlessly satirized Albert Edward, Prince of Wales (later King Edward VII) and the uncle of Kaiser Wilhelm II, as a fat, drunken libertine.[84] In addition, he also produced inflammatory comments on alleged English atrocities, as in the drawing *Der Raubmord in Südafrika* (robbery and murder in South Africa) which appeared on the cover of *Simplicissimus* in 1900.[85] The caption for this illustration read:

(The Queen:) »Don't worry Joe, those men back there won't disturb us, they're my relatives!«[86] The Joe in the drawing, a lanky figure brandishing a long knife, was British Colonial Secretary Joseph Chamberlain. The man in the background wearing a Cossack hat was Nicolas II, Czar of Russia. The figure in a *Pickelhaube*, the spiked Prussian helmet, was Wilhelm II.[87] Queen Victoria's personal and military domination of her Prussian grandson was at the crux of the anti-English sentiment of *Simplicissimus*, and of Paul's vitriolic illustrations concerning the war in Africa.

Though *Simplicissimus* supported the strength and independence of the German government with respect to international affairs and the Kaiser's independence of his grandmother's policies, the position of the journal regarding internal politics was distinctly different. Throughout its history, *Simplicissimus* was consistently critical of the military, the bureaucracy, the power of the church, and the excesses of the capitalist elite. As a consequence, the journal was associated with the political left. During the first years of the twentieth century the political right in Bavaria was dominated by the moralistic and conservative policies of the military and the power of the hereditary monarchy. The contemporary Zentrumspartei (center party) was both religious and particularistic, and sponsored repressive policies such as the notorious Lex Heinze of 1900. This law, named for a Berlin pimp, was intended to counter the morally destructive influence of a broadly defined pornography. As originally written, the law would have imposed harsh punishments upon graphic artists and playwrights whose work was deemed to be obscene. In light of the obtrusive policies of the ostensible center, it was inevitable that the Munich Modernists, and particularly the circle responsible for the pervasive eroticism of *Jugend*, should be driven to the left. Paul summarized his own opposition to the Lex Heinze and its supporters with his drawing *Der Cylinderhut als Feigenblatt* (the top hat as fig leaf) of 1900.[88] He was clearly provoking the censors with this drawing, and the obvious double entendre that it contained. But *Der Cylinderhut als Feigenblatt* was printed amidst a deluge of satirical commentary on the Lex Heinze that appeared in the pages of *Simplicissimus* and other popular publications during 1900, and Paul's provocation went unanswered. Nevertheless opposition to the Lex Heinze was sufficiently widespread to prevent passage of the legislation in its original form, largely as a consequence of the efforts of Paul and other avant-garde artists to draw popular attention to what would have otherwise been an obscure legal proceeding. He played an active role in opposing the policies of the right concerning the Boer War and of the center concerning the Lex Heinze. Ironically, he was equally successful in his opposition to the policies of his own employers.

In his memoirs, Paul noted that while on the staff of *Simplicissimus* he and Thomas Theodor Heine had been supporters of »international« and »radical«, that is to say socialist, politics.[89] Heine was, in fact, internationally regarded as a »rabid social democrat«.[90] Yet the most radical political action in which Paul actively participated during his years in Munich occurred within the offices of *Simplicissimus*, when in 1906 the staff of the journal disputed the absolute authority wielded by Langen. The artistic contributors threatened to establish their own, competing publication if Langen did not offer to share a percentage of the profits earned by the journal. The editor relented, reestablishing his magazine as a corporation. Paul and his coworkers each invested 1400 Marks in Simplicissimus GmbH to become shareholders in the new company.[91] The reorganization of *Simplicissimus* represented a shrewd and profitable commercial undertaking by its staff. Wherever Paul's political sympathies lay in 1906, he himself had become a successful capitalist with an income sufficient to establish himself in a comfortable, middle-class life.[92]

Modern graphic art and modern life

The spirit of reform that Paul and his fellow members of the Munich avant-garde promoted was not confined to individual disciplines, but rather embraced the Jugendstil ideal of the Gesamtkunstwerk: the total work of art. Modern art, modern politics, modern work, modern dress, and modern theater were all perceived as facets of the Gesamtkunstwerk of modern life that was the ultimate goal of the Munich reformers. As a member of this avant-garde, Paul's own artistic efforts quickly assumed the same interdisciplinary character as the broader movement, a trend that would have significant consequences for his later career.

Soon after joining the staff of *Simplicissimus*, Paul began preparing graphic designs for firms that advertised in the journal, or were otherwise supportive of Munich's progressive artists. An early logotype for the printers Michael Huber, completed by 1898, epitomized these designs. It was an exemplary expression of the Jugendstil, combining type design, painterly representation, and purely abstract composition. The serpent in the composition recalled his earliest graphic designs, and their homage to Stuck. However by 1898 Paul had perfected a uniquely personal mode of expression.

In 1901, Bruno Paul designed a poster for the »1. Ausstellung für Kunst im Handwerk« (first exhibition of art in handicraft). His *Reiherplakat* (heron poster), was one of the finest expressions of the Jugendstil aesthetic. It was praised in the magazine *Innen-Dekoration* as thoroughly modern and devoid of any trace of retrospection – even if the heron itself recalled Paul's earlier work for Michael Huber.[93] It became, in fact, an iconic image of the Munich Jugendstil, an embodiment of the spirit of the city's avant-garde. The heron poster was even the subject of an illustration in *Jugend* by Angelo Jank in which it was contrasted with a provincial couple reminiscent of Paul's illustrations for *Agricola*, representatives of a hidebound, conservative society. Paul's mastery of the Jugendstil was reflected in the manifest beauty with which he expressed artistic innovation. He developed this mastery in compositions for *Simplicissimus* such as *Deutsche Weihnachten* (German Christmas) of 1899.[94] Yet the caption for this graceful illustration was bitterly sarcastic: »In solemnity the angel of Christmas floats down to grant peace and good fortune to the Germans. To her regret, she finds nobody at home: the entire nation sits in prison for *lèse majesté*.«[95] Nevertheless Paul himself remained unpunished for this particular offence.

In the same year that Paul designed his heron poster, he created a program cover for the Elf Scharfrichter (eleven executioners), a satirical cabaret inspired by the famous Paris cabaret *Le Chat Noir*. The Elf Scharfrichter were supported by the circle of artists to which Paul belonged: Hirth and Stuck were financial backers, and Wedekind was a member of the ensemble.[96] The format of the cabaret allowed its performers to address issues too controversial or sensitive to be presented in print or on canvas.[97] During the two years of its existence, the Elf Scharfrichter offered scathing criticisms of the hypocritical religious, political and moral attitudes of the Wilhelmine middle classes. Paul may not have been a member of the closed society that sponsored the cabaret, but he was certainly among the inner circle of its artistic supporters, a group that included both Heine and Ernst Neumann.[98]

Paul's program cover for the Elf Scharfrichter was striking for its stark and earnest sensuality. His drawing of a female nude was far more provocative than the unclothed figures that had become a staple of *Jugend*. The cover was a challenge to conventional morality, and particularly to the Catholic center party that had sponsored the Lex Heinze. The old women in the background of Paul's composition, clad in sober black, have been interpreted as an embodiment of the Catholic center, a satirical reference typical of his biting sense of humor.[99] Paul contrasted these figures with his nude subject just as Jank had juxtaposed two bemused provincials with the heron poster. The Elf Scharfrichter cover embodied the union of modern art and modern life, and a condemnation of the mores of the nineteenth century.

Paul also designed a poster for the Elf Scharfrichter in 1903, the last year of the cabaret's existence. He employed the same basic colors as in the earlier heron poster, as well as a derivation of the same idiosyncratic alphabet. Yet the two posters were stylistically distinct. The heron poster, with its exotic, natural forms and gorgeous, muted colors, exemplified the aesthetic of the Jugendstil. The *Scharfrichter* poster, with its hard, bright hues and abstract, geometric background, prefigured Modernist graphic design. Nevertheless, the artistic construction of the later poster was clearly derived from that of the earlier. The ambiguous relationship of figure and ground that Paul established in the Heron Poster by establishing a continuous field of color for the printed border and the legs of the two striding birds also characterized the *Scharfrichter* poster. In the later design, a series of concentric yellow stripes set against the red field effectively suggested a rounded form in space, despite the lack of any device of illusionistic perspective.

The inherent similarities between the two posters revealed underlying trends in Paul's work as an artist. The predominance of abstract, thematic issues over purely stylistic ones characterized both designs. While the two posters were stylistically dissimilar, the alternating use of a continuous red field as figure and ground was central to each composition. As a pair, the posters illustrate Paul's tendency to explore differing interpretations of a central theme, a practice that he perfected as an illustrator for *Simplicissimus*. That he could produce, with equal facility, classic examples of printed art in both the naturalistic vocabulary of the Jugendstil and the abstract, geometric vocabulary of an emerging Modernism illustrates the artistic versatility that was a fundamental characteristic of Paul's work.

These same trends were apparent in Paul's work as an applied artist which, like his poster for the Elf Scharfrichter, originated in the Simpl-Kreis. *Simplicissimus* stood near the center of the Gesamtkunstwerk of modern life that Paul and his colleagues were shaping. The significance of the magazine as a representative of the modern ethos in Munich was raised in 1903 by a dele-

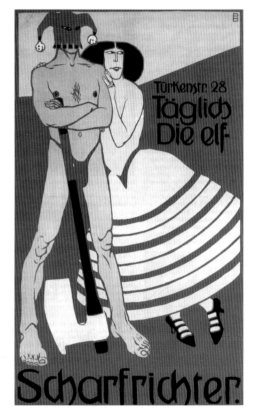

25. Program cover for the Elf Scharfrichter, 1901.
26. Poster for the Elf Scharfrichter, 1903.
27. Poster for the »1. Ausstellung für Kunst im Handwerk« (»Reiherplakat«), 1901.
28. Logotype for the printers Michael Huber, 1898.
29. *Streit der Moden* (Quarrel of the Fashions), 1905. »Above all the reform dress is hygienic, and keeps the body conditioned for the demands of motherhood. As long as you're dressed in those rags, you won't have to worry about that particular embarrassment.«
30. *Deutsche Weihnachten* (A German Christmas), 1899. »In solemnity the angel of Christmas floats down to grant peace and good fortune to the Germans. To her regret, she finds nobody at home: the entire nation sits in prison for lese majesté.«

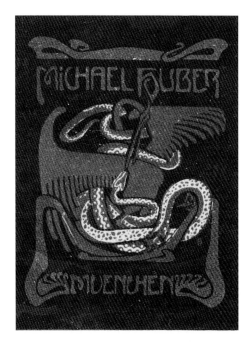

gate to the Bavarian parliament who denounced the pernicious influences of a *versimplicis-simusten Gesellschaft* (Simplicissimusified society); in his diatribe he condemned at a single stroke progressive movements in literature, politics and art.[100] Paul's 1905 illustration *Streit der Moden* (quarrel of the fashions) epitomized the attitudes of this Simplicissimusified society.[101] »Above all the reform dress is hygienic, and keeps the body conditioned for the demands of motherhood«, read the caption, echoing the proponents of the simple, practical Reformkleid. »As long as you're dressed in those rags«, came the reply, »you won't have to worry about that particular embarrassment.«[102] Although Paul himself never designed a Reformkleid, by 1905 he had turned to the applied arts to extend this influence from the public realm of artistic expression to the private domain of daily life.

Bruno Paul and the applied arts

Paul's engagement with *Simplicissimus* and the circle of progressive artists on its staff led directly to his career in the decorative arts, and to his participation in the development of the Kunstge-werbebewegung (applied arts movement). He apparently executed his first furniture designs for his colleague Heine in 1897. Heine had rented an apartment furnished in the heavy, historicist style favored in nineteenth-century Munich. Despairing of his landlord's taste in decoration, he enlisted his friend and fellow *Simplicissimus* illustrator Paul to compose something more in keeping with the spirit of the times. Although there is no surviving evidence to corroborate this story, which Paul himself told in 1966,[103] he was already demonstrating the natural abilities that would foster his success as an architect and a decorative artist shortly after joining the staff of *Simplicissimus*. He soon found a client for his work in the Vereinigte Werkstätten für Kunst im Handwerk (united workshops for art in handicraft).

The Vereinigte Werkstätten für Kunst im Handwerk was incorporated in Munich in 1898 by a group of artists who had participated in the »VII. Internationale Kunstausstellung im Königlichen Glaspalaste in München« (seventh international art exhibition in the royal glass palace in Munich),[104] held in 1897. Paul was a member of the circle of progressive Munich artists who had exhibited at the seventh international exhibition, many of whom belonged to the Sezession. The Sezession fostered an atmosphere of artistic synthesis that inspired members such as Riemer-schmid, Peter Behrens, and Adalbert Niemeyer to expand their work to include the design and production of furniture, metalwork, clothing, and other artifacts of modern life. The spirit of the Gesamtkunstwerk also pervaded the rooms devoted to the applied arts at the VII. Internationale Kunstausstellung. These rooms were among the most popular at the exhibition, and prompted such enthusiastic reviews as the article »Endlich ein Umschwung« (finally a change for the better) in the influential journal *Deutsche Kunst und Dekoration*.[105] The successful inclusion of the applied arts in the seventh international exhibition inspired the foundation of the Ausschuß für Kunst im Handwerk (the committee for artistry in craftsmanship) to promote the continued exhibition of decorative arts at the annual exhibitions of fine art. The very wording of its title, »Kunst im Hand-werk« (artistry in craft), became a rallying cry for the Kunstgewerbebewegung, and a synopsis of its principal objective.[106] On 13 April 1898, its members incorporated the Vereinigte Werkstätten für Kunst im Handwerk G.m.b.H. in Munich.[107] The Vereinigte Werkstätten was dedicated to the development and promotion of the decorative arts through the manufacture and sale of artist-designed housewares, a pragmatic recasting of the original ideals of the applied arts movement. Though Paul is frequently cited as one of the founders of the Vereinigte Werkstätten,[108] the documents of incorporation for the firm indicate otherwise.[109] Nevertheless, he was providing furniture designs for the company within a year of its establishment, and he quickly became one of its most prolific and successful designers.

The Vereinigte Werkstätten manufactured the earliest documented furnishings and interiors designed by Paul. He must have demonstrated his abilities as a decorative artist prior to receiving his first commission from the Werkstätten, but his development as a designer paralleled the history of the firm. Initially he designed in the curvilinear Jugendstil vocabulary of the pieces he exhibited in 1897.[110] The vestibule that Paul designed for the »Kunst-Ausstellung Dresden« (Dresden art exhibition) of 1899 was typical of this early work.

Paul's work for the 1899 »Kunst-Ausstellung Dresden« illustrates the origins of his practice as an applied artist. The paneling, doorcases, and furniture were notable for the linear character of their ornamental embellishments. Paul used opulent and expensive materials in his design, including mahogany, brass, bookmatched black marble slabs, and yellow opalescent glazing. Yet he

31. Room of applied arts at the »VII. internationale Kunstausstellung«, 1897. The room illustrated was furnished by the Ausschuß für Kunst im Handwerk.
32. Vestibule exhibited at the »Kunst-Ausstellung Dresden«, 1899. Executed by the Vereinigte Werk-stätten für Kunst im Handwerk.
33, 34. Cover for *Neue Grobheiten*, 1903.

24

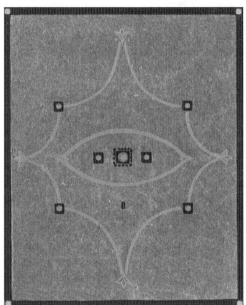

employed these materials in a painterly manner, utilizing them to create a sumptuous visual experience without clear acknowledgement of their differing tectonic capabilities. The graphic quality of Paul's vestibule was summarized in the frieze that he stenciled on the walls. The frieze was entirely two-dimensional, a direct translation of his printed work to an architectural scale. It was clearly related to his book illustrations for Albert Langen, such as his design for the back cover of Peter Schlemihl's *Neue Grobheiten*.[111] Paul had never worked as a sculptor, and his room for the »Kunst-Ausstellung Dresden« lacked the plastic quality of contemporary works by Hermann Obrist or August Endell, who translated graphic conventions to three-dimensional forms.[112]

Yet Paul matured quickly as a designer. He continued to employ the fluid curvilinear forms of the Jugendstil, but he soon abandoned the applied decoration of his projects for the »Kunst-Ausstellung Dresden« in favor of an intrinsic, architectonic ornamentation. In the »Jagdzimmer« (hunter's room) that he designed for the Vereinigte Werkstätten at the end of 1899 he exploited the ornamental qualities of a single material: elm wood. The room included elm paneling, carved elm reliefs, and elm chairs composed of simple members with dramatic compound curves that imparted a muscular vitality. His sparing use of accent materials, including gray-green upholstery and brass lamps, heightened the dramatic effect of the pronounced grain of the wood. The artistic quality of his hunter's room was recognized at the »Exposition Universelle« of 1900 in Paris, where it received a Grand Prix.[113]

Paul's »Jagdzimmer« epitomized his personal style at the turn of the century. The room was exhibited in Munich in 1901 at the »1. Ausstellung für Kunst im Handwerk«, the exhibition for which he designed the heron poster, and at the 1902 exhibition of decorative art in Turin. The armchairs for the hunter's room, produced by the Vereinigte Werkstätten as Model 1744, were particularly successful. A set was sold to King Ferdinand of Bulgaria for installation in Sitnjakowo castle, Paul's first royal commission. He continued to explore permutations of their characteristic splayed form, and produced a number of related designs between 1901 and 1904. The development of the Model 1744 armchair reflected the relentless experimentation that distinguished Paul's work as a designer. Although he did not actually construct his furnishings with his own hands, in working through countless variations of his designs with the artisans who executed them he developed the profound and sympathetic understanding of form characteristic of a master craftsman.

In 1904, Paul designed his »Herrenzimmer für den Regierungspräsidenten von Bayreuth« (office for the head of the provincial government at Bayreuth). The suite of furniture that Paul assembled included Modell 652 and Modell 2531 armchairs derived from the hunter's room of 1899. In the Bayreuth office, however, these characteristically Jugendstil chairs served as a counterpoint to an interior dominated by straight lines and simple geometries similar to the motifs employed in the editorial offices that he designed for *Simplicissimus* in 1903. The editorial offices incorporated a frieze consisting of framed illustrations from the magazine that was echoed in horizontally striped walls and in the severe furnishings, another example of the influence of his graphic work on his projects as an applied artist. He developed the orthogonal motifs of his *Simplicissimus* office in his design for Bayreuth, evoking the final, rectilinear phase of the Jugendstil. The rectilinear aesthetic of the turn of the century originated with the arts and crafts movement, and received its canonical form in the works of the Scottish architect Charles Rennie Mackintosh and the Wiener Werkstätte of Vienna, established by Josef Hoffmann in 1903. Yet while Paul's success as an applied artist paralleled that of Hoffmann,[114] there is little in his Bayreuth office to suggest the influence of Glasgow or Vienna.[115] Instead he drew his inspiration from German design of the late eighteenth century.

Similarities between Bruno Paul's designs and the simple, sturdy classicism of the Biedermeier period, the age of Goethe and Schiller, were the subject of critical comment even before he had fully forsaken the lingering influence of the Jugendstil.[116] Although later historians have tended to focus on the formal qualities of the German classicism of the early twentieth century, contemporary critics adopted a more nuanced assessment of the relevance of the Biedermeier to modern design.[117] A 1905 article by E. W. Bredt in *Dekorative Kunst* entitled »Bruno Paul – Biedermeier – Empire« included an evaluation of the influence of eighteenth-century precedents on Paul's work. Bredt noted that the salons of the late eighteenth and early nineteenth centuries shared a fundamental characteristic of »simple, domestic elegance« with those designed by Paul. »When one examines black-and-white illustrations of Paul's furniture and interiors«, he continued, »the effect of the surfaces and lines alone speaks of a certain coolness that is characteristic of design in the age of Napoleon, although the differing colors of woods, wall coverings and upholstery caution against too close a comparison of the old and the new designs.«[118] This description, which accords perfectly with tendencies that would coalesce in Paul's work after 1908, was illustrated with photographs and drawings of an office he designed for Fritz Esche of Chemnitz in 1903, and photographs of a living room conceived in the same year. These two rooms and their furniture recorded Paul's mastery of the Jugendstil concept of Gesamtkunstwerk, and included such overt references to the union of art and craftsmanship as hammered metal fireplace surrounds that displayed both refined proportions and the physical exertion of their fabrication. These rooms did not incorporate stylistic references to eighteenth-century designs, but rather emulated less tangible qualities perceived as characteristic of Biedermeier interiors. The same was true of Paul's government office for Bayreuth.

The Bayreuth office was exhibited in the United States at the St. Louis International Exhibition of 1904. The room received a Grand Prix, Paul's second major international award. Exhibition audiences were impressed with his work, and unlicensed copies of his housewares were soon being manufactured in the American heartland.[119] In addition, the Philadelphia department store magnate John Wanamaker purchased twenty-one interiors from the German exhibition. It is possible that one of these rooms was Paul's Herrenzimmer.[120] Unfortunately, most of Wanamaker's purchases have not survived, although the colossal bronze eagle that August Gaul cast for the court of honor in the German pavilion is still displayed in the former Wanamaker store in Philadelphia. Paul's work also received critical acclaim in Germany. Hermann Muthesius, writing in *Deutsche Kunst und Dekoration*, stated that »Bruno Paul's room is a museum piece; it points to the desired perfection towards which we are striving«.[121] Critics such as Muthesius admired the office for what was perceived as a new direction in German design after the eclectic Historicism of the nineteenth century and the often overwrought exuberance of the Jugendstil. Paul himself had adopted a typically satiric opinion of these stylistic trends following the St. Louis exhibition, when he illustrated »Die offizielle Berliner Kunst in Saint Louis« (the official art of Berlin in St. Louis) for *Simplicissimus*.[122] By 1904, he was developing a new vocabulary of form characterized by simplicity, clarity, and practicality.

Paul's work for the Vereinigte Werkstätten was not limited to prestigious projects such as the office for Bayreuth. He also designed small housewares for the company, including a series of brass candleholders, as well as affordable furniture for mass production. The 1903 summer exhibition of the Vereinigte Werkstätten was entitled »Die Wohnung für Minderbemittelte« (dwelling for people of limited means). Paul designed a combined living and dining room for the exhibition, a response to the restricted living space of the typical, working-class apartment. The same year, he designed three suites of inexpensive furniture marketed as the »Einfaches Schlafzimmer«, «Einfaches Speisezimmer«, and »Einfaches Wohnzimmer« (simple bedroom, simple dining room, and simple living room). The 1906 Vereinigte Werkstätten summer exhibition, held at the Gasthof Hirsch in Munich, was dedicated to »Die Wohnung der mittleren Preislage« (the moderately priced dwelling). For this exhibit, Paul designed three rooms, a drawing room, office, and bedroom for a four-room, middle-class residence. In 1906, he also designed an inexpensive combination workroom, living room, and dining room. This set of furniture was suited to an even smaller apartment than the dwelling for people of limited means of 1903. It sold for 700 Marks, less than half the price of his contemporary Living Room 24 for the Vereinigte Werkstätten, which included a writing desk, table, side chair, arm chair, table lamp, sofa, bookcase, end table, long case clock, and oval mirror – all for 1700 Marks.

The inexpensive furniture Paul designed for the Vereinigte Werkstätten marked a significant departure from the precedent established by the English firms such as Morris and Company that had pioneered the Arts and Crafts movement. William Morris had clearly inspired the founding of the Vereinigte Werkstätten, and the very name of the firm echoed the »banded workshops« of his 1890 novel *News from Nowhere*.[123] Although the Vereinigte Werkstätten promoted the integration of design and production that was central to the Arts and Crafts movement, the company avoided the fundamental compromise accepted by Morris and his contemporaries. The Vereinigte Werkstätten did not embrace only an ideal of noble craftsmanship that limited its production to a few wealthy clients; on the contrary, the firm readily accepted industrial production of its furniture and successfully promoted its housewares to a broad sector of German society.[124] Advertisements for the Vereinigte Werkstätten appeared in design magazines such as *Innen-Dekoration* and *Dekorative Kunst*, but also in *Simplicissimus*. It is telling that all six of the Vereinigte Werkstätten advertisements published in *Simplicissimus* during 1904 featured Paul's projects exclusively.

Paul was initially identified as a »Kunstmaler« (art painter) in the Vereinigte Werkstätten advertisements, a reminder of the calling that had drawn him to Munich eight years before. By 1904, however, he was a prolific designer of furniture and interiors as well as an illustrator. Other than

35. »Jagdzimmer«, 1899. Executed by the Vereinigte Werkstätten für Kunst im Handwerk.
36. »Herrenzimmer für den Regierungspräsidenten von Bayreuth«, 1904. Executed by the Vereinigte Werkstätten für Kunst im Handwerk. Note the kidney-shaped desk, an adaptation of the classic Heppelwhite writing table.
37. *Die offizielle Berliner Kunst in Saint Louis* (The Official Art of Berlin in St. Louis), 1904.
38. First- and second-class waiting room for Nuremberg main station, 1905. Executed by the Vereinigte Werkstätten für Kunst im Handwerk.

his work for *Simplicissimus*, he painted very little. His evolving attitude towards the fine art of painting was already suggested in a cover illustration from 1898 entitled »Wilhelm der Schweigsame« (William the Silent).[125] In this technically advanced illustration,[126] Paul contrasted a photographic reproduction of a historical portrait with characters and a background of his own composition – acknowledging the discord between the traditional art of portraiture and the realities of modern life. Only the wealthy purchased paintings in any quantity; Paul's projects for the Vereinigte Werkstätten, like his illustrations for *Simplicissimus*, found a far broader audience.

In 1905, Paul designed the interiors of the first and second class waiting room of the main railway station in Nuremberg.[127] His designs for Nuremberg represented a new challenge to the young artist, that of responding to the strict functional and economic demands of a commercial enterprise. The first and second class waiting room was to be furnished as a café-restaurant, and required a far larger number of identical tables and chairs than any previous project Paul had undertaken. Such a room was typically furnished with the ubiquitous Thonet bentwood chairs, which were lightweight, durable, and inexpensive.[128] However, Paul did not elect to use bentwood chairs in Nuremberg.[129] Instead, he designed a series of simple, carved chairs assembled in a variety of configurations from standardized components. While the use of common elements to produce a range of furnishings echoed the manufacture of Thonet's bentwood chairs, the solid materiality of Paul's design made a far more explicit reference to the ideals of high culture than the comparatively utilitarian designs produced by Thonet. The translation of cultural identity to objects of mass production was intimated by a 1906 article in *Dekorative Kunst* by Paul Johannes Rée that praised the Nuremberg waiting room as an example of the best achievements of contemporary interior design.[130]

Paul had the opportunity to justify the accolades accorded his Nuremberg waiting room in 1906 when he participated in the »3. Deutsche Kunstgewerbe-Ausstellung Dresden« (third German applied arts exhibition in Dresden). He exhibited three complete rooms. The first was the office from Bayreuth, displayed as a study, albeit differing subtly but significantly from the one presented in St. Louis in accordance with Paul's developing taste.[131] In Dresden, the details and furnishings of the office were simplified. For instance, Paul replaced the elaborate motif of the ceiling coffers of the original installation with a pattern of concentric squares. He also revised the stepped configuration of the corner cabinet with its wooden buttresses integrated with the paneled walls in favor of a lower version with a strong horizontal cornice. A stark square table with a leg at each corner replaced the pedestal table displayed in 1904, and he substituted refined and elegant leather seats for the complex Modell 652 chairs in the earlier room. Only the paneling, the frieze, the pendant light fixtures, and the carpet remained unchanged. The other rooms exhibited by Paul in Dresden, a vestibule and reception room for the marble quarries of Kiefersfelden in the

39. »3. Deutsche Kunstgewerbe-Ausstellung Dresden«, 1906.
40. »Arbeitszimmer« displayed at the »3. Deutsche Kunstgewerbe-Ausstellung Dresden«, 1906.
41. Dining room displayed at the »3. Deutsche Kunstgewerbe-Ausstellung Dresden«, 1906.
42. Festival decoration of the Schwere-Reiter-Kaserne, Munich, 1906.

Bavarian Alps and a dining room for the Vereinigte Werkstätten, displayed the same self-confidence and maturity as the reworked office.

The Dresden exhibition was a significant event in the history of modern design in Germany, as a consequence of policies adopted by the organizing committee led by the architect Fritz Schumacher. Schumacher developed a selection process that favored the designs of independent artists rather that the potentially artistically indifferent products of established manufacturers. Paul's work was prominently displayed in Dresden, evidence of his fundamental agreement with the Kunstgewerbebewegung promoted by Schumacher and his circle, which included Muthesius, Peter Bruckmann, Wolf Dohrn and J. A. Lux. These men would withdraw from the Fachverband für das Deutsche Kunstgewerbe (alliance for the German applied arts) over their support of Schumacher and his ideals, prompting the establishment of the German Werkbund.

The artist as architect

Bruno Paul's introduction to the practice of architecture occurred through the Vereinigte Werkstätten, as a logical extension of his projects for furniture and interiors. Soon after it was founded, the firm offered the planning, construction, and furnishing of entire houses. The company archives contain photographs of architectural models of three small houses that Paul conceived in 1905, his earliest known designs for entire buildings. They are identified as an »Angebautes Wohnhaus mit Atelier« (enlarged house with studio) and a »Landhaus mit Atelier« (country house with studio) by Bruno Paul, and a »Landhaus« by Bruno Paul and F. A. O. Krüger.[132] These were apparently speculative projects; although a similar design was built in Bonn as Haus Prym.

Paul's designs for small artists' houses with attached studios immediately suggest the most famous examples of the type built in Germany during the first years of the twentieth century: the residences designed for the Darmstadt Künstlerkolonie (artist's colony) by Behrens and Joseph Maria Olbrich. Paul's houses were superficially similar to those built in Darmstadt, with roughcast walls and asymmetrical massing derived from the projects of the architect-members of the English Arts and Crafts movement. The influence of English design on progressive German housing was particularly pronounced following the publication of Muthesius' Das englische Haus in 1904.[133] The suggestion of Fachwerk, the German equivalent of English half-timber construction, on both of Paul's models certainly suggested the influence of Das englische Haus, while the horizontal bands of windows, low eaves, and chimney pots of the small country house recalled the contemporary work of Voysey and his followers. Details of Paul's models also echoed the characteristic rural houses of the Oberlausitz, the »Umgebindehäuser« that he had known as a child. Yet despite such concurrences, Paul's designs were uniquely his own.

Paul's model for a house with studio offers a significant insight into his development as an architect. The house was to be ornamented with a series of panels containing elongated lozenges defined by inward-curving arc segments. Paul employed this same motif in his designs for the »3. Deutsche Kunstgewerbe-Ausstellung« (third German applied arts exhibition) where it occurred, in various forms, in art glass panels, lighting fixtures, mirror frames, a decorative frieze, and various pieces of furniture.[134] Considering the time required for the Vereinigte Werkstätten to

execute Paul's contributions to the Dresden exhibition, it is likely that he was designing them in parallel with the preparation of his model houses. At the time he was clearly interested in a formal vocabulary that he employed, with equal facility, in a variety of artistic media. This practice again recalls the ideal of the Gesamtkunstwerk, the artistic synthesis characteristic of the Jugendstil that was a central theme in Paul's early work as an applied artist.

Paul's first published architectural project was even more closely related to his interior designs than his apparently unexecuted series of artist's houses. In 1906, he received a commission to decorate the stark façades of the Munich barracks of the heavy cavalry regiment »Prinz Karl von Bayern«, the Schwere-Reiter-Kaserne, for a visit by Kaiser Wilhelm II. Paul adapted another of the motifs he had employed in Dresden, that of an orthogonal grid interrupted by a single lozenge as a focal element, in the wooden architectural ornaments that he conceived for the barracks. The effect of his ornaments, installed like pilasters against the smooth façade of the existing building and adorned with ribbons and garlands, was soberly festive, monumental, and classical.[135]

When Wilhelm II arrived in Munich on 12 November, he found Paul's decorations very much to his liking. According to Paul's recollection, the Kaiser halted his motorcade as it passed the barracks and personally commended the designer.[136] Despite the satires on the official taste of the Hohenzollern monarchy that regularly appeared in the pages of Simplicissimus, the Kaiser himself maintained an educated interest in architecture.[137] His admiration for Paul's work illustrates the extent to which the artist had engaged the aesthetic sensibilities of mainstream culture. Notwithstanding the inherent irony of the meeting between the autocratic sovereign and the Simplicissimus illustrator, Paul's brief reception by Wilhelm II in 1906 facilitated his appointment to a professorship in Berlin the following year.

A new direction

By 1906, Bruno Paul had emerged as one of the most prominent modern artists in Central Europe. His fame had been established through his illustrations for Simplicissimus, published over the span of a decade. The vibrant cultural milieu of turn-of-the-century Munich that had provided Simplicissimus with its creative vitality inspired Paul to explore the limits of his own artistic abilities. He continued to draw and paint, but also designed metalwork, furniture, textiles, and entire interiors for the Vereinigte Werkstätten für Kunst im Handwerk for which he received international acclaim. As an applied artist, Paul contributed to the definitive character of the Jugendstil, and then to its transcendence. In 1906 his work was increasingly cited as a harbinger of a new direction in German design. Paul's designs for furniture and interiors ultimately led him to architecture, a discipline in which all of his interests could be conjoined. His first executed commissions demonstrated his natural talent for design on an architectural scale.

Despite his splendid accomplishments, Paul had never realized the objective that had brought him to Munich as a student. He had not become one of the »Malerfürsten« of the city, and it was obvious that he never would. Characteristically, he confronted this realization by seeking a new challenge towards which to apply his restless intellect. Paul was ready to leave Munich when an opportunity arose in 1906.

3. The reconquest of a harmonious culture: 1906–1912

Two events of lasting importance to Bruno Paul's professional career occurred within a single year: his appointment to direct the Unterrichtsanstalt of the Kunstgewerbe-Museum in Berlin and his participation in the establishment of the German Werkbund. Both evoked a common theme: the ideal of a harmonious culture embodied in the reconciliation of artistic principles with the production of the artifacts of daily life. Paul related this ideal of cultural harmony to the precedents of Biedermeier Neoclassicism. In the period following his appointment to the Berlin school of applied arts, he developed a design vocabulary in his buildings and interiors that recalled the simple elegance of the middle-class aesthetic of the last years of the eighteenth century. For Paul, this aesthetic represented more than formal language; it embodied the reform of the applied arts in Germany and the re-establishment of the more equitable relationship between patrons, artists, and craftsmen that had existed prior to the industrialization of the nineteenth century.

Paul sought to renew this relationship in Berlin through his reform of the curriculum of the school of applied arts, as well as in his designs for furniture and interiors. After his move to Berlin, he also established an independent architectural practice. His work as an architect, which largely consisted of prestigious residential and commercial projects, extended the aesthetic program of his furnishings to the scale of entire buildings. Nikolaus Pevsner, in his seminal 1936 book *Pioneers of the Modern Movement from William Morris to Walter Gropius*, concluded that Paul's aesthetic program was able to »effect a change of taste throughout the county, which Gropius, the most uncompromising German innovator, might not have been able to bring about«, and praised the »comfort, cleanliness and abolition of tawdry fuss« characteristic of Paul's work.[138] This work reflected a significant direction in the history of progressive design in Central Europe, that of a pragmatic Modernism attuned to the needs and desires of the middle classes. It was this Modernism that sustained the often-fractious German Werkbund in the years prior to the War, and which played a central role in shaping its ideological positions.

Paul's appointment to the Berlin school of applied arts

On 7 December 1906, the Prussian government appointed Bruno Paul to head the school of applied arts in Berlin, officially the Unterrichtsanstalt des königlichen Kunstgewerbe-Museums (educational institution of the royal museum of applied arts).[139] At the time, the museum was located in the 1881 building later known as the Martin-Gropius-Bau, an elegant structure in the style of Schinkel's celebrated Bauakademie,[140] and a Historicist extension to the west, the Museum für Völkerkunde (museum of ethnology). The school of applied arts was east of the museum, in a Neo-Baroque building overlooking the gardens of the Prinz-Albrecht-Palais.[141] It had not had a permanent director since December 1904, when Professor Ernst Ewald died in office following a protracted illness that had long deprived the school of effective leadership. Although Paul was chosen as an artist rather than an administrator, he began to reform the curriculum of the school as soon as he accepted the office of director – transforming the institution into one of the most emulated and admired schools of art in Central Europe. A brief notice in the journal *Kunst und Handwerk* commemorated the transition in his career: »Bruno Paul was appointed the director of the royal school of applied arts in Berlin; thus bringing to conclusion an affair that has excited general interest in many quarters. The director's post having been vacant for approximately two years, the successor to this preeminently responsible position has been an open question, colored by abundant rumors concerning the likely contenders; Bruno Paul's appointment has garnered universal admiration, even if the loss of such an outstanding artist is painful for Munich. Paul may prove as successful a director of the Berlin school as he is an artist.«[142] In fact, Paul's success in Berlin would soon eclipse his achievements in Munich.

Paul's opportunity to reform the school of applied art originated with two of the most significant artistic advisors to the government of Kaiser Wilhelm II: Hermann Muthesius and Wilhelm Bode.[143] In 1904, Muthesius had been appointed a »Geheimrat« (privy councilor) in the Prussian government upon the completion of an eight-year attachment to the German Embassy in London. Muthesius originally went to London to study the principles of design and design education that had facilitated the global success of British industry and commerce. As a privy councilor, he was responsible for reorganizing schools of art throughout the state of Prussia, and he responded to this charge by appointing prominent and successful artists to positions of leadership. Within a year of his return to Berlin he had already appointed the architect Hans Poelzig to direct the school of applied arts in Breslau, and Paul's Munich colleague Peter Behrens to lead the school in Düsseldorf.

Wilhelm Bode was the director of the Prussian state museums, including the museum to which the Berlin school of applied arts was attached. In 1906 he attended the »3. Deutsche Kunstgewerbe-Ausstellung« specifically to seek a candidate to succeed the late director, Ernst Ewald. He later recorded that upon examining the exhibits he selected Paul, who had »cast off the bad habits of the Jugendstil« in favor of a compelling and personal interpretation of historical precedents. By 1906 the vocabulary of Art Nouveau had already lost its aura of contemporaneity.[144] Nevertheless Bode recalled his apprehension upon approaching Wilhelm II with his recommendation that a member of the staff of *Simplicissimus* receive a royal appointment. Indeed, the Kaiser himself had studied at the school of applied arts as a boy,[145] and had been personally tutored by Ewald. Moreover the school had enjoyed the particular patronage of his mother Victoria, who had been Kaiserin of Germany for ninety-nine days in 1888 prior to the premature death of her husband, Kaiser Friedrich III. However, Wilhelm's autocratic personality inadvertently ensured Paul's success. »I know nothing of *Simplicissimus* and care to learn nothing of your candidate«, the Emperor proclaimed, declaring that he would act on the strength of Bode's recommendation.[146] As a consequence, Paul relinquished his position on the staff of *Simplicissimus*, published his final illustrations under the pseudonym Ernst Kellermann, and entered the service of the Prussian government. Nevertheless his appointment was the subject of considerable comment, epitomized by a verse from a poem penned by the critic Alfred Kerr: »Bruno Paul caused quite a fuss / Drew for *Simplicissimus* / Yesterday a malefactor / Now applied-arts school director / Anton Werner ›The state's disgrace!‹ / (A change of pace – a change of pace!)«.[147]

Prior to Paul's appointment, the school of applied arts in Berlin provided conventional instruction in the minor arts, offering classes in architectural drawing, sculpture, metalwork, painting, and graphic design. In addition, the faculty operated educational workshops to teach engraving, printing, enameling, woodcarving, decorative painting, and embroidery, as well as offering evening classes for the training of apprentices. The curriculum reflected the needs of nineteenth-century industry, a situation that Pevsner decried for the reactionary spirit and emphasis on historic ornament emphasized in the education of its students.[148] But Paul was not inclined to maintain the status quo. He moved his family to Berlin in early 1907, and assumed his office with clear ideas for the reform of the school of applied arts, aspirations derived from his personal experiences in Dresden and Munich.

As director, Paul promoted revisions to the curricula for the training of craftsmen, de-emphasizing classroom study in favor of increased training in the school's workshops or the private practices of its professors. He expressed the belief that this change would result in the education of craftsmen better suited to the needs of modern industry.[149] He also addressed the difficult question of the education of women at the school, which accommodated a large number of female students who were nevertheless excluded from the advanced courses that would have prepared them for professional employment. Paul began by denouncing the mass acceptance of female students, proclaiming that the school should only accept those who demonstrated genuine artistic ability and could hope to pursue independent careers.[150] His own daughter Hilde, who was seven years old when he moved to Berlin, would later benefit from his willingness to train capable young women. Indeed, his policies would eventually lead to the admittance of women to all of the school's programs, and to an essential parity between the opportunities available to male and female students. This parity was encouraged by Paul's imposition of more selective admission criteria for both male and female applicants to the school. He strongly believed that practical experience and natural ability were essential prerequisites to an education in the applied arts.

In 1907, Paul stated that »A practical training in commercial operations is the precondition of every healthy school of applied arts. Each pupil should know the techniques and materials of a trade before he enters the school.«[151] He did not, however, believe that any given student should be proficient in a specific trade, rather that each should have a basis of practical experience on which to build. This conviction originated in his own career as an artist, as well as in the Jugendstil ideal of artistic synthesis.

Paul's students began their studies in the Vorschule (introductory curriculum) that preceded admittance to one of the Fachklassen (subject courses) in an individual discipline. The introductory curriculum was organized into four classes, one each for architecture, sculpture, painting, and graphic and commercial art. Paul reorganized the Vorschule so that all of the four courses were taught concurrently. This schedule allowed all students in the introductory curriculum, regardless of their intended vocation, to work together and to learn from one another. In 1907, Paul expressed his belief in the shared experience of sculptors, furniture designers, graphic artists, decorative painters, commercial draftsmen, and engravers, thereby establishing the fundamental principle of his reforms.[152]

Along with his obligations as director of the school of applied arts, Paul assumed responsibility for teaching one of the advanced courses for architecture, Fachklasse 1c. The advanced classes at the school were organized around the professional activities of their instructors, and students worked on the private commissions received by their professors. Paul praised this arrangement soon after his arrival in Berlin, noting that the students in the advanced classes and the workshops had the opportunity to gain practical experience working on actual projects under the guidance of their teachers.[153]

In addition to his Fachklasse, Paul established an independent architectural practice in Berlin. His private office was very much an adjunct to his studio at the school of applied arts, which was staffed with eager if inexperienced students working without monetary compensation. The rate of turnover among his paid staff was relatively high, with staffing levels fluctuating in response to the volume of work being produced. A similar condition existed at Behrens' Berlin office, though he did not have the advantage of unpaid student assistants after leaving his academic position in Düsseldorf in 1907 to become the artistic advisor to AEG. Several well-known architects of the second generation of European Modernists worked for both Paul and Behrens in Berlin. The best known is Ludwig Mies, who worked briefly for Paul during 1907. In addition, Paul Thiersch, appointed to be Paul's assistant in 1907, had previously worked for Behrens in Düsseldorf. After Thiersch opened his own office in 1909, Paul hired Adolf Meyer, another former Behrens employee. He also retained Thiersch to lecture at the school of applied arts, exemplifying the close relationship between his private practice and his official position as director of the school.

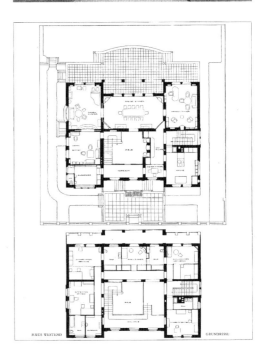

The first architectural works of Paul's Berlin practice

Paul's first architectural project in Berlin was Haus Westend, built in the fashionable district of Charlottenburg in 1908 for Hans Schuppman, one of the directors of the Vereinigte Werkstätten. Paul designed the house during 1907, soon after his arrival in the capital. The project exemplified his confidence and natural ability as an architect, although the building was closely related to his furniture and interiors. Schuppman intended his house to be an advertisement for the Werkstätten, a demonstration of the full range of services offered by the firm. Paul responded with a design derived, like his contemporary furnishings, from Biedermeier models. Yet Haus Westend was not a Historicist building. Paul reduced the formal vocabulary of the late eighteenth century to its essential characteristics: simplicity, consistency, and formal discipline. These timeless qualities were antithetical to the decorative exuberance of the Jugendstil. In forsaking the restless ornament of the turn of the century, Paul abandoned the pursuit of a synthetic modern style. Instead he developed a language of typical and normative forms, derived from a dateless Classicism. In so doing, he created a modern architecture of flexibility, functional efficiency, and proportional elegance.

Haus Westend is notable for its incorporation of architectural characteristics that would be present in Paul's work throughout his long career. The public façade of the house, the elevation facing Kaiserstraße,[154] reflected an elegant, disciplined formal vocabulary immediately reminiscent of the middle-class architecture of the first quarter of the nineteenth century. The simple forms of the façade, rendered in pebble roughcast and articulated with classically-proportioned casement windows without shutters, a row of attic dormers, and a single concession to Empire grandeur in the stone embrasure of the centrally-located door, recalled such well-known monuments of German classical design as Goethe's house on the Frauenplan in Weimar.[155] The garden façade displayed a looser interpretation of the tradition of German Classicism. The portico facing the garden featured a complex stepped roof with undulating ridgelines, a charismatic expression of the innovation that Paul derived from the vocabulary of Biedermeier Classicism.

Haus Westend differed most significantly from its early-nineteenth-century precedents in its plan, which was that of a modern middle-class house with integrated sanitary and service facilities in place of the detached kitchen and servants' quarters and absent indoor plumbing of the prosperous homes of the preceding century. The incorporation of contemporary amenities posed a significant design challenge in that the smaller symmetrical house plans of the age of Schinkel, exemplified by such iconic buildings as the pavilion at Charlottenburg palace, made no accommodation for kitchens, toilets or baths. At Haus Westend, Paul located such auxiliary functions

behind the street façade, where tall windows illuminated some of the smallest rooms in the house. The principal interior spaces, the central dining room and flanking Herrenzimmer and Damenzimmer (study and drawing room) on the main floor and the owners' bedrooms on the floor above, all adjoined the more secluded garden front of the house. The ordered composition of the main façade reflected the differing functions accommodated by the plan. Thus the two front windows in the kitchen were paired with three smaller windows in the slightly projecting bay of the garderobe in the opposite wing of the house. The ordering of the façade was sufficiently strong to balance the asymmetrical configuration of the windows, which adds a dynamic element to what would otherwise have been a distinctly severe elevation.

Paul's plans for Haus Westend embodied a response to the aspirations of many successful Berliners of the first decade of the twentieth century. The design was comfortable and convenient, luxurious without being pretentious, and elegant without being immodest. The house was well built, and exquisitely tasteful. Although Haus Westend was Paul's first significant architectural commission,[156] it was confidently and masterfully conceived. Amidst the eclectic historicist and Jugendstil villas that fronted Kaiserstraße in Charlottenburg, he built a modern suburban house that reflected the ideal of harmonious culture embodied by his furniture and interiors. In so doing, Paul established himself as a favored architect of Berlin society.

Paul created a new and versatile typology with his design for Haus Westend, a stylistic vocabulary that was applicable to domestic projects of widely divergent function and scale. In 1909, for example, he designed a country house north of Berlin for the banker Paul von Mendelssohn-Bartholdy: Schloß Börnicke. While significantly larger and more complex than Haus Westend, Schloß Börnicke incorporated the same formal conventions as the earlier house. Again Paul subverted strict bilateral symmetry to the functional efficiency of his plan. As a consequence, the elevations of the house exhibited an inherent tension between the order suggested by the formal vocabulary of German Neoclassicism, and Paul's informal and domestic distribution of architectural elements. He achieved a similar balance in his integration of the new Schloß into the parks and gardens of its predecessor. »Bruno Paul's artistic ability to bind architecture and nature into a unified composition is exemplified by this rebuilding«, his assistant Joseph Popp later wrote, »whatever was dull or uninteresting was improved, the best of the old work was preserved and organically incorporated into the new.«[157] In the house itself he successfully combined the functional flexibility of the English free style, popularized in Central Europe with the publication of Muthesius' *Das englische Haus*, with a quiet, classical dignity. Schloß Börnicke was an ideal home for an enlightened member of the aristocracy. It was also an emphatically modern house, commissioned in part to display Mendelssohn-Bartholdy's collection of contemporary paintings. Van Gogh's celebrated 1889 still life *Vase with Fourteen Sunflowers* hung in the hall of Paul's Schloß Börnicke, in a niche with a sofa, table and side chairs that he designed to accompany it. Yet Paul's work was by no means limited to the social stratum of the Mendelssohn-Bartholdys.

At the same time that Paul was working on Schloß Börnicke, he designed a much smaller house in Berlin for the prominent Social Democratic politician Dr. Heinrich Braun. Epitomizing the fluency that Paul had achieved as a residential designer, Haus Braun was a simple, practical building, elegantly proportioned and skillfully detailed. The house combined a cool precision reminiscent of Schinkel with a functional efficiency derived from the vernacular tradition of domestic design. The balance that Paul achieved between seemingly contradictory influences had a profound influence on his students, among whom was the young Ludwig Mies. Mies' first executed project, the Villa Riehl, was a direct counterpart to Haus Braun, and borrowed freely from Paul's practice. Despite its many naïve characteristics, Villa Riehl prefigured Mies' mature work in its abstracted classicism, pure geometries, and dynamic symmetry – all features he derived from Paul. As well as providing inspiration to his students, projects such as Haus Braun contributed to the ubiquity of the Neoclassical villa as a suburban housing type in pre-war Berlin.

The significance of Haus Braun, and indeed its particular influence on Mies, lay in the rationale that underscored its composition. As an architect Paul was, effectively, an autodidact. He was not immersed in the classical tradition as a student: as a successful designer he deliberately chose this vocabulary for his architectural projects. Moreover he specifically selected the Classicism of the eighteenth century, rather than the antique classicism which he knew well from his time at the Munich academy,[158] and which paralleled the language of his own work as an illustrator. Eighteenth-century Neoclassicism provided Paul with a model solution to problems similar to those that beset architectural practice in the first decade of the twentieth century, namely the imposition of order and clarity upon changes wrought by the introduction of new materials and techniques, unprecedented functional requirements, and unfamiliar societal demands. This model offered a response to modern problems, and held the promise of a correspondingly modern architecture. Paul was certainly not alone in turning to the precedent of eighteenth-century Classicism for the development of a modern vocabulary of design. This was the cause advocated by Paul Mebes' influential book *Um 1800: Architektur und Handwerk im letzten Jahrhundert ihrer traditionellen Entwicklung* (around 1800: architecture and craftsmanship in the final century of their traditional development), which was published in 1908. However Paul, who was studying eighteenth-century prototypes long before the introduction of Mebes' book, proved particularly successful accomplishing the transformation of such precedents. Haus Braun clearly indicated the path of these transformations.

In addition to designing residential projects, Paul also established himself as a commercial architect. In 1910 he designed a façade and interiors for an office building planned by the architect Kurt Berndt for 36 Unter den Linden, the celebrated avenue leading from the Brandenburg Gate to the Berlin Schloß. Paul's façade for the building, the Zollernhof, was immediately evocative of the formal vocabulary of Haus Westend, with attenuated, severely molded bands of masonry on-

Villenkolonie Zehlendorf - Kl.-Machnow

Landhaus Braun
Architekt: Prof. Bruno Paul

ly suggesting the proportions of a classical order. The Zollernhof diverged from the precedent of Paul's earlier domestic projects in the sculptural embellishment of the façade. Heroic nude figures, carved from the same stone as the ashlar veneer, stood between the paired windows of the tall attic. A band of heavy swags set beneath shells and rosettes, realistically carved with unblemished fruit, crowned the shop windows opening onto the street. By the standards of Wilhelmine Berlin, the sculptural program of the Zollernhof was modest; it was not, however, an element of Paul's original project. He added the sculpture at the instigation of the Kaiser, who believed that the severity of the initial design was unworthy of Unter den Linden. In fact, Paul provided a retouched and simplified photograph of the Zollernhof for inclusion in Joseph Popp's weighty monograph *Bruno Paul* of 1916. The original photograph, showing the additional sculptural embellishment of the actual building, was later published in Gustav Adolf Platz's seminal *Die Baukunst der neuesten Zeit* of 1927,[159] the first thorough compendium of Modernist architecture in Germany. Paul had embellished his original design at the same time that Adolf Loos was obliged to revise the elevations of his office building for Goldman & Salatsch on the Michaelerplatz in Vienna (which, incidentally, also appeared in *Die Baukunst der neuesten Zeit*), and in response to a similar imperial objection.[160] Neither architect was pleased to have done so. Nevertheless in a 1913 article in *Deutsche Kunst und Dekoration*, Paul stated of the Zollernhof: »It is instinctive, from nowhere, in the shadow of Messel.«[161] This deference to Alfred Messel, designer of the Wertheim department store and the foremost commercial architect in contemporary Berlin, is typical of Paul's self-effacing assessments of his own work. The sharply delineated stereotomy of the Zollernhof was considerably more abstract than Messel's buildings, notwithstanding the recollection of Biedermeier domesticity in the eyebrow dormers of its steeply pitched tile roof. If Paul believed himself overshadowed by Messel, he was nevertheless responsible for introducing a new rationalism to the architecture of central Berlin.

At the same time Paul was designing the Zollernhof, he was also preparing drawings for a palatial house commissioned by Adolf Gans for Königstein im Taunus, a small country town in the mountains north of Frankfurt. Haus Hainerberg, as the building was named, provided a compelling demonstration of the flexibility of Paul's architectural vocabulary. Haus Hainerberg itself was conceived as a grand country house, and might have been mistaken for an eighteenth-century Schloß but for the distinct clarity and abstraction of individual architectural elements and the tension between order and asymmetry typical of Paul's work.[162] The project included the design of a complex of service buildings at the edge of the property, including stables, storage, and accommodations for staff. At Haus Hainerberg Paul employed the same architectural vocabulary in his humblest and grandest residential designs, without compromising the propriety of either. The complex of buildings that he designed in Königstein embodied the ideals of modest wealth and noble labor, an equitable relationship between social classes, and a harmonious German culture.

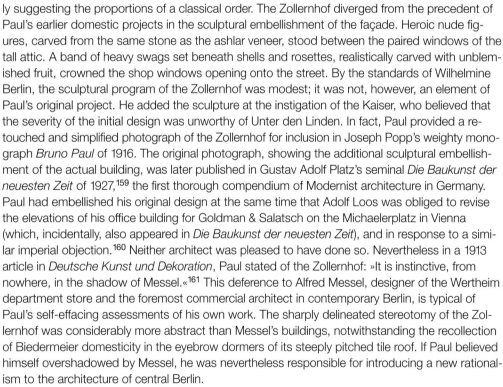

By the eve of the First World War, Paul's aesthetic sensibilities had made him a profoundly successful architect. He had established himself as a favorite of Berlin society, and designed a number of large and costly houses in the capital. Among his most important clients during this period was Paul von Mendelssohn-Bartholdy, for whom he designed a large house in the Berlin suburb of Wannsee as well as an office building for the Mendelssohn-Bartholdy Bank on Jäger-straße in central Berlin. Paul also designed houses in Wiesbaden, Cologne, and Duisburg, establishing a reputation in the Rheinland that would eventually lead him to establish an office in Cologne, directed by Franz Weber. His commercial projects prior to the First World War included the Heilanstalt Pützchen, a sanatorium built in the suburbs of Bonn in 1911, but which closed after Germany's defeat of 1918. However Paul's plan, which reflected his interest in the relationship of architecture and landscape, survived the reconstruction of the former Heilanstalt in 1925,[163] and, indeed, is preserved in the configuration of the Sankt-Adelheid-Gymnasium which presently occupies its site. In 1912 Paul designed the Nellinistift of the Rose-Livingston-Stiftung in Frankfurt, a home for elderly women dedicated the following year. Such projects, published in contemporary journals, constitute the recognized body of Paul's works from this period prior to 1914. Yet the few surviving records from Paul's classes at the school of applied arts indicate that his published works represent a mere fraction of the total number of projects for which he was commissioned. [164]

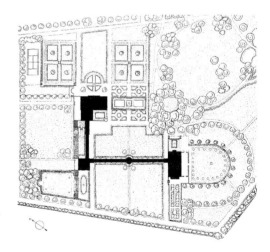

In addition to his private projects, Paul received prestigious commissions from the imperial government – although he never received the favor of the Kaiser himself. His best-known building from the era prior to the First World War was such an official project, the Völkerkunde-Museum (later the Asiatisches Museum) in Dahlem. Wilhelm von Bode described the project in the 1915 *Jahrbuch der preußischen Kunstsammlungen* (yearbook of the Prussian art collections). »For the style of the building«, Bode wrote, »a connection with the monumental eighteenth century estates of Brandenburg was desired; not only for the sake of tradition or out of consideration for the proximity of Potsdam, the most beautiful townscape in Prussia, but also because of the way in which the individual buildings of a large estate relate to one another.« He continued by recounting his desire that the museum building should be as simple and practical as possible. »Paul's plan met this requirement«, he concluded, as »both the overall plan and the individual buildings made the desired association with Prussian buildings of the second half of the eighteenth century, and presented a tasteful solution that met the desires of the departmental curators of the Asiatic museum.«[165] In spite of Bode's description of the stylistic program for the new museum, Paul's design was clearly developed from the precedent of Haus Hainerberg. The war delayed construction of the museum, however, and when it was finally completed in 1921, it was the last and grandest of Paul's architectural expressions of the »zweites Biedermeier«, the reinterpretation of the simple, practical aesthetic of German Classicism that he had been instrumental in promoting as a style for the new century.

54. Heilanstalt Pützchen, Bonn, 1912.
55. Heilanstalt Pützchen, Bonn, 1912. Condition in 1925, following the construction of the main building of the Sankt-Adelheid-Gymnasium on the site of Paul's colonnade.
56. Heilanstalt Pützchen, Bonn, 1912. Plan.
57. Asiatic Museum, Berlin-Dahlem, 1921.
58. Rose-Livingston-Stiftung, Frankfurt, 1913.

Paul and the Werkbund

Paul's move to Berlin in 1907 coincided with the events that predicated the founding of the Deutscher Werkbund. Although the Werkbund was formally established in Munich on 5 October, 1907, its origins can be traced to the »3. Deutsche Kunstgewerbe-Ausstellung« in Dresden, which was organized by the architect Fritz Schumacher on behalf of the government of King Friedrich August of Saxony. Schumacher's selection process for the exhibition favored the works of individual artists over the production of established firms working in the historical styles. Condemning the notion of the applied arts as a business, he organized an exhibition that celebrated the applied arts as art.[166] In early 1907 Muthesius followed the Dresden exhibition with a series of lectures at the Berlin Handelshochschule (business college), where he had been appointed to a professorship. In his inaugural lecture, he denounced the same firms that had been slighted by Schumacher's selection process the year before. The subsequent publication of Muthesius' lecture produced the storm of controversy that he had desired. The June 1907 annual meeting of the Fachverband für die wirtschaftlichen Interessen des Kunstgewerbes (association for the economic interests of the applied art industries) precipitated a direct confrontation between the supporters and opponents of Muthesius. This confrontation resulted in the resignation of the progressive faction within the Fachverband, and prompted the establishment of the Werkbund four months later.[167]

The original membership of the Werkbund consisted of twelve prominent artists and twelve applied art firms. Paul was one of the twelve artists, as were Peter Behrens, Theodor Fischer, Josef Hoffmann, Wilhelm Kreis, Max Läuger, Adalbert Niemeyer, Joseph Maria Olbrich, Richard Riemerschmid, J. J. Scharvogel, Paul Schultze-Naumburg, and Fritz Schumacher. The firms included the Vereinigte Werkstätten, the Deutsche Werkstätten of Dresden, and the Wiener Werkstätte.[168] At the ceremonial foundation of the Werkbund in Munich, Schumacher proclaimed the principal objective of both the new organization and the German nation as a whole to be »the reconquest of a harmonious culture« (die Wiedereroberung einer harmonischer Kultur).[169] This objective mirrored the Gesamtkunstwerk of modern life developed in fin-de-siècle Munich, and the majority of the original members belonged to the Munich Sezession, or to its successors in Vienna and Berlin.[170] Consequently the Werkbund was an extension of a culture that Paul had helped to define, and its ideology reiterated his own program of reform. Indeed, he served on the executive committee of the Werkbund in the years prior to the First World War, and exerted considerable influence over the development of its policies.

The twelve founding corporate members of the Werkbund demonstrated the pragmatic objectives of the organization, described by Ludwig Deubner as »the co-operation of art, industry and handicraft by means of education, propaganda, and concerted action«.[171] Muthesius was the most committed sponsor of the alliance between the association and commercial enterprise. When he returned to Berlin in 1904, he brought with him the conviction that German standards of design compared unfavorably to those of Great Britain, and that fundamental reforms to the practices of German industry and the German educational system would be required before the country could compete effectively in the international market. The Werkbund became the primary focus of his efforts to elevate the standing of German design. In 1908 Paul designed a new line of standardized furniture for the Vereinigte Werkstätten, the Typenmöbel, that expressed his commitment to the Werkbund and its ideals.

Typenmöbel

The Vereinigte Werkstätten introduced Paul's Typenmöbel in 1908. Although Typenmöbel literally means type-furniture or typical furniture, the term »standardized furniture« may be closer to the intent of the name, insofar as the concept of a standard simultaneously implies both exemplary and normative status. The Typenmöbel was a range of mass-produced furniture, as well designed as the individual pieces that Paul conceived for private commissions, yet intended to be readily affordable. Paul intended his Typenmöbel to be versatile and flexible in its use, so that any number of different groupings could be composed from the various pieces produced. In 1936, Pevsner described Paul's Typenmöbel in terms of a foreign industrial precedent, stating that »the idea came from America, where it had been in use for some time for bookcases«.[172] Although there are obvious similarities between the commercial production of shelving in standardized sizes and the uniform proportional and dimensional system maintained throughout the Typenmöbel range, Paul's furniture represented something far more significant than a European adaptation of American industrial practices. As the first Typenmöbel catalog proclaimed, the furniture was intended to establish an alternative to the »stylistic confusion of the last forty years: the frivolity of Renaissance, Gothic, Baroque, Empire, Rococo, Egyptian-Hellenic-Assyrian-Style, Louis XVI and Jugendstil«.[173] The Typenmöbel was conceived in »simple, standardized forms that could be adapted to differing tastes and differing floor plans«. The individual pieces were not »resplendent with superfluous decoration«, but designed with »solid forms and equally solid workmanship«.[174] In short, the Typenmöbel represented a new way to furnish a middle-class German home.

The first Typenmöbel catalog, published in 1908, emphasized the modernity of the designs. Paul himself conceived the cover for the catalog, including the Vereinigte Werkstätten trademark he designed and registered the same year. The bold geometries, simple coloration, and innovative alphabet that he employed in the cover epitomized avant-garde graphic design. The catalog illustrations were simpler still. They consisted of photographs with laconic captions, arranged objectively on the individual pages. The borders, printed in pale green, provided a spare elegance. Paul's catalog embodied the union of the fine and applied arts that was central to his program of reform, and provided a perfect counterpart to the furniture that it illustrated.

Paul's Typenmöbel included all of the pieces necessary to complete a living room, dining room, bedroom, nursery, or study with a matched set of coordinated furnishings. The line incorporated a remarkable number of elements, ninety-nine individual pieces upon its introduction: beds, sofas, bookcases, and desks in a range of sizes, as well as chairs, dressers, a buffet, a variety of tables, and even a long case clock. Typenmöbel could be purchased in several finishes, including varnished walnut, mahogany, oak, and lacquered spruce. All of the pieces were produced in accordance with a consistent aesthetic program and, in the larger elements such as the bookcases and shelving, to a modular system of dimensions. As a result, pieces with the same finish could be combined to create an effectively unlimited number of harmonious ensembles. Indeed, as the photographs in the 1908 Typenmöbel catalog demonstrated, it was possible to tastefully furnish a house entirely with Paul's standardized furniture.

Paul's Typenmöbel was intended to be simple, practical, and inexpensive. Nevertheless it could not be classified as »Arbeitermöbel«, or furniture for the working classes: Typenmöbel was furniture for a middle-class home.[175] The Typenmöbel dining room illustrated in *Dekorative Kunst* in 1908 consisted of a square table, two armchairs, two side chairs, a buffet, and a credenza. In the period prior to the First World War, when the average income of a working class German family was between 900 and 3000 Marks, a Typenmöbel dining room in stained oak cost 969 Marks.[176] Typenmöbel was not merely too expensive for most working class homes, it was also designed for a different social environment. For example, the elements of the Typenmöbel dining room suite paralleled those of the most exclusive groupings produced by the Vereinigte Werk-

59. Typenmöbel catalog, circa 1908.
60. Typenmöbel catalog, circa 1908. Cover. Paul also designed the company logo for the Vereinigte Werkstätten.
61. Typenmöbel dining room, 1908.
62. Dining room in Paul's residence, Berlin, 1907. An interior of the apartment on Grolmanstraße in Charlottenburg. Just visible at the left of the image is the frame of one of a number of Japanese prints that Paul hung in his dining room.

stätten, including the dining room exhibited by Paul at the »3. Deutsche Kunstgewerbe-Ausstellung« of 1906. Such rooms reflected social rituals that did not occur in the average working class apartment or rural home of 1908. When Paul designed a suite of »Arbeitermöbel« in 1906, he included furnishings for a combined living, working, and dining room in deference to the modest standard of living typical of the Wilhelmine working classes. In contrast, the Typenmöbel dining room suite resembled the furnishing of his own dining room in Berlin, the dining room of a prominent royal professor.

Paul conceived his Typenmöbel as simplified versions of the expensive handmade suites of furniture that he was designing for the Vereinigte Werkstätten. Nevertheless the serially-produced Typenmöbel represented a viable option for the furnishing of a typical middle-class home, and as such reflected a new and important development in European interior design. Paul's Typenmöbel marked the first occasion on which progressive design was successfully promoted, on the scale of mass production, to middle-class customers.[177] The role of the middle classes in supporting modern design, and of commercial interests in fostering this support, was growing in the years prior to 1908. In 1902, and again in 1905, the Wertheim department store in Berlin staged significant exhibitions of modern interior design to widespread public interest.[178] The Typenmöbel could be distinguished from the artist-designed interiors displayed at Wertheim in 1905, or in Dresden the following year, by its relative neutrality. Although the Typenmöbel was radical in its simplicity, its transformation of classical forms, and its modes of production and distribution, it was also elegantly restrained. The furniture that Riemerschmid and Pankok designed in the first decade of the twentieth century still manifested the lingering Jugendstil ideal of the Gesamtkunstwerk.[179] Their compositions suggested that any element of disharmony in the attire, the demeanor, or the possessions of the household would compromise the integrity of the whole. Significantly, Paul never designed a Typenmöbel room as such, only rational, practical, and flexible suites of furniture that would have to be combined with fabrics and accessories from other sources.[180]

Paul developed the Typenmöbel in parallel with his work as an architect and designer. His interiors for the doctors' and patients' rooms at the Heilanstalt Pützchen were furnished with Typenmöbel, and he did not hesitate to utilize pieces of his standardized furniture for commissions that were otherwise completed with custom designs.[181] Moreover, Paul utilized aesthetic motifs from the Typenmöbel in his architectural commissions. The service buildings at Haus Hainerberg incorporated the ornamental lozenges of the Typenmöbel buffet, as well as the fundamentally modular composition of his standardized furniture. Although Paul did not promote his service buildings as standardized houses (Typenhäuser), they were certainly not far removed from such a description. Like the Typenmöbel, they belonged to the Werkbund ideal of harmonious culture.

Reforming the artifacts of daily life

In 1909, Paul completed the interiors of the Villa Feinhals in Cologne, a project begun by Olbrich in 1908. Had Olbrich lived, he would have designed the interiors of the house himself, but he died prematurely while his drawings were still incomplete and the house was under construction. The client, Joseph Feinhals, selected Paul to complete the work. Feinhals owned the company that made Manoli cigarettes, and was a prominent supporter of the Werkbund.[182] Paul was a personal friend, and one of the few artists considered capable of succeeding Olbrich.[183]

The interiors Paul conceived for Villa Feinhals reflected the harmonious culture embodied in typical forms, and included elements of Typenmöbel for the garden furnishings, as well as modular kitchen cupboards that were almost identical to the Typenmöbel buffets.[184] Paul's dining room for the Villa Feinhals included a table and chairs that were also closely related to items from the Vereinigte Werkstätten catalog, and to the simple dining room furniture installed in Haus Westend the previous year. Yet much of his furniture for Villa Feinhals did not conform to the ideal of standardization as emphatically as did the kitchen and dining room suites. The garden room furnishings especially demonstrated a more idiosyncratic approach. The furniture for this room consisted of individual designs, notwithstanding their subsequent listing in the Vereinigte Werkstätten catalog. The garden room chairs, Modell 12137, combined formal simplicity, refined detailing, and emphatic coloration. There was an inherent tension in their design, reflected in the juxtaposition of architectonic, fluted front legs with brass bases and capitals and zoomorphic rear legs with a subtle yet muscular curvature. The same apparent tension existed in the carved arms, which combined sweeping upper surfaces with straight vertical elements and an inward curving volute at the point of support. Such features clearly recalled the precedent of eighteenth-century English furniture such as that produced by Robert Gillow of Lancaster and his apprentice, George Hepplewhite. Nevertheless the Modell 12137 chairs bore approximately the same relationship to Georgian prototypes that the Typenmöbel chairs did to Biedermeier originals. In both instances Paul accepted an eighteenth-century model as the expression of a type that he subsequently developed in accordance with contemporary methods of production and with his own personal aesthetic program. Critics noted the references to eighteenth-century precedents in the completion of the Villa Feinhals, but credited Paul with creating a »modern environment for modern man« characterized by the calm and simple refinement of its design.[185]

Joseph Feinhals was one of a number of prominent capitalists who embraced Paul's understanding of the needs of the »modern man«. As early as 1905, Countess Ottilie von Faber-Castell, heir to the clebrated pencil company founded by A. W. Faber in 1761, hired Paul to execute a suite of rooms in the castle designed for her family by Theodor von Kramer in 1903. The successful execution of Paul's modern interiors within the Faber-Castells' otherwise historicist Schloß Stein

established significant precedents in his career, with respect both to the prestigious nature of the commission and to the endorsement of his aesthetic sensibilites that it entailed. In 1907, Paul received a commission from Baron Jan Viktor von Wendelstadt to design three rooms for Schloß Neubeuern, which was being rebuilt by Gabriel von Seidl. As he had for Schloß Stein, Paul completed a suite of rooms, and their furnishings, with simple geometric ornamentation typical of his contemporary work. Once again, his interiors were distinguished by their inherent modernity. In 1909, Paul designed a dining room for Robert Bosch, who had commissioned an Italianate villa in Stuttgart from the architects Carl Heim and Jakob Früh. Paul's interior for the Villa Bosch demonstrated the ascendancy, even among prominent circles of German society, of the practical modernity that he espoused.

In addition to prestigious interiors for private clients, Paul provided designs for a series of relatively modest commercial projects. These interiors, like the service buildings for Haus Hainerberg, demonstrated Paul's success in developing a vocabulary of form that could be applied across multiple social strata, a characteristic of cultural harmony. Several of his commercial interiors were published, including the Staege coffee sales room and the Café Kerkau, both furnished by the Vereinigte Werkstätten in Berlin in 1909. The two interiors displayed the influence of the Villa Feinhals, particularly in the patterns of multiple frames that were a favorite motif of Olbrich and the Viennese Secessionists, and which Paul adopted for his work in Cologne. The same pattern appeared in the plaster ceiling of the Café Kerkau, although the interior as a whole owed little to Vienna. Paul created an individual design that was praised for its »essential qualities, functional expression and material beauty«, qualities typical of his contemporary work.[186]

In spite of Paul's success as a designer of interiors, he continued his relentless stylistic experimentation rather than perpetuating proven and popular forms. In 1910 he designed a series of display rooms for the Vereinigte Werkstätten in Berlin, with furniture that displayed the same slender, refined aesthetic as the garden room furnishings for the Villa Feinhals. Georgian furnishings continued to provide Paul with the inspiration for a more refined development of the Biedermeier.[187] He touched on the process of his adaptation of historical models in a 1907 synopsis of his objectives for the school of applied arts. »By detailed study of exemplary works of art from significant moments in the history of craftsmanship«, he wrote, »a pupil ought to develop a sense for the logical handling and application of materials and for the beauty of form that arose during periods of artistic perfection.«[188] The process he described was certainly applicable to the furnishings displayed in 1910, which embodied the logic and grace of Georgian prototypes in wholly original compositions.

The furniture Paul derived from eighteenth-century English models retained the simplicity and refinement characteristic of all of his work. He was, as he noted in 1907, not interested in the style of historical precedents, but rather their embodiment of timeless principals of composition.

Accordingly, Paul simultaneously explored a spectrum of design vocabularies throughout his career, ranging from the severe and utilitarian to the delicate and ornate. The archives of the Vereinigte Werkstätten alone contain over 3,000 individual designs he produced between 1897 and 1928. He developed early proposals for starkly minimalist furniture, including a purist folding chair conceived in 1907. The dining room suite he designed for Haus Herxheimer in Frankfurt in 1911 included another remarkably prescient piece, the buffet listed in the catalogs of the Vereinigte Werkstätten as Modell 12314. Although the base of the buffet was assembled from solid mahogany, it was surmounted by a series of tubular metal stanchions, most likely brass, supporting sheets of plain float glass from unadorned corner brackets. This composition of metal and glass would still have been regarded as inherently modern a quarter century after its introduction, when these materials were once again of interest to the avant-garde. Yet Paul also produced extraordinarily late Jugendstil works, including a series of chandeliers with arms in the form of smiling serpents reminiscent of his *Unterwelt* cover of 1896. One such chandelier, designed for the living room of Haus Hainerberg in 1912, remained in Deutsche Werkstätten catalogs into the 1920s. Nevertheless, throughout his career the majority of his designs fell between the extremes of severity and exuberance.[189]

Interiors for Norddeutscher Lloyd

By 1906 Heinrich Wiegand, director of the Norddeutscher Lloyd (North German Lloyd) shipping company of Bremen, concluded that the interiors of his ocean liners should reflect the inherent modernity of the best contemporary decorative art. He considered a group of young artists, lead by Bruno Paul, Henri van de Velde, Peter Behrens, Otto Eckmann, and Richard Riemerschmid, to champion the renewal of both European art and European culture.[190] Of these artists, Wiegand selected Paul as the most suitable (geeignetsten) to assume responsibility for the interior design of the Norddeutscher Lloyd liners.[191] The position that Wiegand offered was both prestigious and lucrative, a great opportunity both for Paul and for the Kunstgewerbebewegung. However, his offer came too late, after Paul had accepted the still greater honor of leading the school of applied arts in Berlin.

Neverheless, Wiegand persisted in his desire to commission modern interiors for his ships. In 1906 he announced a contest for the design of first-class cabins for the new liner *Kronprinzessin Cecilie*. The winners included, unsurprisingly, both Paul and Riemerschmid, as well as Joseph Maria Olbrich. Paul's cabin, executed by the Vereinigte Werkstätten in a vocabulary reminiscent of his work for the »3. Deutsche Kunstgewerbe-Ausstellung«,[192] was a striking departure from the Neo-Baroque interiors characteristic of earlier Norddeutscher Lloyd vessels.[193] When he wrote the article »Passagierendampfer und ihre Einrichtungen« for the 1914 Werkbund yearbook, Paul

67. Display room for the Vereinigte Werkstätten, Berlin, 1910. Note the Japanese prints on the walls.
68. Haus Herxheimer, Frankfurt am Main, 1911. Dining room.
69. First class cabin for the Norddeutscher Lloyd liner *Kronprinzessin Cecile*, 1906.
70. Express steamers of the Norddeutscher Lloyd at Bremerhaven, circa 1910. In the left foreground are the nearly identical liners *Kronprinzessin Cecile* and *Kaiser Wilhelm II*, in the right foreground is *George Washington*.
71. Solarium of the Norddeutscher Lloyd liner *George Washington*, 1910.

dismissed the snobbery and furniture-magazine banality (»Möbelmagazin-Banalität«) of the »Norddeutscher Lloyd style« of the nineteenth century. By contrast, his first-class cabin was simple and elegant. Following his designs for *Kronprinzessin Cecilie*, he designed a smoking room for the postal steamer *Derfflinger* of 1907 and a dining room and salon for the Genoa–New York liner *Prinz Friedrich Wilhelm* of 1908. A Norddeutscher Lloyd publication described how »with a desire to eradicate the purposeless character of the interior decoration and appointment of steamships, the North German Lloyd resolutely took the advanced step of inviting the leading architects for interiors to design and fit up the interiors of the *cabines de luxe* of the *Kronprinzessin Cecilie*«. The brochure stated that in the competition organized by the line, »Prof. Bruno Paul easily established his supremacy, and it naturally followed that he be entrusted with the modern designing of the interiors of the North German Lloyd's steamships *Prinz Friedrich Wilhelm*, *Derfflinger*, and finally the magnificent *George Washington*.«[194] Paul's commission to complete the principal public rooms of *George Washington* provided him with an opportunity to address a uniquely modern design challenge.

Paul's designs for *George Washington* reflected a significant opportunity for the ideology of the Werkbund. The ship was the largest yet constructed in Germany, and a symbol of national opposition to British domination of maritime commerce. *George Washington* represented the first op-

portunity offered to a leading member of the Werkbund to design the major public rooms of a North Atlantic liner. Paul's interiors, assembled by the Vereinigte Werkstätten in Bremen, exhibited an understated elegance derived from disciplined design and meticulous craftsmanship, as well as the judicious use of costly materials. In addition to exquisite woodwork and vibrant textiles, Paul employed simple accents of polished stone. The gilt framed mirrors and stone veneers of the »Repräsentationsraum« illustrated in the Werkbund yearbook of 1914, evoked traditional conceptions of luxury without the imitative qualities of the »Norddeutscher Lloyd style«.

Paul's designs for *George Washington* were widely exhibited. The reading room was displayed in Munich in 1908 where, as the company noted, it was »most favorably commented upon«.[195] The same year the first class salon of the ship was exhibited in the »Schiffsbauausstellung Berlin« (Berlin shipbuilding exhibition) for which Behrens executed his first architectural commission for AEG. In addition, the Norddeutscher Lloyd published a small book in English in 1910 to promote *George Washington* to American travelers.[196] According to this publication, the ship represented »the culmination of applied art«. »It is a steamship of individuality«, Norddeutscher Lloyd proclaimed, »admired by all for its attractiveness, its purity of design, its beautiful lines and the rich, soft harmony of colors in the inlays of woods and finishes«. The brochure described the interiors of the ship as »restful, luxuriously elegant and artistic«, spaces in which »all unnecessary elaboration has been eliminated«. These qualities were characteristic of Paul's work. His interiors for *George Washington* constituted a prominent international success for the recently-established Werkbund.

The touring exhibition »German Applied Arts«

Photographs of Paul's interiors for the Norddeutscher Lloyd were included in the 1912 touring exhibition »German Applied Arts«, organized for display in the United States by the museum director Karl Ernst Osthaus.[197] Paul's work was represented by photographs of the hall and solarium aboard *George Washington*, the exterior of Haus Westend, and a boudoir from the Villa Feinhals.[198] He also contributed the graphic work *Peasant Woman*,[199] eight different wallpaper patterns manufactured by Otto Schütz, and two different linoleum designs manufactured by the Delmenhorster Linoleum Fabrik »Anker-Marke«. In addition to Paul's work, the selection of wallpapers in the exhibition included patterns by Behrens, Hoffmann, Riemerschmid and Max Läuger, who had designed the gardens for Villa Feinhals. According to the exhibition catalog, Paul and his colleagues »through decorative construction and color arrangement in clear accentuation of the character of the paper, created modern wall papers which bring light and beauty also into the little dwellings of the townspeople and workmen«[200] – a reiteration of the aspirations of the Werkbund in the form of a cultural renewal predicated on the union of artistic design and industrial production.

The touring exhibition »German Applied Arts« opened in Newark to widespread popular acclaim, before traveling to St. Louis, Chicago, Indianapolis, Cincinnati, Pittsburgh, and New York. Contemporary observers compared the exhibition to the Armory Show,[201] the International Exhibition of Modern Art displayed in New York between 15 February and 15 March of 1913 which has been credited with introducing the American public to Marcel Duchamp and European Modernism. More insightful commentators noted that the Touring Exhibition exemplified the modern movement in the applied arts, which was recognized as originating fifteen years previously – with the emergence of the Jugendstil.[202] It is perhaps fortuitous that American observers regarded 1897, the year that Paul began his professional career, as the origin of the modern movement. He was specifically cited in American newspapers as one who had »developed the arts of both exterior and interior decoration to keep pace with the times«.[203] The touring exhibition »German Applied Arts« consolidated his position as a leading exponent of an incipient international Modernism.

The 1912 exhibition was a celebration of the artistic individualism that Osthaus supported. He wrote the catalog so that the names of artists were given precedence over the titles or descriptions of their works. Nonetheless, reviews of the exhibition generally focused on the quality of the designs displayed, which demonstrated, in the words of a reporter for the *New York Herald*, »what can be done to impress an artistic standard on the everyday life of a people«.[204] This assessment underscored the success of the Werkbund, both in Germany and abroad, in achieving the objectives that Schumacher proclaimed at its founding, and to which Paul had so successfully given form.

72. Thirteen-armed candelabrum, 1901. Manufactured by the Vereinigte Werkstätten and exhibited in Dresden in 1906, in a room designed by F. A. O. Krüger. Compare this room with Paul's »Arbeitszimmer« from the same exhibition.
73. Paul's official residence, Berlin, 1914. Salon.
74. Bruno Paul, circa 1914.
75. Paul's official residence, Berlin, 1914. Living room of the new residence of the director on the grounds of the school of applied arts.

Paul's residence in Berlin

In 1914, Paul rebuilt his official residence in the buildings of the school of applied arts on Prinz-Albrecht-Straße, a project that epitomized his artistic beliefs. The furniture that he designed for this, his own home, reflected the elegance, refinement and cultural harmony of his commissioned interiors on the eve of the First World War. Paul's living room embodied the timeless virtues of anthropometric proportions, signified by the conscientious use of the antique orders, by the inclusion of rare and inherently beautiful materials such as mahogany, crystal, and marble, and in the harmonious and muted coloration of painted, stained and dyed surfaces.

The interiors that Paul designed for his residence also demonstrated the position that he himself had attained in Berlin society. As a royal professor he was numbered among the »hoffähig«, the privileged circle entitled to appear at court. In addition to his own work, his residence contained etchings by Piranesi, Tang bronzes, and European antiques. Such symbols of refined culture reinforced Paul's identity as a person of taste and of means. His personal life echoed his material success; he was a frequent traveler and an accomplished horseman.[205] Moreover, the former *Simplicissimus* illustrator had attained the dignity of official recognition. He had been admitted to the Prussian royal academy in 1907.[206] In 1911, he received the Prussian order of the red eagle (Roter Adlerorden), an honor bestowed by the Kaiser for service to the crown.[207] By 1914, he had fulfilled the parental aspirations that had dispatched him to Dresden in 1896. The rebellious spirit of youth had led him to a lofty position in the Prussian civil service, material prosperity, and the patronage of the imperial government.

In addition to artifacts of aristocratic culture, Paul displayed venerable objects of his own design in his Berlin residence. The thirteen-armed candelabrum that he designed for the Vereinigte Werkstätten in 1901 was prominently displayed. Despite such symbols of continuity, Paul's residence also indicated emerging changes in his career. His furnishings were not produced by the Vereinigte Werkstätten, but likely by the Berlin firm Herrmann Gerson, purveyors of furniture to the imperial court. Moreover, many of the pieces Paul conceived for his own home reflected a far looser interpretation of the solid, practical elegance of eighteenth-century designs than his earlier work. By 1914 Paul was seeking a cultural ideal more expressive and elaborate than simple, Biedermeier Classicism. This search prefigured the next phase in his artistic career.

4. War and revolution: 1912–1920

Although Paul and his colleagues in the Werkbund succeeded in promoting the quality and marketability of German design, the loose aesthetic principles of the organization never coalesced into a coherent style. The competitive challenges of the open market were increasingly reflected in Paul's own designs in the years prior to the First World War, as he labored to consolidate his position as a leader of the avant-garde. By 1912, his work had embodied the influence of Biedermeier Classicism for seven years. After successfully advancing the »zweites Biedermeier« as the characteristic vocabulary of progressive German design, Paul sought to maintain his position as an arbiter of popular taste by reinvigorating his personal style.

During the years immediately before and after the war, Paul's designs evinced a relentless formal experimentation. Just as he had never completely forsaken the influence of the Jugendstil, so he retained his commitment to the material simplicity and functional elegance of German Classicism. Yet Paul explored innumerable themes and variations in his furniture and interiors, continuously expanding the formal vocabulary of his earlier work through the development of new designs. His architectural projects from the second decade of the twentieth century followed the precedent of his furniture designs. His buildings continued to draw from the tradition of eighteenth-century Classicism, although their references to historical models became looser and increasingly abstract.

The development of Paul's personal style paralleled his reform of the curriculum of the Berlin school of applied arts. By 1912, he had held the directorship for five years, and he had established himself in the vanguard of the movement to reform artistic education. He continued to shape the organization of his school both through the appointment of new staff and the promotion of professors whose ideas agreed with his own. Paul encouraged collaboration between the members of the faculty, and he actively sought their participation in the completion of his own projects. When the war suspended his private practice, Paul turned his attention to the theoretical objectives of his educational reforms. During the war he wrote a series of articles elaborating his theories on the future of artistic education and the applied arts. These essays, among the few theoretical works that he published, identified the basic principles that would shape the development of his school in the first years of the Weimar Republic.

Educational reform

In 1912 Paul was still living in the apartment on Grolmanstraße in Charlottenburg where he had moved with his wife Maria and their young daughter Hildegard in 1907.[208] Despite his daily commute across Berlin to his office on Prinz-Albrecht-Straße, his private life had become virtually indistinguishable from his role as director of the school of applied arts. He traveled widely on behalf of the school, representing his administration and its reforms at conferences and exhibitions throughout Central Europe. He ran his architectural studio from Prinz-Albrecht-Straße, working in concert with his students and his fellow professors. The curriculum of the school was an extension of Paul's private practice; as he implemented his reforms, he shaped the administration of the school and the composition of its faculty in the image of his own professional success.

Paul officially taught a »Fachklasse« in architectural design, in accordance with the terminology of the Kunstgewerbeschule. Even his earliest students referred to his atelier, however, using the French name associated with academic instruction.[209] The change in nomenclature, which would not be officially recorded in the curricula of the school until 1921, is indicative of the direction of his reforms. He had himself been an academy student, and was influenced by the academic model of artistic education. Nevertheless his primary motivation in the organization of his classes was teaching students in the pragmatic discipline of professional practice. Paul's students worked long hours on his architectural and interior projects, learning the techniques of design through direct experience under the guidance of their professor. In accordance with Paul's reforms, only the most capable students were admitted to the advanced courses offered by the school. His students demonstrated confidence and ability in their work, and several of them, including Julius Bühler and Otto Scholz, had drawings published in *Moderne Bauformen*.[210] Colored illustrations by his students Bruno Scherz, Julius Cunow, and Bernhard Fech were included in the book *Farbige Raumkunst: 120 Entwürfe moderner Künstler*.[211] Their work reflected Paul's stylistic influence, but also the competence and self-discipline required of a successful architect. Students of painting, sculpture, and drawing worked in similarly academic settings, where the distinction between the fine and applied arts was gradually dissolved.

In his teaching plan for the school year ending in 1911, Paul proclaimed his determination that his professors should »consult with their students as frequently as possible on the practical details of their own private commissions«.[212] Moreover, he intended that these private commissions should conform to his own progressive inclinations, rather than mindless duplication of historical models that had characterized the German schools of applied arts in the nineteenth century. Although Paul believed in the value of historical precedents, he did not advocate the perpetuation of historical styles. Accordingly, he sought practicing modern artists of refined technical ability to lead the advanced classes at his school.

The Prague-born painter, print-maker, and photographer Emil Orlik, a professor at the school of applied arts since 1905, embodied the qualities that Paul sought in members of his faculty. Orlik belonged to the circle of progressive artists working in Berlin, and was an active member of the Sezession movement. The characteristic style of his graphic art was inspired by an extended journey to Japan in 1900, where he printed woodcuts that were enthusiastically exhibited in Dresden, Berlin, Brno, and Vienna upon his return. Orlik was, in the words of the critic Ludwig Hevesi, the »most-Japanese European artist« at a time of widespread enthusiasm for Oriental art.[213] As a teacher, he helped inspire the increasing interest in geometric abstraction that would become characteristic of twentieth-century graphic art. He also inspired Bruno Paul. Photographs of Paul's apartment on Grolmanstraße, published in *Dekorative Kunst* in 1908, show several Japanese prints prominently displayed among his possessions. Whether or not Orlik prompted the acquisition of these prints, which do not appear in earlier photographs of Paul's home in Munich, the two professors clearly agreed in matters of aesthetic principle. As a consequence, Paul sought Orlik's collaboration on many of his architectural commissions. He also facilitated the transformation of Orlik's class in commercial and publishing art into an atelier in the model of his own.

The Berlin Sezession, to which Paul and Orlik belonged, contributed to Berlin's ascendance over Munich as the center of the arts in Germany. The Sezession also provided a forum for artists whose opinions paralleled Paul's own, including the painter Emil Rudolph Weiß.[214] Like Orlik, he had been a professor at the school of applied arts under Ewald. When Paul assumed the directorship of the school, Weiß was responsible for the advanced classes in decorative painting and pattern design. His elegant, impressionistic style possessed a classical simplicity that appealed to Paul. In 1911, Weiß painted the walls of a salon in Schloß Börnicke, another example of the professional collaboration that Paul encouraged among the members of his staff. In 1915, Paul devoted one of his few published articles to the subject of Weiß and his architectural painting, writing: »Now the ways and means are in the hands of both the mature leaders and the young seekers, and they are all promoting the same objective: The development of a decorative painting that will correspond to the nature and the needs of our time.«[215]

In addition to advancing the careers of members of Ewald's staff whose ideas were sympathetic to his own, Paul was able to appoint new faculty members as he consolidated his influence on the curricula of the school. In 1909, he hired Ludwig Sütterlin to teach the evening classes in handwriting. The circumstances of Sütterlin's appointment illustrate the efforts made by the leadership of the Werkbund to influence the German educational system. In October 1909 Wolf Dohrn, managing director of the organization, wrote Paul a letter recommending Rudolf Koch for the vacant teaching position for handwriting and script. Paul, who clearly envisioned the vacancy in a broader context than the teaching of handwriting, replied that Koch did not have enough experience as a printer. Moreover he already had an ideal candidate in the person of the »efficient Sütterlin«.[216] Sütterlin was responsible for the development of the Sütterlin Kurrent or Sütterlinschrift, a simplified script that was taught throughout Prussia.[217] In addition to his interest in the reform of German handwriting, Sütterlin was a successful applied artist, a prolific graphic designer as well as a craftsman in glass and leather. He was also a painter, and the catalogs of the school referred to him as Maler (painter) Sütterlin.[218]

The sculptor Joseph Wackerle was another of the multi-talented artists Paul recruited to join the faculty of the school of applied arts. Like Orlik and Weiß, he made periodic contributions to Paul's buildings and interiors. In 1909, he worked with Paul on the interiors of the Café Kerkau[219] as well as the reception room of the Imperial Chancellery, one of Paul's most prestigious commissions.[220] He also carved the entry doors for Villa Feinhals.[221] Wackerle worked with equal facility in wood and stone, bronze, gold, and porcelain, displaying a multitude of talents that accorded perfectly with Paul's ideal of creative ability. From 1910, he led the classes for decorative sculpture at the school of applied arts.

76. Dining Room 66, 1912. Produced by the Vereinigte Werkstätten.
77. Haus Leffmann, Cologne, 1913. Living room.
78. Haus Leffmann, Cologne, 1913. Dining room.

By 1914, Paul presided over a faculty that reflected his ideals of modern art. The leading professors in this distinguished company all possessed abilities that transcended individual disciplines and the customary distinctions between the fine and applied arts. Professional collaborations between Paul and his professors were common, and indeed the ideal of collaboration was central to the curriculum of the advanced courses. Paul's own students participated in the completion of the majority of his published projects. Those admitted to his atelier generally worked on his projects seven and one half hours per day, six days a week, learning by repetitive practice under the supervision of their professor and his assistants.[222] Although their working hours were long, the students remembered their experiences in Paul's atelier fondly, and many of them would remain in contact with one another for decades afterwards. In addition to gaining practical experience through participation in actual projects, the students received general instruction in the practice of architecture. The archives of the school of applied arts include a receipt for a series of photographs that Paul purchased from Chicago for use in his classes. These photographs included sketches by Frank Lloyd Wright, as well as nine images of his Avery Coonley House of 1908, a recent American project that Paul evidently admired.[223] As a consequence of Paul's own interest in contemporary developments in the arts, the graduates of his school were not merely technically proficient, but familiar with the broader context of contemporary design. They were also exceedingly competent. In 1914 Paul sent one of his students, K. E. M. Weber, to the United States to oversee German participation in the »Panama-Pacific International Exposition« in San Francisco on his behalf. Unwilling to return home following the declaration of war, Weber began a new career in California, where he became one of the first European Modernists to succeed in the new world.[224] Weber, who had worked on the drawings for Haus Hainerberg, was typical of the students in Paul's atelier. He was admitted on the basis of intelligence and innate ability, comprehensively trained in the practice of design, and then encouraged to pursue his own development as an artist.

Furniture and interiors: 1912–1914

In the years before the First World War, Paul expanded the vocabulary of the »zweites Biedermeier« to include forms and materials unprecedented in eighteenth-century models. In 1912 he designed a suite of furniture that heralded this new direction, Speisezimmer Nr. 66 (dining room) for the Vereinigte Werkstätten. The chairs for this suite of furniture emulated Biedermeier precedents in their scale and proportions, but incorporated idiosyncratic details such as the molding of their backs, each of which featured an undulating curve broken by a pronounced stagger. This striking feature was accentuated by the finish of the chairs: white lacquer with dark green, striped uphol-

stery. The matching buffet continued the theme established by the chairs in the central element of its undulating plan, which echoed the broken curve of their backs. This dining room has been described as Baroque; its elements reflected a stylistic experimentation that paralleled the transformation of the disciplined aesthetic of the Renaissance during the seventeenth century.[225] Nevertheless there was nothing extravagant or bizarre about the room. The basic form of the chairs was as simple and practical as any that Paul had designed, notwithstanding their color. In 1908 he had designed the least expensive elements of the Typenmöbel line, the pieces fabricated from soft, characterless spruce, to be painted rather than stained, while the furniture he designed for individual commissions utilized costly and beautiful woods, finished and stained in order to emphasize their intrinsic qualities. Speisezimmer Nr. 66 introduced a new emphasis on color to Paul's expanding design vocabulary. This emphasis was, in fact, characteristic of modern interior design in the second decade of the twentieth century, a fact that is often overlooked as a consequence of the paucity of color images surviving from the period. In addition to their emphatic coloration, the broken curve of the chair backs for Speisezimmer Nr. 66, and the undulating form of the buffet, would soon become favored elements in Paul's design vocabulary.

The interiors that Paul designed for Haus Leffmann in Cologne, an architectural project that he began in 1912, were as innovative as the earlier Speisezimmer Nr. 66. The interior of Mrs. Leffmann's living room (Wohnzimmer der Dame) epitomized Paul's formal experimentation. The basket-like wicker sofa had few precedents in Paul's work, although it was elegantly proportioned and finely detailed. Finished in patterned stucco, the striking chimneypiece suggested a traditional tile stove expanded to an architectural scale, while the white and pale gold dining room incorporated equally unexpected features, including doors paneled with flowing ogee curves and a white lacquer chandelier festooned with strands of robust beads. The geometric exuberance of the dining room corresponded with the progressive tastes of the owner, who hung Picasso's *L'acteur* of 1904 in the center of the room. This painting was, and indeed remains, notable for its emphatic use of colors in a raw juxtaposition of turquoise, scarlet, and earthy browns. In 1921, Max Creutz described the »singular experience« (»einzigartiges Erlebnis«) of the Leffmann's dining room, which he perceived as a perfect setting for Picasso's painting.[226]

While Paul was supervising the construction of Haus Leffmann, he prepared for the first major exhibition organized by the Werkbund, scheduled to open in Cologne during the summer of 1914. He conceived some of his finest interiors for the Gelbes Haus (yellow house), a model home at the exhibition furnished by Herrmann Gerson of Berlin.[227] The dining room of the house contained Paul's most innovative designs, a suite of mahogany furniture finished in a striking turquoise lacquer. The dining room buffet translated the undulating plan of the buffet from Speisezimmer Nr. 66 into a three-dimensional form.[228] The expressive forms of the furniture echoed the architectural treatment of the interior: vestiges of a classical ordering were limited to the free, attenuated forms

framing the built-in cupboards in the corners of the room and to ceiling coffers reduced to a filigree pattern of simple moldings. The architectural features of the room were dominated by Orlik's painted decoration, including a large floral still life that complemented Paul's turquoise furniture in its brilliant coloration.

Paul also designed the dining room carpet for the Gelbes Haus, a circular composition executed by Herrmann Gerson in blue, red, and green. Dominating the carpet was a zigzag pattern, an element shared with the tables and chairs of the salon, a room that featured decorative carvings by Joseph Wackerle. Paul employed a related zigzag motif on the walls of the Bierhalle (beer hall) that he furnished for the Werkbund exhibition. The prominence of the zigzag motif in Paul's interiors presaged the popularity of this pattern during the 1920s, but it was only one of a number of motifs with which Paul experimented in Cologne. The chairs in the beer hall illustrated the fundamental shift in his design process embodied in his work for the 1914 exhibition. While Paul's earlier mass-produced chairs – including the chairs for the Nuremberg waiting room and the Typenmöbel chairs – were designed in accordance with a process of simplification and abstraction of established furniture types, the chairs for the beer hall resulted from an additive process. The downward curve of their stretchers and their spherical finials were not essential to the ladderback chair as a type; they were stylistic elaborations.

Paul's interiors for the Weinhaus (wine house or wine restaurant) located adjacent to the beer hall in Cologne were equally idiosyncratic. The wine restaurant incorporated features that were purely ornamental: trapezoidal panels above the framed mirrors on the walls, broken curves in the lattice panels between the dining areas, and the swelling, baluster shaped colonettes. Such features imparted an atmosphere of exoticism to the interior that was enhanced by the decoration provided by Orlik, who painted flowering plants on the barrel vaulted ceiling of the dining hall and finished the smaller Nebensaal (lower hall) with an atmospheric landscape that clearly recalled his travels in the Orient. The decorative features of the wine restaurant contrasted with its furnishings, which were among the most austere Paul ever designed, simpler even than the Typenmöbel. The chairs, in particular, were elegantly fabricated, with no ornament other than their subtly curved backrests and lustrous dark finish.

Notwithstanding the experimental features of Paul's beer hall and wine restaurant, he designed his most prescient interior at the Cologne exhibition for the Gelbes Haus. In this room, the entry hall, he employed the same juxtaposition of severity and exuberance that characterized his restaurant designs. The room, a rotunda with corner niches, derived from the era of Schinkel. But the stripped classical detailing of the room, and the starburst motifs of the stucco ceiling and the patterned stone floor, seem, at least in retrospect, more consistent with the decorative arts of 1925 than of 1914. Yet the interior of the entry hall was typical of his contemporary work. Characteristically, the room was dramatically colored, with the moldings and the furniture finished in green and black. Yet the simple, elegant settees still suggested the influence of Biedermeier design, while the sculpted figures by Wackerle epitomized the harmonious collaboration that Paul had so successfully promoted at his school.

Architectural practice on the eve of the World War

In the years immediately prior to the war, Paul designed a series of houses for prominent members of German society that paralleled the stylistic experimentation and subversion of historical references characteristic of his contemporary interiors. These houses shared topological features with his earlier work: steep tiled roofs with prominent dormers and elegantly symmetrical garden façades ultimately derived from Haus Westend. After 1912, however, Paul turned away from the close reliance on eighteenth-century precedent that characterized his earlier domestic projects. Though he remained devoted to the typology of the Biedermeier suburban villa, his references to German Neoclassicism became increasingly abstract as he experimented with the geometric composition of his residential designs.

The house in Cologne that Paul designed for the factory owner Paul Leffmann in 1912 embodied the emerging trends in his architectural work. The elevations belonged to the same family of forms as earlier projects, but the extreme simplicity of the garden façade suggested a shift in Paul's work. Although the composition of this façade was topologically similar to that of Haus Herxheimer of 1911, in the later house Paul significantly reduced the articulation of the walls, highlighting their prismatic qualities. In addition, he set the windows of the garden façade so close together that their shutters overlapped, creating a horizontal emphasis in contrasting to the vertical configuration of the individual casements. In the majority of his earlier houses, he had established a tension between symmetry and asymmetry in the composition of their elevations; for Haus Leffmann he designed rigidly symmetrical façades that derived their interest from an internal, geometrical tension between horizontal and vertical elements. In addition, he left the brickwork of the walls unplastered, utilizing Dutch clinkers with variegated colors and irregular surfaces that provided a counterpoint to the simple massing of the building. Haus Leffmann demonstrated the decreasing significance of historical types in Paul's architectural work in favor of the formal experimentation that also characterized his contemporary designs for furniture and interiors.[229]

In 1913, Paul designed two houses, Haus Röchling in Duisburg and Haus Herz in the Berlin suburb of Dahlem, both formally derived from Haus Leffmann. Although both houses recalled the Classicism of the eighteenth century, Paul utilized antique columns and Biedermeier eyebrow dormers as isolated elements, subsidiary to the primarily geometric ordering of his façades. Like Haus Leffmann, Haus Röchling and Haus Herz were not published until the 1920s, by which time the abstract qualities of their façades were becoming increasingly commonplace.[230]

The simplification and abstraction apparent in Paul's residential projects on the eve of the war culminated in his architectural projects for the 1914 Werkbund exhibition: Gelbes Haus, beer hall, and wine restaurant. Like all of the buildings constructed for the exhibition, Paul's projects were intended to be temporary, and consequently were fabricated from wood with a thin veneer of cement plaster, rather than the masonry that he preferred.[231] Yet the temporary nature of the exhibition did not preclude a high standard of design. Paul's projects enjoyed three of the most visible sites available, facing the city of Cologne across the Rhine, with the beer hall and wine restaurant flanking the central axis of the exhibition, and Theodor Fischer's main hall. The wine restaurant was linked to Behrens' festival hall on the north side of the axis, while the beer hall was paired with Hoffmann's Austrian pavilion to the south. Characteristically, the beer hall and the wine restaurant were conceived as a balanced pair rather than identical compositions, despite their symmetrical placement relative to the central axis of the site. The Gelbes Haus was located adjacent to the beer hall, on a terrace above the Rhine. Notwithstanding the important sites that Paul secured for his three projects at the 1914 exhibition, the buildings he designed were notable for their simplicity and restraint.

Bruno Paul and the 1914 Werkbund debate

Paul retained his position on the executive committee of the Werkbund during the planning of the 1914 Cologne exhibition. The committee continued to reflect the diverse nature of the organization. It included established artists such as Riemerschmid and Hoffmann; commercial interests represented by the committee chairman Peter Bruckmann, Behrens of the AEG, and Karl Schmidt of the Deutsche Werkstätten; the museum director Karl Ernst Osthaus; and the young architect Walter Gropius, the most recent appointee. The committee also included van de Velde and Muthesius, who held the office of vice chairman. The heterogeneity of the committee echoed the composition of the Werkbund itself, which had grown increasingly diffuse and unmanageable

84. Haus Leffmann, Cologne, 1913. Exterior.
85. Haus Herxheimer, Wiesbaden, 1912. Exterior.
86. Haus Rochling, Duisberg, 1914. Exterior. Built for the Norwegian Consul.
87. Werkbund Exhibition, Cologne, 1914. Overview. The exhibition ground seen from the city of Cologne, on the opposite bank of the Rhine.
88. Werkbund Beer Hall, Cologne, 1914. Exterior.

with the rapid increase in its membership after 1907.[232] Muthesius hoped that the 1914 exhibition would provide an opportunity to reestablish the coherence that had characterized the Werkbund at its foundation. Accordingly he drafted ten theses, extensions of Schumacher's call for the reconquest of a harmonious culture, with the expectation that they would be enthusiastically embraced at the seventh annual meeting of the Werkbund, scheduled in conjunction with the 1914 exhibition. Insofar as Paul was concerned, Muthesius was absolutely correct.

Muthesius drafted his theses to emphasize the significance of standardization (Typisierung) to the cultural and commercial goals of the Werkbund. Although he referred to the ideal of a harmonious culture, the bent of his theses was effectively pragmatic, concerning the advancement of quality and marketability in the products of German industry. Muthesius distributed copies of his theses a week before the annual meeting to ensure their acceptance. The reaction was quite the opposite, and the theses provoked an open rebellion by a small group of artists including Osthaus, Gropius, Hermann Obrist, August Endell, and Rudolf Bosselt. This vocal opposition rallied behind van de Velde, who quickly composed a series of countertheses in response to Muthesius' planned address. Van de Velde denounced standardization and advocated individual artistic expression as the guiding principle of the Werkbund. Muthesius softened his address in the interest of the unity of the organization, but the rebels did not relent. Their public confrontation marked a turning point in the history of the Werkbund, the dissolution of the idealistic brotherhood founded in Munich by Paul and his fellow apostles of the applied arts.[233] Nevertheless the debate between Muthesius and van de Velde set the stage for the future development of the Werkbund and its ideology, as the shifting relationship between the rationalization necessary for efficient mechanical production and the creative expression of individual artistic intent emerged as one of the principal determinants of European Modernism.

The 1914 debate has come to symbolize the confrontation between the proponents of a broadly-defined classicism – represented by Muthesius, Paul, and Fischer – and an emerging avant-garde championed by van de Velde and including Gropius, Bruno Taut, Meyer, and Hans Poelzig.[234] However, the actual context of the debate was more complex. Although there was a stylistic component to the confrontation, a purely stylistic analysis of the debate does not withstand scrutiny. The classicism of the 1914 exhibition embraced manifold interpretations, including the Biedermeier models adopted for Muthesius' Hamburg–Amerika pavilion, the idiosyncratic vocabulary of Behrens' festival hall, and the cool efficiency of Paul's wine restaurant, beer hall, and Gelbes Haus. In contrast, the theater designed by van de Velde and Obrist[235] constituted the swan song of the Jugendstil, which many informed observers had long regarded as both ossified and old-fashioned. The model factory designed by Paul's former assistant Meyer and his partner Gropius was stylistically innovative, despite the classicism of its axial, hierarchical plan and sculptural ornamentation. Such apparent inconsistencies demonstrate the extent to which the debate between Muthesius and van de Velde cannot be accepted solely as a matter of artistic principle, or as a consequence of political polarization among the members of the Werkbund.[236] Questions of the commercial imperative of standardization in the interest of efficient industrial production versus a cherished freedom of artistic expression were directly relevant to the objectives of the Werkbund in 1914, yet their resolution proved more difficult to codify than to embody. Paul's work in Cologne occupied a middle ground between the polemical positions of Muthesius and van de Velde, a position that was characteristic of the exhibition as a whole.

By 1914, when Paul completed his projects for the Cologne exhibition, he had supplanted the vocabulary of the »zweites Biedermeier« with an expanded conception of harmonious culture. In his work for the Vereinigte Werkstätten, Paul emerged as an early proponent of rational design for industrial production, a principle that he extended to his architectural projects. Nevertheless, the standardization that he promoted in his practice provided a basis for his relentless formal experimentation. Though he accepted a discipline based on the Western classical tradition, the simplicity, clarity, and order of his work permitted him freedom of formal expression without compromising the virtues of quality and taste admired by his patrons. Paul had discovered classicism for himself, and made the classicism of reform his own.

The balance Paul struck between standardization and individual expression was, in fact, characteristic of the Werkbund in 1914. At the Cologne exhibition the Deutsche Werkstätten exhibited its own range of Typenmöbel based on a similar pragmatic compromise.[237] A description of the Deutsche Werkstätten Typenmöbel published in the *Studio Yearbook of Decorative Art* for 1914 proclaimed that the individual parts »of which there are something like 800 different kinds, can be made in large quantities and with the most advantageous employment of machine labour; while the extensive range of combinations ensures to the complete article an individuality and character

89. Cover for the first issue of *Wieland*, 1915.
90. Cover for *Wieland*, 1915. »Ivan Ivanovich: Better German barbarism without beatings than Russian culture with them.« The men depicted are Russian prisoners of war, represented as conscripted peasant soldiers.
91. Calendar illustration from *Wieland*, 1918.

of its own«.[238] Some twenty artists provided designs for the Deutsche Werkstätten Typenmöbel, including three members of the executive committee of the Werkbund: Behrens, Hoffmann, and Niemeyer. Paul did not contribute to the competing range of furniture introduced by the Deutsche Werkstätten, but continued to expand his own Typenmöbel line in a similar manner.

The war years

Only one month after the opening of the Cologne exhibition, Serbian nationalists assassinated the Austrian Archduke Franz Ferdinand in Sarajevo. Though most Germans initially believed that the military confrontation that followed would quickly end, the exigencies of war soon curtailed most of Paul's work and severely disrupted the operation of his school.

At the beginning of the war, the buildings of the Berlin school of applied arts were appropriated by the military for use as a hospital. The school was restricted to a third of its former area; medical personnel and wounded soldiers occupied the majority of the studios and lecture halls. Students and members of the faculty and staff were called to military service. In the first year of the war alone, 144 students and 25 staff members were sent into uniform, and many of them never returned. Among those killed in 1914 was Peter Kollwitz, son of the artist Käthe Kollwitz.[239] By the second year of the war, 20 students and 3 staff members had fallen in combat, and every class at the school was affected. Bernhard Fech, a student in Paul's atelier who had completed the drawings for the Gelbes Haus in 1914, was killed in the trenches the following year.

In 1914 Paul assumed editorial responsibility for *Wieland*, an illustrated weekly magazine of art and literature.[240] A patriotic endeavor published in support of the central committee of the German Rotes Kreuz, *Wieland* was initially patterned after the weekly format and graphic style of *Simplicissimus* and *Jugend*. Throughout 1915, Paul contributed regular illustrations to the magazine, much as he had done for *Simplicissimus* years before, and many of his drawings for *Wieland* echoed his youthful work. Their loose visual style and biting sarcasm could have graced the pages of *Simplicissimus*, although Paul's graphic style had softened since his Munich years. The majority of his early drawings dealt directly with the war; some were bellicose and patriotic, others were more reflective. For his editorial work Paul received the Rotes Kreuz medal, third class, from the government in December 1915.

After less than a year of publication, the editorial staff of *Wieland* adopted a monthly format. By the third year of publication, the magazine bore few similarities to the frequently satirical patriotic journal that appeared in 1914. Indeed, by 1917 it was dedicated to fashion and popular culture, and characterized by a self-conscious avoidance of significant reference to the progress of the war. Paul continued to submit drawings, with decreasing regularity, but wrote a number of articles for the journal, in which he presented his opinions concerning art and education.

The April 1917 issue of *Wieland* featured the article »Künstlerlehrzeit« (An artist's apprenticeship), Paul's first and most concise public synopsis of the objectives of his educational reforms. While emphasizing the significance of well-organized schools in order to provide artistically talented students with a fundamental education in the crafts, he contended that technical and craft schools »must become fully conscious of their important function and renounce all traces of artistic dilettantism. ... The more thoroughly and resolutely these schools implement the training of their students in the crafts«, he concluded, »the closer they will come to fulfilling their proper function.«[241] The fundamental implications of these statements are identical to the objectives that German reformers, beginning in 1896, extrapolated from the English Arts and Crafts movement: that there is no intrinsic distinction between fine art and applied art, that the process of creating an object with one's own hands is the root of artistic expression, and that the objective of art education is not the proliferation of artists, but the service of the greater society.[242] In »Künstlerlehrzeit«, Paul addressed each of these issues in proposing a system of artistic education. He brought the Berlin school of applied arts ever closer to this ideal by making practical experience a prerequisite for admission and by expanding the role of the preliminary classes in the individual crafts while elevating the advanced classes – and especially his own class in architecture – to the status of ateliers. Although the war temporarily curtailed his reforms, »Künstlerlehrzeit« outlined his objectives.

In May 1917, Paul published a second essay in *Wieland*: »Architektur und Kunstgewerbe nach dem Kriege« (Architecture and applied arts after the war). He described the ultimate goal of his reforms: the implementation of a new and higher standard of design. Paul praised an emerging architecture that would »cast aside the stylistic memory of earlier epochs as it accepts the realiza-

Einzelnes Kriegergrab, Straße Soly=Smorgon   Bruno Paul

tion that good architecture is not based on the selection of motifs, but on the arrangement of the building elements and the proportions of all of the individual parts, eventually producing a standardization of expressive forms«. The recognition of these fundamental concepts, he argued, would end the stylistic confusion that beset German design. After the war, he predicted that Germans would »experience the building of public places and streets that hold each other in mutual respect and of a worthy city hall that represents its municipality and is not reduced to wretchedness by its location between a pompous commercial building and a splendid beer palace«. Commercial buildings would no longer appropriate the solemnity of churches and temples, and nothing would be presented by a building that was not »precise and appropriate«. Paul proclaimed the conditions of precision and propriety as the »natural prerequisite of efficient objectivity«. The number of precise and appropriate buildings that had already been completed in Germany offered the promise that post-war architecture would not only »atone for the sins of the last half century«, but also »attain the maturity and uniformity that it previously enjoyed«.[243]

Despite the optimistic tone of Paul's articles concerning the future of German art, he was deeply affected by the war. His essay »Kriegergräber im Osten« (war-graves in the East) was the most elegiac of his published works. Paul had given considerable thought to the subject of war-graves as a member of the Landesberatungsstellen für Kriegerehrungen (state advisory commission for war memorials): drawings of military graves, many in his own hand, are preserved in the archives of his school in Berlin.[244] School records also indicate that he made two visits to the eastern front in November and December of 1915 in conjunction with his work for the Landesberatungsstellen, during which he spent three weeks among the troops in the face of the approaching winter. Afterwards he described a lonely gravesite with a soldier's handwritten memorial to a fallen companion, »enclosed with staves of birch, as a touchingly simple monument to self-sacrifice unto death, at the same time a memorial of faithful camaraderie«. He described the humble grave becoming »with each decade more beautiful, more serious and more expressive a monument to the devotion of German men to their fatherland«, an embodiment of the ideal soldier's noble and selfless dedication to duty.[245] Paul clearly felt a personal connection to the sacrifices of war. In editing the five-volume series Kriegergräber, Beiträge zu der Frage: Wie sollen wir unsere Kriegergräber würdig erhalten (war-graves, answers to the question: how shall we keep our war-graves worthy) on behalf of the state advisory commission), he included an illustration of a memorial to Bernhard Fech, his fallen student.

The shortages of materials and labor during the war restricted Paul's activities as an architect and designer. He began few new architectural projects during the war years, and production of his furniture came to a standstill. He did undertake several small and patriotic commissions, however, the best known of which was the ceremonial chain of office forged in iron for the Oberbürgermeister of Göttingen in 1917 to replace a gold original melted down and donated towards the costs of the war.[246] Paul also continued to work on several projects that had been initiated prior

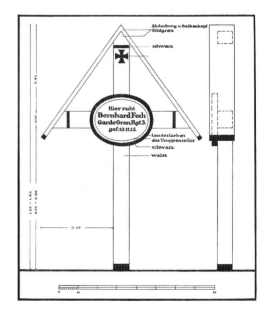

to the commencement of hostilities, including the Völkerkunde-Museum in Dahlem and Haus Friedwart in Wetzlar.

Haus Friedwart was Paul's only architectural project completed during the war years, and provided his first opportunity to develop for a private commission the aesthetic motifs that he introduced at the Cologne exhibition. A local architect in Wetzlar, Jean Schmidt, began the design of the house for the industrialist Ernst Leitz before the war. Located high on the slope of Wetzlar's castle hill, the site overlooked both the Leitz optical-equipment factory and the core of the medieval city. While the house was under construction, Leitz selected Paul to complete the project. Idiosyncratic features of the house without parallels in Paul's previous work, including the awkward entry portico, apparently originated in Schmidt's plans. The tall mansard roof with its ranks of dormers, and the completion of the interiors, resulted from Paul's intervention.

Haus Friedwart is one of the few early projects by Paul for which original drawings have survived. The drawings illustrate Paul's transformation of Schmidt's initial design, exemplified by a rendering of the entry hall in which Paul inserted an abstractly-patterned metal grill within a semicircular fan light of historicist aspect. The large drawings were gracefully rendered in pencil, with as much emphasis on the effects of light and shadow and on the material properties of different surfaces as on the design of individual elements. Erasures and amendments to the rendered drawings demonstrate the extent to which Paul's training as an artist informed his work as an architect. He conceived his furniture and interiors as volumes in light, rather than as pure geometric forms. Yet he worked in a scale approximating the 1:10 preferred by both the Vereinigte Werkstätten and the Deutsche Werkstätten for working drawings, emphasizing the close relationship between his artistic perspectives and the technical documents prepared for the execution of his designs.[247] As completed, Paul's interiors for Haus Friedwart were remarkably faithful to his presentation drawings.

The drawings for Haus Friedwart also illustrate the creative experimentation that followed Paul's participation in the 1914 Cologne exhibition. As he had in Cologne, Paul collaborated with Emil Orlik in Wetzlar. Orlik conceived the railing in the stair hall with a climbing pattern of exotic leaves that provided a counterpoint to the simple, geometric paneling of the adjoining walls. The overall effect of the hall was similar to that of the wine restaurant of 1914, with a self-conscious exoticism enriching, but not overwhelming, a composition of clarity and restraint. Other interiors for Haus Friedwart stressed Paul's developing interest in color as an element of design. While his kitchen furniture was ostensibly simple and functional, a pragmatic response to a utilitarian program, Paul finished the individual pieces in a pale blue lacquer with slate blue accents, effectively concealing the details of their wooden construction. For the upstairs hall at Haus Friedwart, Paul designed a series of simple oak and wicker furnishings completed in brilliant vermilion lacquer. A contemporary critic referred to the red hall as an »attack on the senses«, its brilliant color a di-

chotomy of »ecstasy and terror«.[248] Nevertheless these emphatically colored furnishings for Haus Friedwart were typical of Paul's contemporary work, as epitomized by his interiors for the Gelbes Haus. Although this furniture was both practical and confortable,[249] the expressive forms and muted exoticism that Paul employed in its design signified his departure from the stolid classicism of the Biedermeier.

Haus Friedwart was the last of Paul's buildings built before the end of the war. While he was working on the house in 1916, however, he was one of twelve prominent architects invited to participate in a design competition for the Haus der Freundschaft (house of friendship) in Constantinople, a symbol of the alliance between Germany and the Ottoman empire. The Werkbund organized the contest, and selected prominent architects to submit designs. Four of the twelve – Paul, Behrens, Riemerschmid, and Endell – had made their names in Munich prior to the turn of the century; in addition to these respected artists, three of the more radical members of the Werkbund – Gropius, Poelzig, and Taut – were invited to submit designs.[250] The competition was organized such that the twelve entrants would also constitute the jury, and would themselves select a winner. Paul's entry did not fare well in the competition, however, and was eliminated in the first round of voting. His proposal, an urban palazzo of Mediterranean influence with a severe façade of seven bays and an elegant colonnade,[251] was the simplest of the entries; despite its practical virtues, however, Paul's design did not inspire the enthusiasm of his colleagues. His austere and practical classicism no longer projected the aura of reform that it had a decade earlier.[252] In 1916, Paul was forty-two years old and, for the first time in his life, seemed no longer on the cutting edge of artistic development.

Revolution

Despite *Wieland's* optimistic tone, conditions in Berlin became increasingly desperate after 1917. Paul and his family had to subsist on basic foodstuffs that were strictly rationed; former luxuries such as coffee, tea, cocoa, and tobacco existed only as unpalatable ersatz replacements. The British blockade of German ports was slowly but surely strangling the national economy. Popular discontent with the progress of the war and the conduct of the imperial government was becoming endemic.

The revolution in Russia marked a turning point in German history, and indeed for Bruno Paul himself. Revolutionary fervor was growing in Berlin during the first months of 1918, and inspired Karl Liebknecht and Rosa Luxemburg's Spartakusbund to call a general strike in the capital. The government managed to suppress the strike, but the discontent that had fostered it grew more intense as the spring offensive mounted by the German armies in the west became a humiliating rout, and Austria-Hungary sued for peace. By October, Germany was forced to acknowledge defeat. In November the last imperial chancellor, Max von Baden, announced the Social Democrat Friedrich Ebert as his successor and proclaimed the abdication of the Kaiser. Yet workers and soldiers throughout Germany were soon in open revolt. Berlin plunged into months of unrest punctuated by bloody factional conflict and political murder. One social group, however, was conspicuously absent from the conflict that accompanied the foundation of the Weimar Republic: the affluent middle classes that had been Paul's principal patrons. Germany emerged from the First World War as a deeply polarized society in which the centrist, middle-class ideology of the last decade of the monarchy seemed to have disappeared from the political process.

The radical tone of German politics in the first years of the Weimar Republic inspired a similar revolutionary zeal among the circle of avant-garde artists a generation younger than Paul. Even as rival political factions fought in the streets of Berlin, two radical artists' associations were established: the Novembergruppe (November group) and the Arbeitsrat für Kunst (work council for art).[253] The two organizations, which merged in December 1919, promoted a utopian, socialist program for reforming the role of the artist in society, with Gropius and Taut as two of the leading figures – and principal propagandists – of the movement. Many of the points that Gropius and Taut made in their manifestoes for the Arbeitsrat für Kunst echoed Paul's agenda for the reform of the school of applied arts in Berlin. But Taut's demands – for the revocation of the privileges accorded to artists in government service, the dissolution of the state schools of art, and the establishment of a completely democratic system of education in which students were free to elect their professors – challenged the fundamental bases of the reforms that Paul had implemented. Though established architects such as Paul Mebes joined the Arbeitsrat für Kunst or the Novembergruppe, Paul himself did not. He received an invitation from Gropius to register as a member

98. Haus der Freundschaft, Constantinople, 1918. Project.
99. Dining room for the Deutsche Werkstätten incorporating chairs from the Paretz dining room, 1921.

of the Arbeitsrat, but he filed the mimeographed letter, unanswered and with the reply card still attached.[254] His disinclination to join with the young radicals was not the result of a fundamental opposition; he simply disagreed with the polemical nature of both the Arbeitsrat für Kunst and the Novembergruppe. He had achieved a position of influence and authority through his diligence and diplomacy. Although his membership in the re-established (and no longer royal) Prussian academy was confirmed in January 1919, by the founding of the Weimar Republic, Paul was no revolutionary.

In the midst of the political and artistic crises that followed the war, Paul attempted to resume his career in private practice. As normal life slowly returned to Berlin, he hoped to repeat the success of his Typenmöbel of 1908 by designing a new series of standardized furniture in 1920. The 1920 Typenmöbel was produced by a company in Berlin, the Typen-Möbel Gesellschaft mbH Zoo-Werkstätten, founded a year earlier.[255] Paul designed three suites of furniture for the Zoo-Werkstätten: the Paretz dining room, Potsdam study, and the Rheinsberg bedroom, all named for Prussian castles. Marketed as middle-class furniture for daily use (bürgerliche Gebrauchsmöbel) without reference to the affordability of the 1908 originals, it found few buyers in the desperate postwar economy. The Paretz dining room alone cost 16,600 Marks, the Potsdam study cost 22,074 Marks, and the Rheinsberg bedroom 23,814 Marks for stained mahogany or 16,307 Marks with a lacquer finish. The prewar price of a complete Typenmöbel dining room from the Vereinigte Werkstätten was only 969 Marks, still more than the yearly income of many working-class families.

The few surviving images of the 1920 Typenmöbel show pieces with simplified massing and ornamental elaboration, not unlike Paul's work for the 1914 Werkbund exhibition. The 1908 Typenmöbel line featured elegant surfaces clad with quartered, bookmatched veneers with intarsia borders, while the 1920 designs featured large, severely detailed planes of wood with naturalistic carved ornament. The 1920 Typenmöbel was as original as its predecessors, yet its applied decoration echoed the qualities of traditional, period furnishings. It embodied a modernity suitable for a traditional home. Yet the limited market for middle-class furniture for daily use compelled the Typen-Möbel Gesellschaft mbH Zoo-Werkstätten to revise its business strategy and change its name, becoming the Vereinigte Zoo-Werkstätten in 1923. The fault was not entirely Paul's, though he had clearly misjudged the health of the postwar economy. Nevertheless the chairs from the Paretz dining room were adopted by the Deutsche Werkstätten as their Modell 115, and remained in production throughout the 1920s.

The revolution of 1918 caught Paul completely off guard. Although he had supported the Socialists during his days as a student at the Munich academy, he had become a respected royal professor, and an agent of the Prussian government. Unhappy with conditions in the capital following the dissolution of the monarchy, Paul considered resigning from the school of applied arts in Berlin to accept a post in Munich, where he hoped to work closely with his former colleague Riemerschmid.[256] In his letters to the Bavarian government, he recalled the »happy Simplicis-simus days« (fröhliche Simplizissimuszeiten) of his youth, offering a clue to his motivation for con-sidering a return to Munich. But in December 1920 he elected to stay in Berlin, reluctantly citing the social and professional obligations that precluded his relocation.[257] Yet conditions in the capi-tal were hardly ideal. Well into the 1920s, Paul was obligated to pencil out the word »royal« (kö-niglich) from his letterhead as his cash-starved school economized by continuing to use the sta-tionary printed for it by the Prussian government before the war. Paul also remained busy with the Landesberatungsstellen für Kriegerehrungen, as the defeated country struggled to honor its fallen youth.

Reform and the culture of revolution

In the years before the war, Paul had moved slowly and deliberately towards a new mode of artis-tic expression. If the pace of his artistic development was measured, it was with good reason. Paul had composed the reception room for the Reichskanzler and planned a major new museum for Berlin. He had also begun to supply designs to the firm that provided furniture and interiors to Wilhelm II and the Kaiserin Auguste Viktoria. Following his successful projects for simple, inexpen-sive furnishings for the working classes and his reinvention of the bürgerlich home, he began the process of reforming the taste of the aristocracy. In so doing, Paul sought to influence every stra-tum of German society, creating a genuine style for the twentieth century commensurable with the epochal styles that preceded the historicism of the nineteenth century and the synthetic modernity of the Jugendstil. The unexpected revolution of 1918, and the disastrous war that had instigated it, prevented the realization of his aims.

The social and political influence of the German aristocracy largely dissolved during the winter of 1918–19. Although Paul lost any hope of himself being ennobled for his efforts, as Stuck and Bode had been,[258] the disappointments of 1919 did not prompt him to join the artistic revolution. He recognized that many of the practical reforms promoted by the revolutionaries echoed his own published theses; he also realized that the utopian aspirations of the new avant-garde were a poor substitute for actual commissions. While a new generation of visionary designers pub-lished artistically brilliant proposals such as Taut's crystalline »Alpine Architecture« and Mies' translucent office tower for the Berlin Friedrichstraße, Paul continued his successful practice as an architect. He built prolifically between 1920 and 1925, and many of his projects were pub-lished.[259] Ironically one of these projects, a façade for the Kunstmessehaus Dülk (Dülk exhibition center for the arts), adapted the scheme for a severe, seven-bay palazzo that he had unsuccess-fully proposed for the Haus der Freundschaft. He had stated in 1916 that his design for Istanbul could just as well be constructed in Berlin, and he was correct.[260]

Paul was at the height of his abilities in 1920. He was forty-six years old, and had belonged to the exclusive circle of Germany's foremost artists for a quarter century. Yet he was aware that a younger generation of artists was beginning to challenge his position of leadership by appropriat-ing the revolutionary fervor that had swept the country in 1918. The ascendancy of the new gener-ation indicated a fundamental shift in German design. Although Paul never regained his reputation as a stylistic innovator after the revolution, he would play a central role in the dissemination of the modern design of the interwar years.

5. Consolidation and renewal in the Weimar Republic: 1920–1925

During the 1920s, Paul sought to reestablish his position of artistic leadership, which had been challenged in the early years of the Weimar Republic by a new generation of designers who embraced the ideals of social and aesthetic revolution. The younger generation of German designers included Gropius, Mies, Taut, and Mendelsohn, the leaders of a new modern movement propagated by revolutionary rhetoric. Paul, ever taciturn, was lost in the cacophony of manifestoes, programs, and irregular periodicals that accompanied the ascendancy of the new generation.[261] Yet he was unwilling to be forgotten.

Paul's return to professional prominence was heralded by a shift in his aesthetic sensibilities, and a reorganization of the school of applied arts. He belatedly accepted the formal vocabulary of Expressionism, the loosely defined aesthetic that characterized the projects of the younger generation of German architects after the war. Though Paul never abandoned the grace and refinement of his earlier work, he proved himself a capable Expressionist designer, largely as a consequence of his own experiences with the Jugendstil twenty-five years before. In a period when little was being built in Germany because of the unsettled political and economic circumstances of the new republic, Paul built and published a number of Expressionist projects, reestablishing his credentials as a modern designer as he approached his fiftieth birthday.

The 1924 reorganization of the school of applied arts marked a high point in Paul's career. In the early years of the Weimar Republic, the establishment of the Bauhaus reinvigorated debate on the reform of artistic education. The Bauhaus was formed, at least in theory, through the amalgamation of the school of applied arts and the academy school in Weimar, realizing the union of fine and applied arts that Paul had been advocating since 1907. When the Prussian government acted on his advice and merged the Berlin school of applied arts with the school of the state academy, Paul assumed a position analogous to that occupied by Gropius. As head of the new Vereinigte Staatsschulen für freie und angewandte Kunst (unified state schools of fine and applied arts), Paul was at last able to complete his program of reform.

Architectural Expressionism

An architectural parallel to the Expressionist movement in literature emerged prior to the Werkbund exhibition of 1914, when Bruno Taut built his »Glashaus« as a challenge to the calm classicism promoted by Paul and the majority of his colleagues on the executive committee. Yet even in his own Gelbes Haus, Paul incorporated the exotic motifs and prismatic forms characteristic of Expressionist design. This aesthetic became increasingly prominent after the war, as artists sought to forge a cultural identity distinct from that of the former Empire. Radical groups such as the Arbeitsrat für Kunst fostered the development of an Expressionist architecture. Although Paul did not support the revolutionary idealism of organizations such as the Arbeitsrat, he was determined to align his own work more closely with the tastes of the emerging avant-garde. Yet he maintained his allegiance to the middle-class clientele that he had cultivated under the monarchy. Though the members of this commercial and industrial class lacked a decisive political voice within the new democracy, they retained the resources to continue building during the years of unrest.[262] Moreover, they allowed Paul to maintain the momentum of his career at a time when commissions were few and far between. This momentum transformed his work from his wartime experimentation into the Expressionism of the Weimar Republic.

In 1921, Paul completed his first wholly and overtly Expressionist building, Haus Fraenkel in the Hamburg suburb of Blankenese. Its composition was largely unprecedented in Paul's work, although several details recalled his earlier Haus Friedwart. He sheathed its exterior walls with a veneer of uncoursed sandstone, a material that was not suited to classical detailing and which he had not previously employed. He crowned the sandstone walls with an emphatic, outward arching cornice with a smooth plaster surface. The sculptural profile of the cornice, which followed the plan of the projecting semicircular bays on the garden façade of the house, belonged to a vocabulary of fluid, sculptural forms that was arousing considerable interest in 1921. Mendelsohn's Einstein Observatory in Potsdam, which employed similar undulating forms, was completed the same year. But in Haus Fraenkel the plastic detailing was limited to a single element of a design that was, in its fundamental form, simple and conventional. Despite the singularity of the design in the context of Paul's own work, when the house was published during 1923 in *Deutsche Kunst und Dekoration*, the critic Hans Rolffsen praised the restrained elegance of its exterior, and its

tranquil site above the river Elbe.[263] The harmonious relationship of the house and its natural setting was of particular interest to Paul after the war. At the time he designed Haus Fraenkel, Paul was a member of the editorial staff of *Gartenschönheit*, a widely popular magazine dedicated to the artistic garden and the integration of the landscape and the built environment.[264]

»The interior of the house«, Rolffsen wrote, »was another world.« Certain details, such as the pair of carved entrance doors, perpetuated the Biedermeier tradition of Paul's earlier houses. The stair hall of the house recalled Haus Friedwart, with a wooden railing roughly carved with twining vines, but here the carved vines abandoned all vestiges of Naturalism in favor of a fantastic pattern of heavy, thick elements carved in the round.[265] A black lacquer finish heightened the surreal effect of the railing. Paul designed the majolica stove for the music room with similarly exaggerated vegetal forms, a motif inspired by the same Rococo models that Poelzig emulated in the interiors of his Großes Schauspielhaus.[266] Despite its fantastic form, Paul's stove projected a quiet dignity; it was elegantly proportioned and beautifully detailed. The quality of this stove, which was typical of all of the internal details of the house, contributed to an interior that Rolffsen deemed to be a »world of the most exquisite taste«.[267] The interior was also a world of the most recent taste that incorporated, in details such as the chevron pattern of the veneers in the paneled hall, the exaggerated angularity that characterized the final phase of architectural Expressionism. In the interiors that Paul designed for Haus Fraenkel, he embraced the latest trends in German design, albeit without polemical intent. Unlike the majority of Expressionist projects, the comfortable home that he conceived for the Saxon industrialist Fraenkel was modern, without promoting a revolutionary social or political ideology.

In 1922, Paul helped to organize the »Deutsche Gewerbeschau« (German trade exhibition) in Munich, the epitome of the Expressionist movements in architecture and the decorative arts. He collaborated in his administrative efforts with Karl Schmidt of the Deutsche Werkstätten, his Werkbund colleagues Pankok and Fischer, and his former employees Redslob and Thiersch. In addition to his administrative responsibilities, he designed a series of architectural elements for the exhibition, in projects that effectively employed abstract, geometric elements within a fundamentally classical framework. His garden terrace was typical of his work for the »Gewerbeschau«, displaying the topology and the harmonious proportions of a classical portico, but with dramatically tapered piers in place of columns. The same wedgelike forms appeared inverted above the display cabinets on the rear wall of the terrace, creating a rhythmic pattern, while the display cabinets themselves reflected a motif employed throughout his designs for the trade exhibition. The profile of the cabinets reappeared on an architectural scale in a pavilion for the Deutsche Werke, which took the form of an attenuated pyramid atop a cubic base. Paul echoed this form in a series of freestanding cabinets for the Vistra company, which in profile reproduced a form that Paul had employed in the design of built-in shelving for both Haus Friedwart and Haus Fraenkel. At the Trade Exhibition, he translated this pattern into dramatic, sculptural forms.

In a description of the »Gewerbeschau« published in *Dekorative Kunst*, Joseph Popp noted that Paul was the only artist at the exhibition to translate the »angles, points and serrations« of cubism into compelling three-dimensional forms that worked »without any applied ornament, only form and color«. He particularly admired the way in which Paul employed the »simple motifs of a slender pyramid and boxes with open and closed surfaces, of different sizes and in varying spatial relationships« to establish such differing experiences as the »almost bizarre mood« of the array of cabinets and the weightless, airy proportions of the terrace.[268] The effects he created were startling. Yet like all of Paul's best work, his Expressionist designs for the trade exhibition were simple, logically consistent, conscientiously detailed, and flawlessly executed.

In the year of the trade exhibition, Paul designed a house in Cologne for the banker Otto Kaufmann. In certain details, Haus Kaufmann was closely related to the exhibition designs. The columns supporting the balcony on the garden façade possessed the same abstract qualities as those for the contemporary garden terrace, although not their striking attenuation. Similarly the massing of the house itself, which was even simpler than the Gelbes Haus of 1914, suggested the pure geometries of the trade exhibition. Although Haus Kaufmann was similar in composition to the earlier Haus Leffmann, Paul did not articulate its brick walls with pilasters or shelter its dormers beneath vestigial pediments. The absence of such familiar details suggested a fundamental shift in Paul's interpretation of the middle-class residence as a building type.

Despite its idiosyncratic detailing, Haus Kaufmann still belonged to the tradition of the Biedermeier suburban villa that Paul had adopted before the war. In Haus Kaufmann, he reduced this type to the essential form of a central, prismatic block with largely symmetrical fenestration, flanked by balanced but asymmetrical subsidiary elements. But he dissociated this typology

103. Artist unknown, cover design for *Gartenschönheit*, 1922.
104. »Deutsche Gewerbeschau«, Munich, 1922.
Pavilion.
105. »Deutsche Gewerbeschau«, Munich, 1922. Display cabinets.
106. »Deutsche Gewerbeschau«, Munich, 1922. Exterior of the garden terrace.

107. Haus Kaufmann, Cologne, 1923. Dining room.
108. Haus Neven-Dumont, Cologne, 1924. Exterior.
The subject of one of the few articles that Paul wrote
about his own work.
109. Vanity from the Deutsche Werkstätten bedroom
suite Number 180, 1921.
110. Deutsche Werkstätten armoire model 7843, 1923.
111. Deutsche Werkstätten Plattenhaus H 1018, Hellerau, 1925. Dining room.

rom the vocabulary of Neoclassicism. Paul used correctly proportioned antique orders at Haus Friedwart,[269] employed attenuated Corinthian columns at Haus Fraenkel, and at Haus Kaufmann substituted simple rectangular piers for antique columns as he turned away from the language of Neoclassicism in favor of a more abstract formal vocabulary.

While Haus Kaufmann was under construction, Paul designed another suburban villa in Cologne for the publisher and newspaper editor Dr. Kurt Neven-Dumont.[270] Although the garden façade of the house suggested the abstracted classicism of Haus Kaufmann, the detailing did not. The slope of the tile roof was broken by a step, creating a horizontal band pierced by tiny, triangular dormers. The broad eaves sheltered stark plaster walls articulated only through the placement of simple, shutterless windows. The prominence of the central block of the house was challenged by the integration of subsidiary elements, which concealed its fundamental symmetry. A projecting triangular bay was the most notable feature of the street façade of the house. The front door was modestly sheltered by a simple cantilever, and flanked by fixtures with pyramidal caps like the display cases for the 1922 trade exhibition.

Paul wrote one of his few published articles on Haus Neven-Dumont, the 1928 essay »Ein Kölner Wohnhaus« (a house in Cologne). He described the prismatic form of the house, noting the triangular bay in the street façade, which provided the residents an unobstructed view of both entrances to the house. He referred to this characteristic feature of the house as its »nose«, providing an accent to its principal elevation. Of the exterior as a whole, Paul argued that »it works only through the proportioning of the built elements and each individual component, and asserts itself in its surroundings as one would expect of a good and distinguished house«, notwithstanding its Expressionist details. The ideals of harmony and propriety remained undiminished in his residential work, and not merely as aesthetic criteria. »Just as the owners and their guests will gather together around the blazing fireplace in winter«, he wrote, »so will the open loggia be the most commonly used room during the summer.« »There they will sit down to meals or to tea«, he continued, »and spend their evenings in the open air, sheltered from the rains, into October.«[271] This domestic idyll epitomized Paul's objectives as a residential architect: the creation of order, comfort, and convenience.

Furniture and interiors

Paul's belated interest in Expressionism did not reflect a coherent system of aesthetic principles, and he produced few purely Expressionist interiors. His designs for the trade exhibition were a notable exception, though the crystalline forms that he conceived for Vistra bore little relation to

his earlier domestic designs. Nevertheless, he exhibited a dining room at the trade exhibition, executed by the Deutsche Werkstätten in a vocabulary that was only slightly less abstract than the Vistra displays. The pattern of mullions in the vitrine, which also appeared in the chair backs and the matching buffet, was the most striking feature of the design. While the patterns recalled the Chinese-inspired metalwork for Haus Friedwart, their looser patterning also suggested the Neo-Plasticism being developed concurrently in the Netherlands by the leading contributors to the magazine *De Stijl*: Piet Mondrian, Theo van Doesburg, and Gerrit Rietveld. But Paul's interest in Neo-Plasticism was limited.

In 1923, Paul designed a bedroom suite, no. 180, for the Deutsche Werkstätten. The sinuous forms of the individual elements were typical of his Expressionist interiors. The complex carved supports for the vanity mirror, with their sculptural profiles, introduced a characteristic ambiguity. With pure, sculptural forms suggesting musculature or swelling vegetation, the suite introduced an unexpected and psychological motif into an otherwise conventional interior. Indeed, the basic elements of Paul's bedroom no. 180 were simple and practical. Many of the pieces derived from his standardized designs, including an armoire that differed only in detail from the Typenmöbel of 1920. Yet the bedroom introduced emphatically Expressionist elements to the middle-class interior.

Paul's interiors for Haus Kaufmann were similarly conceived. The dining room chairs epitomized his contemporary furniture, displaying ornamentation that was both dramatic and innovative. The carved backs, with flowing forms suggestive of rising flames or growing vegetation, broke with historical precedents, while retaining the comfortable proportions of traditional furniture.

Though Paul's carved wood chairs for Haus Kaufmann were technically conservative, he also experimented with new materials and new modes of production. When the Deutsche Werkstätten developed a new press for laminating veneers, he responded with a series of designs that exploited the new technology, including his wardrobe Modell 7843, introduced by the Deutsche Werkstätten in 1923. The undulating surface of the wardrobe was one of Paul's favorite motifs, exaggerated to perform a structural function. The doors were composed of very thin veneers, creating a panel that was both lightweight and flexible.[272] At the same time, their complex shape provided necessary rigidity to a piece of furniture constructed from less than one third the material required for a traditional design.[273] Despite their functional form, the stained and brightly polished doors of the wardrobe produced a dramatic visual effect of unusual elegance. The Deutsche Werkstätten exhibited an example in 1925 at the »Il Mostra Internazionale della Arti Decorative«, the second Monza Biennale. Paul was himself impressed by the aesthetic possibilities of laminated veneers, and would frequently employ the technique in his furniture and interiors.

In 1924, Paul conceived a series of furnishings for a prefabricated model house that he designed for the Deutsche Werkstätten. The majority of the furnishings for the model home, the Plattenhaus (panel-house) H 1018, were practical and simple. Many of the chairs for the house, however, followed the pattern established by Paul in his earlier Expressionist interiors in the transformation of a traditional furniture type to create an unexpected effect. The relationship of the chair arms and their supports was purely sculptural, an experiment in the juxtaposition of seemingly abstract forms.[274] Nevertheless, the Plattenhaus chairs were one of his final Expressionist designs for serial production.

Expressionism and the middle class

During the 1920s, the vast majority of Paul's clients were members of the middle class. Before the war he had conceived both inexpensive furniture for factory workers, and exquisite individual pieces for the aristocracy. But, for differing reasons, these two markets effectively disappeared in Germany after 1918. In their absence, Paul committed himself to the needs of the social stratum to which he himself belonged.

Paul's architectural projects were commissioned by members of the so-called old middle class, the sector of German society traditionally identified by the possession of real property. Originally composed of landowners, artisans, and professionals, the old middle class had expanded following the unification of 1871 to include the increasingly prosperous industrialists, commercial entrepreneurs, and publishing magnates of the Gründerzeit. Paul's clients, including the factory-owner Fraenkel, the banker Kaufmann, and the publisher Neven-Dumont, belonged to the post-1871 expansion of the old middle class, and their opinions were accordingly progressive.

The Expressionism that Paul promoted to his successful, capitalist clients was notably devoid of revolutionary political intent. In this regard, his designs of the 1920s paralleled a broader historical trend. The Expressionist movement had associated itself with the rebellious spirit of 1918, and for a time loose organizations including the Novembergruppe and the Arbeitsrat für Kunst championed an aesthetic closely aligned with their aspirations for the new republic. In 1920, for example, Berlin residents and theatergoers of every political persuasion enthusiastically received Robert Wiene's Expressionist masterpiece *The Cabinet of Dr. Caligary*, notwithstanding the radical pacifism of the original script. The public embraced the modernity of the film, without committing to its revolutionary intent. Expressionism became synonymous with contemporaneity, a transformation that was also reflected in Paul's own work.

Initially, as had been true of his Jugendstil designs, Paul's Expressionist furniture was too costly for any but the most successful purchasers. His Modell 180 bedroom, for example, cost 7,263 Marks following the stabilization of the German currency in 1925.[275] At that time, the average monthly salary of a German office worker was approximately 160 Marks. Few office workers, members of the so-called new middle class of white-collar employees, could afford such furnishings. Nevertheless, Paul's next bedroom for the Deutsche Werkstätten, Modell 181, sold for 880 Marks.[276] Although still relatively expensive, this bedroom suite was within the means of the more prosperous members of the new middle class.

The inexpensive furnishings that Paul designed with Expressionist details during the early years of the Weimar Republic did not produce the commercial success of the Wilhelmine Typenmöbel. Their intended customers, the Angestellten, were impoverished by the economic turmoil that followed the events of 1918.[277] Yet the new middle class endured, and many of its members purchased luxury items such as the bedroom number 181 as a symbol of their aspiration to the social status enjoyed by the old middle class. In a 1922 publication on the middle-class home, Alexander Koch stated that the house should reflect the personality of its owner as the »cloak and very image of his soul«.[278] Paul did not share the Marxist hope that a proletarian consciousness would awaken within the Angestellten.[279] Instead, he provided them the opportunity to express the soul of a broadly-defined social status that transcended the pre-industrial distinction of the old and the new middle classes, and that was characterized by an essential modernity.

This essential modernity was reflected most clearly in a commission that Paul received from the Berliner Straßenbahn-Betriebs-GmbH, or BStBG, the company that provided streetcar service in the German capital. He was retained to provide the artistic design of the T24/B24 streetcars.[280] More than 1,200 of these vehicles were built between 1924 and 1926, and their design set the standard for all subsequent Berlin streetcars constructed prior to the Second World War. Although Paul was not involved in the mechanical or structural design of the T24/B24 streetcars, he exerted considerable influence over their form. In addition, he was responsible for their livery: chrome yellow (postgelb) overall with a broad white band containing the windows. The vibrant colors and simple, rational forms of Paul's streetcars were once so ubiquitous in Berlin that his contribution to the unique character of the city's streetscapes was unparalleled. However the interiors of the T24/B24 streetcars were more impressive still.

One detail of the interiors of Paul's T24/B24 streetcars can stand for the character of the whole. The handholds at the end of each of the seats had a complex undulating form. Their general appearance is typical of the 1920s: an Expressionist flourish to an otherwise simple and functional element. However, Paul conceived these handholds to serve a specific purpose. A sketch by his assistant Sergius Ruegenberg, who worked on the drawings for the T24/B24, illustrated how the form of the handholds would permit their simultaneous use by several passengers – which, in fact, is precisely how they were employed. Similarly expressive forms appeared in the frames of the sliding doors at the ends of the passenger compartment and in the handles for the operable windows. Paul was obsessed with the functional characteristics of such forms, Ruegenberg recalled. He remembered Paul demanding a piece of modeling clay, »after crushing it in his hand, the organic form of the door handle remained ... There's nothing more functional than this, in contrast to what I was drawing six months later, for Mies.«[281] As a whole, the interior of a T24 or B24 streetcar was simply, rationally, and elegantly designed. Ruegenberg, for his part, learned much in Paul's office. He went on to prepare the drawings for Mies' Tugendhat House, and his Barcelona Pavilion.

Seifhennersdorf

In 1923, the city council of Seifhennersdorf, Paul's childhood home, sponsored a design competition for a new town hall. The programmatic requirements for the new town hall were modest in light of the worsening inflation. The competition program specified three principal objectives. The construction of the new town hall should result in the improvement of the public square adjacent to the existing village church; the plan should permit access to the town offices from each of the two public streets adjoining the site, as well as separate access for subsidiary building functions; and the architectural design should be deferential to the adjacent church, and should reflect the traditional character of local building types.[282] Notwithstanding the humble terms of the program, the competition attracted widespread interest in a year that presented many German architects with few opportunities. Although Paul's own office was relatively busy during 1923, he prepared a design for the Seifhennersdorf competition.

Unfortunately Paul's design for the Seifhennersdorf town hall, which was accorded honorable mention in the competition, has been lost. First prize went to Professor Jost of the Technische Hochschule in Stuttgart[283] in collaboration with Architect Burlage of Leipzig.[284] Jost, a former associate of Paul Schultze-Naumburg, was an experienced designer of public buildings for small communities.[285] His simple, efficient scheme for Seifhennersdorf provided the Rathausplatz between the town hall and the church with the form it retains to the present day. Jost's design was clearly influenced by the traditional architecture of the Oberlausitz, and satisfied the third requirement of the competition program by incorporating features such as the characteristic extended dormers of local farmsteads. His project did not provide direct access to the town offices from both of the streets as required by the program, but it did meet the fundamental needs of the town council.

113. Rathaus and war memorial, Seifhennersdorf, circa 1929. Drawing by Adolf Schorisch.
114. Wedding chamber, Seifhennersdorf, 1925. Drawing by Adolf Schorisch.
115. War memorial, Seifhennersdorf, 1929.

Although Paul's design did not win the competition for the new town hall, the city government retained him to assist in the execution of Jost's project, rather than Burlage. Paul exerted only a limited influence over the implementation of Jost's plans, but he completed the most prominent interiors for the new town hall, including the wedding chamber, committee room, cashier's office, mayor's office, and Ratskeller.[286] These rooms, with furnishings described in the Festschrift published for the dedication of the town hall as »simple, clear, purposeful and therefore beautiful«, epitomized his work of the 1920s.[287] Despite the vernacular character of the town hall, several of Paul's interiors received comment for their modernity, including the committee room with walls patterned in pale gray zigzag stripes.[288] The wedding chamber, which provided ample opportunities for symbolic elaboration, was likely the most coherent of all of his Expressionist interiors.

This tiny wedding chamber was the most refined of Paul's interiors for the Seifhennersdorf town hall. Though the room was intended for the performance of civil marriages, he provided it with an atmosphere of quiet sanctity. He designed a relief for the altar-like podium consisting of a linked pair of rings, then continued this motif of conjoining forms throughout the room. The windows were patterned with twining vines echoing the pointed arches of a medieval church. Paul continued this ecclesiastical symbolism in the carpet, a gift from the Seifhennersdorf weaving school, with patterns of interlacing crosses. The chairs incorporated carved backs that repeated the theme of harmonious union in their simple, elegant form. They were Paul's most confident Expressionist furnishings, as a consequence of their relevant and immediate symbolic content.[289]

In 1927, Paul completed a second project for Seifhennersdorf, a war memorial located in the square between the town hall and the parish church.[290] The monument was assembled from carved blocks of stone consisting of flat panels listing the 262 citizens of Seifhennersdorf lost in the war, and relief sculptures created by Professor Raemisch in Berlin. The relief panels depicted scenes of combat, evacuation of the wounded, a soldier's funeral, and the mourning wives and mothers of the fallen in a continuous frieze that formed the capital »S« for Seifhennersdorf. When viewed obliquely, the »S« was not readily apparent, and the monument appeared as interlocking blocks of masonry, with the flat panels recessed behind the surface of the frieze blocks. Paul himself selected the site for the memorial between the church and the town hall to remind to the people of the village of their common interest in the sacrifice of their fellow townsmen,[291] but also to establish an oblique approach to the monument in order to emphasize the complexity of its form.

Paul's war memorial demonstrated his acceptance of the aesthetic principles of the new avant-garde. It provided a counterpart to the monument to Karl Liebknecht and Rosa Luxemburg designed concurrently by his former student Mies. Mies' monument was dedicated on 13 June 1926, and had apparently been designed around the time he joined the Gesellschaft der Freunde des neuen Rußland (society of friends of the new Russia), in January of that year.[292] Paul was working on the Seifhennersdorf war memorial as early as April 1926, although it was not dedicated until 1929. Viewed obliquely from the corner of the Rathausplatz, Paul's monument clearly belonged to the same formal vocabulary as Mies': an abstract composition of projecting and receding masses. But Paul's monument was not an abstract sculpture, and its form was closely related to its symbolic function. The capital »S« was both a reference to the specific purpose of the monument as a commemoration of the honored dead of Seifhennersdorf, and a counterpoint to the meandering frieze with its more general reference to the futility of war. The frieze framed the memorial panels, which were recessed within it; the capstone protected the sculpted frieze from the weather, and projected beyond it. The form of Mies' monument was far more loosely related to its function.[293] Moreover the Liebknecht-Luxemburg Monument proved imperfectly suited to its

role as a memorial, demonstrated both by the inscription »Ich bin Ich war Ich werde sein« (I am, I was, I will be) that was originally installed and subsequently disappeared without a trace, and by the stainless steel Communist star and flagpole that Mies uncomfortably superimposed upon the irregular brick surface. In contrast, Paul's memorial was a unified design, with inscriptions integral to its composition. Nevertheless he designed the Seifhennersdorf memorial to express the same visceral condemnation of the politics of force as the Liebknecht-Luxemburg Monument, and similarly to commemorate the aspirations of the common man. »War brings destruction and oblivion, while peace fosters life and the blessings of productive labor«, proclaimed the dedicatory Festschrift for the inauguration of Paul's project, »concord nourishes, discord consumes – this is what the monument proclaims to us.«

Bruno Paul successfully adapted the formal vocabulary of the younger generation of German Modernists to his own practice, but not at the expense of his own established mode of design. He transformed the final phase of architectural Expressionism, complete with its prismatic recollection of Soviet Constructivism, to his own purposes. The Seifhennersdorf war memorial was his most successful Expressionist project, precisely because its programmatic requirements were more receptive to the formal, psychological, and sociopolitical tendencies of the broader Expressionist movement in painting and sculpture than were those of his architectural commissions. But Paul's memorial exhibited a lucidity and coherence that recalled the simplicity, efficiency, and perspicuity of his earlier work.

By 1927, Paul had reestablished himself in the circles of the avant-garde. His reemergence as an innovator was encouraged by the stabilization of the Mark in 1925, which precipitated new construction throughout the republic. More significantly, the Prussian government belatedly provided him with the opportunity to realize the educational objectives that he had outlined in 1907.

The Vereinigte Staatsschulen für freie und angewandte Kunst

In early 1924, the Prussian ministry of science, art, and education merged Paul's school of applied arts with the art school of the Prussian academy. The union of the two institutions proceeded in accordance with the recommendations Paul laid out in his 1919 article »Erziehung der Künstler an staatlichen Schulen« (the education of artists in the state schools).[294] But the ministry, to which Paul was appointed an advisor in 1922, did not pursue his suggestions until the desperate state of the German economy compelled it to act.

The ministry decreed that director Kampff of the academy school should be dismissed, and Paul appointed to replace him as the head of a combined institution entitled Vereinigte Staatsschulen für freie und angewandte Kunst (unified state schools of fine and applied art). He was immediately confronted with the difficult tasks of relocating the school of applied arts to the buildings of the academy school in Charlottenburg, and of eliminating redundant faculty positions. The decision of the ministry provoked a storm of protest over the fate of the venerable academy school, which had been established in 1696. The academy students initiated many of the protests over the loss of prestige that they perceived to accompany amalgamation with the school of applied arts. The academy professors, who faced the prospect of being pensioned off at the height of the inflation, joined the students in protest. Fritz Stahl, a reporter for the *Berliner Tageblatt*, incited popular support for the academy's students and faculty. He claimed to hold Paul in the highest regard,[295] but blamed the Prussian ministry for an arrogance that would have been inconceivable under the monarchy.[296]

Paul was wary of the aspirations of members of his new staff, perceiving Hans Poelzig, who had led an atelier at the academy since 1922, as a particular challenge. Although five years older than Paul, Poelzig had aligned himself with the young radicals in the early years of the Weimar Republic. Moreover, he had been elected president of the Werkbund in 1919, and promptly rekindled the debate of 1914 by emphatically denouncing the artistic value of the typification promoted by Muthesius. Instead he proclaimed that objectives of the Werkbund must be »firmly rooted in craftsmanship and art, not in industry and technology«.[297] For Poelzig, craftsmanship was a spiritual construct, an ethical principle derived from a medieval ideal. Paul was fundamentally opposed to Poelzig's conception of the Werkbund, and actively sought to limit his influence in the Vereinigte Staatsschulen. Paul feared Poelzig's ordination as »pope of architecture« in the new institution, and wrote a letter to the Prussian ministry of science, art, and education, in which he outlined an organizational structure for his school that would prevent such a thing from occurring.[298] An administration patterned after the universities, he maintained, would allow the effective

implementation of his educational objectives, while assuaging his opposition within the academic faculty.

Paul organized the Vereinigte Staatsschulen around three departments: architecture, fine art, and applied art. At the end of 1924 the new school had 539 students, of whom 401 attended classes full time. Of this total, which was balanced nearly equally between men and women, 40 were students of architecture, 121 of fine art, and 240 of applied art.[299] The number of students decreased in subsequent years as the school established a manageable population, but Paul continued to preside over a institution far larger and more complex than its closest contemporary parallel, Walter Gropius' Bauhaus.

Paul versus the Bauhaus

When the Prussian ministry of science, art, and education merged the schools of academic and applied art in Berlin it fulfilled an aspiration that Wilhelm von Bode had promoted since the turn of the century, and which Paul had made his own. The merger of the two schools also echoed events in Weimar during the spring of 1919, when the Staatliches Bauhaus was established from the local school of applied arts and the former Großherzogliche Hochschule für bildende Kunst. Van de Velde had directed the school of applied arts in Weimar since its establishment in 1906. When he was obligated to leave Germany as an enemy alien during the war, he left a short list of potential successors that included his principal allies in the 1914 debate: Obrist, Endell, and Gropius. Gropius emerged as the strongest candidate to succeed van de Velde. However his appointment was delayed by the closure of the Kunstgewerbeschule in 1915, and his own military obligations. In 1919 Gropius received an offer from the revolutionary government of the short-lived Freier Volksstaat Sachsen-Weimar-Eisenach[300] to head the school of the academy of fine art, which had continued in operation during the war. He presented a counterproposal to the government, recommending the merger of the academy school and the school of applied arts, which at the time existed only in name. In March the government approved Gropius' plans, and his appointment as director of the new institution, soon renamed Bauhaus.

In a speech before the parliament of Thuringia in Weimar on July 9, 1920, Gropius represented the Bauhaus as the logical culmination of the educational reforms begun in German schools of art at the end of the nineteenth century.[301] In a sense, he was justified in making this claim, since the Bauhaus embodied the merger of fine and applied arts that had been promoted by the Werkbund since 1907. Gropius cited the support of the directors of »the most important art institutes in Germany and Austria« as evidence of the significance of the Bauhaus to the broader movement for artistic reform. Paul, »director of the great school of arts and crafts in Berlin, advisor to the Prussian government before the war«, appeared with Fischer, Schumacher, and Riemerschmid in the list of notable architects that Gropius cited as supporters of his program, notwithstanding the fact that they were among the leading advocates of the standardization that he had opposed at the 1914 Cologne exhibition.

Although Gropius quoted Paul in his speech to the parliament of Thuringia, he only did so in order to promote his own reputation. Gropius cited Paul's December 1919 article »Erziehung der Künstler an staatlichen Schulen« in a manner that suggested that Paul's article had been written as a response to the April 1919 Bauhaus program. Gropius did not concede that Paul had made the same suggestions concerning unified instruction in the fine and applied arts in his wartime article »Künstlerlehrzeit«, begun (according to a 1917 letter from Paul to Geheimrat Pallat of the Wilhelmine ministry of culture) in 1912[302] and had been advocating this principle in the teaching plans of his school since 1907. Moreover, Gropius disclaimed the dissolution of van de Velde's school in October 1915. Indeed, the professors of the grand ducal academy of art rebelled against Gropius' leadership in 1920, and seceded en masse. Thus the Bauhaus did not, in actual fact, represent the union of van de Velde's school of applied arts with the school of the grand ducal academy, but rather a wholly new institution of Gropius' creation.

As director of the Bauhaus, Gropius deliberately positioned himself to succeed Paul as the leader of the reform movement in German art education. In a discussion with the council of Bauhaus masters on 9 December 1921, he proclaimed that the spirit of collaboration at his school »should not be conceived as it was in the previous generation«, among whom he specifically included Paul, but was intended to »clear the way for the creative energies of the individual and to establish an objective foundation on which individuals will be able to collaborate«.[303] It is unclear precisely how Gropius intended the collaboration of the Bauhaus to differ from the practice of the Berlin school of applied arts, which had been so effectively demonstrated at the Cologne exhibition.[304] The intent of his statement was obvious: that a new avant-garde had emerged in German design and intended to distance itself from the accomplishments of the preceding generation of artists.

Paul himself had little sympathy for Gropius and his visionary program of artistic reform, and was unwilling to relinquish his preeminence as a reformer. In a 1924 letter to the Prussian ministry of science, art, and education, he evoked the biting sarcasm of his youth in response to the organization of the Bauhaus and its spiritual association with the vanished system of guilds. »On the other hand, ›council of masters‹ sounds like something from the medieval legend of the ›Sängerkrieg auf der Wartburg‹«, he wrote. »tata tati tatatä-ta or Staatliches Bauhaus – tätä tätä – and it sounds unmodern (unmodern) and pathetic«, he continued, »it is ultimately inconsequential whether one prefers a ›council of masters‹ to a ›council of teachers‹.«[305] For Paul, the Bauhaus was an expression of revolutionary enthusiasm like the Arbeitsrat für Kunst, prepossessed with the exhilaration of progress unbounded by practical responsibility. He knew that Gropius had never actually confronted the challenge of reconciling the fine and practical arts, or developed a comprehensive curriculum, or forged a consensus within a diverse and antagonistic faculty. He saw, more clearly than anyone else in Germany, what Gropius had not achieved.

In 1936, Pevsner concluded that the Bauhaus and Paul's Vereinigte Staatsschulen had been the two most important schools of art in the Weimar Republic. He was an enthusiastic supporter of Gropius, whom he proclaimed the »greatest living German architect«. He also praised the »atmosphere of youth, conquest, thrill« that pervaded the Bauhaus in emulation of the passionate and revolutionary spirit of its founder.[306] But Pevsner was troubled by the shortcomings of Gropius' program. Despite the heroic ideal of architecture as the pinnacle of artistic expression, the Bauhaus did not include a formal department of architecture while Gropius was director. In fact the teaching of architecture at the Bauhaus only really began in 1927, under Hannes Meyer. Pevsner also noted Gropius' lack of interest in painting, the traditional epitome of the fine arts.[307] In the absence of focused instruction in architecture or painting, the early Bauhaus failed to realize the unification of the fine and applied arts to which Gropius had aspired.

By contrast, Pevsner praised Paul's Vereinigte Staatsschulen for restoring the »balance between painting and sculpture on one side, and handicraft and design on the other«. Paul had been emulating academic models of instruction in the curricula of his school of applied arts since 1907. When he assumed the directorship of the schools of the Prussian academy in 1924, he was able to bring his reforms to their logical conclusion. »When I relocated from the cramped quarters of Prinz-Albrecht-Straße to the larger buildings of the academy«, Paul wrote, »the union of education in the fine and applied arts that I had been planning did not await confirmation.« In fact, he continued, it resolved itself immediately.[308] Pevsner praised Paul for providing »art education of the highest standard for students of painting as well as of pottery or bronze founding« with the

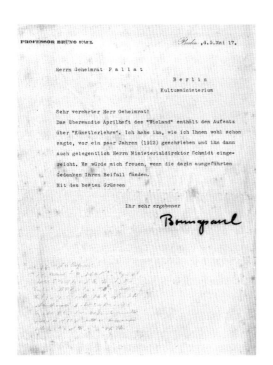

same preparatory courses given to all pupils. Although Paul did not share Gropius' revolutionary zeal, Pevsner acknowledged that the Vereinigte Staatsschulen remained unique as a consequence of a system »too consistent and drastic« for the conservative factions in artistic education. Nevertheless Pevsner concluded that the Vereinigte Staatsschulen, unlike the Bauhaus, »represented a success in almost every respect«.[309]

Renouncing Expressionism

By 1925, Germany was settling in to a period of austere stability under a revalued currency. The fantastic designs conceived by Bruno Taut and the members of the Gläserne Kette that had embodied the aesthetic ideals of the Expressionist movement seemed increasingly irrelevant. Nevertheless the ornamental qualities of the few emphatically Expressionist projects that were actually constructed, including Poelzig's Großes Schauspielhaus in Berlin, did produce a lasting influence on European artists. The vocabulary of modern design that was celebrated at the »Exposition des Arts Décoratifs et Industriels Modernes« held in Paris in 1925 derived in part from the tradition of German Expressionism, specifically from the mannered and aesthetic Expressionist vocabulary that Paul himself had promulgated.

Ironically, Paul did not participate in the Paris exposition. The organizing committee, intent on promoting the ascendancy of French design and mindful of the political ramifications of the Ruhr crisis of 1923–24, dispatched invitations to Germany too late for an effective response. Paul's Munich colleague Behrens designed a crystalline winter garden for the exhibition, but he did so for the Austrians. Though the French had hoped to demonstrate the superiority of their artistic accomplishments, many of the modern interiors displayed in Paris recalled the abstract classicism of Paul's work for the Cologne exhibition of 1914. He made the most of this renewed interest in such precedents by founding the Richmodishaus für Kunst und Handwerk in Cologne with capital invested by the Deutsche Werkstätten. Paul planned the headquarters and sales rooms for the firm in 1925, and provided designs for furnishings and interiors. The Richmodishaus sold copies of the office from the Gelbes Haus, as well as of the famous blue dining room. The firm also sold new designs in the same style, characterized by undulating surfaces and brightly colored finishes, including a red dining room that was displayed at the third Monza Biennale in 1927. Although Paul was willing to capitalize on the French style of 1925, he was unwilling to return to the aesthetic that he had favored during the previous decade. He was equally reluctant to commit himself to an Expressionism that had largely run its course. Instead he began to explore, as did many of his students, the Neues Bauen, the »New Building« that would become synonymous with European Modernism.

When the school of applied arts relocated to the academy buildings on Hardenbergstraße, Paul was obligated to establish a new home for his family in Charlottenburg. He moved with his wife and daughter into a building that he had purchased and renovated in 1920 at Budapester Straße 45, a fashionable address in the shadow of the Kaiser Wilhelm memorial church, overlooking the Berlin Zoo.[310] There he began a new life, and entered a new phase of his career. Prior to the war, Paul had been a leader of an avant-garde committed to the reform of popular taste; by 1925, he had emerged as a reformer of the avant-garde and a champion of mainstream modernity.

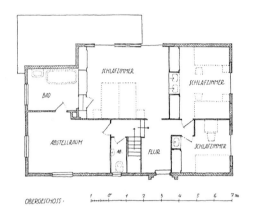

OBERGESCHOSS.

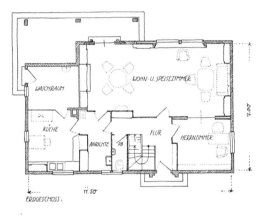

ERDGESCHOSS.

6. Pragmatic Functionalism and the timeless German building arts: 1925–1932

In 1924, G. F. Hartlaub organized an exhibition in Mannheim entitled »Die neue Sachlichkeit«, or the New Objectivity. The term Neue Sachlichkeit was soon applied to the »Neues Bauen«, the New Building, that would eventually be commemorated as the International Style. Paul was only fifty years old in 1924, and considerably more successful and experienced than the younger architects responsible for the promulgation of the New Building. Yet he retained the ability to recognize and appropriate emerging trends that had served him so well throughout his career. As popular interest in Expressionism waned, he committed himself to the new style. Paul's projects of the late 1920s, however, were still profoundly influenced by his own professional experience, and by the ideals of comfort and convenience he had fostered during three decades of architectural practice. His work epitomized a pragmatic Functionalism that represented an alternative to the polemical objectivity of the Neue Sachlichkeit.

The Plattenhaus H 1018

In 1925, two years before the inauguration of the Weißenhofsiedlung, Paul introduced his Plattenhaus H 1018, or panel-house H 1018, at the exhibition »Wohnung und Siedlung« in Hellerau. Although the furnishings he designed for his Plattenhaus in 1924 were Expressionist in character, the building itself embodied the aesthetic of the New Objectivity. The tiny building was a composition of prismatic volumes, ostensibly flat-roofed elements devoid of conventional architectural ornament. As in all of Paul's residential designs, the street façade was the most rigorously ordered, notwithstanding its asymmetry.[311] The remaining elevations of the house were functionally designed, with small rectangular windows aligned in accordance with the internal distribution of rooms.

Paul designed his Plattenhaus to be assembled from prefabricated components manufactured by the Deutsche Werkstätten. The house was composed of approximately one hundred individual elements, predominantly plywood panels. Externally it was finished with Eternit (asbestos-cement), applied to produce a smooth finish that emphasized its simple, prismatic geometries.[312] The system of construction was similar to that employed in earlier wooden houses produced by the Deutsche Werkstätten, but Paul's Plattenhaus could be assembled from far fewer components than other models of comparable scale. This simplicity belied the spatial complexity of the design, with rooms of differing ceiling heights fitted together within the cubic volume of the exterior.[313] He intended his design as a departure from the largely traditional, rural housing types offered by the Deutsche Werkstätten. »The exterior form of the new house is composed to fit into the urban environment«, proclaimed the catalog published in conjunction with the introduction of the Plattenhaus H 1018, »and this cosmopolitan character is also expressed in the interior.«[314]

Internally, Paul's Plattenhaus echoed the topology of his earlier middle-class homes. By eliminating the two-story stair hall and minimizing the floor area devoted to circulation, he was able
to retain features of his larger houses that were unusual in a building the size of the Plattenhaus
H 1018, which had a total floor area of only 153 square meters. The tiny study, which featured a
fireplace, built-in shelving, and elegant hardwood paneling, was representative of Paul's inten-
tions for the house. It blurred the distinctions between architecture and cabinetry, a characteristic
shared with his 1924 Haus Auerbach in Berlin-Dahlem. The interiors of Haus Auerbach featured
built-in furniture, hidden lighting, and undulating wall surfaces shaped from laminated veneers.
While the interiors of the Plattenhaus H1018 were far simpler, it was undeniably a small, efficient
middle-class home, reflecting middle-class standards of comfort and convenience.

The Plattenhaus H 1018 appeared in the catalogs of the Deutsche Werkstätten together with
a complete line of Plattenhäuser, largely of traditional design, ranging in size from the 55 square
meter H 122a designed by Eugen Schwemmle through Richard Riemerschmid's 285 square meter H 287. Copies of Paul's Plattenhaus H 1018 could be purchased for 15,520 Marks: less than
the cost of a typical masonry house of similar quality, but more than the majority of the prefabricated houses sold by the Deutsche Werkstätten.[315] The Werkstätten produced large numbers of
wooden houses in traditional and vernacular styles, but it apparently never sold a second Plattenhaus H 1018 – there was simply no market for such a dwelling during the years of economic uncertainty.[316]

Although Paul remained committed to the New Building, he recognized that technological and
stylistic innovation could only be sustained through the patronage of appreciative clients. In the
context of Paul's career, which was characterized by his relentless development of themes and
variations, his single Plattenhaus was a failure – notwitstanding its technical sophistication and its
frequent publication.[317] Yet as a genuine and affordable product of mechanical production, the
house accorded perfectly with the objectives of the celebrated 1927 Werkbund exhibition »Die
Wohnung«, the Stuttgart Weißenhofsiedlung. However, Paul did not participate in the exhibition
organized by his former student Mies van der Rohe. His name was not included in the list of invi-
tees compiled by Mies and his collaborators, and his efforts were directed elsewhere. He had received a commission to coordinate German participation in the »III Mostra Internazionale delle Arti
Decorative«, the third Monza Biennale. The biennale opened two months earlier than »Die Wohnung«, and Paul's attention was focused on Monza. If he had an opinion regarding the Weißenhofsiedlung, he never expressed it publicly. With his Plattenhaus he had already demonstrated a
viable prototype for inexpensive, mass-produced modern housing. Despite professional enthusiasm for his design, the free market would not readily sustain such innovation.

The architecture of modern commerce

The stabilization of the Mark in 1925 initiated a resumption of the commercial construction that
had largely been forsaken during the inflation. Paul, who had maintained a successful architectural practice during the lean years that followed the revolution of 1918, took immediate advantage
of the economic stabilization. He invested his own money in the Richmodishaus, the Cologne
bureau of the Deutsche Werkstätten, and designed the offices and salesrooms for the company.
Paul's design included the insertion of tall display windows into the ground floor of an existing
Neoclassical building adjacent to the Neumarkt in the center of the medieval city. His modifications transformed the character of the building, eliciting the praise of Richard Heyken in *Deutsche Kunst und Dekoration*: »The historical beauty of the building was not only preserved, but
enhanced by the rhythmic insertion of the high shop windows into the smooth façade.«[318]

Following the completion of the Richmodishaus in 1927, Paul prepared a design for the Sinn
department store in Gelsenkirchen. The site, on the commercial Bahnhofstraße near the central
station, had none of the historic character of the Neumarkt in Cologne. Paul took advantage of
opportunities afforded by this location and designed an emphatically modern building. Conceiving
the elevations of the Sinn store in horizontal bands, he designed continuous strip windows of
green opalescent glass, contrasting them with the white-painted spandrels. The ground floor was
dominated by a strip of windows 3.2 meters high, which included a single curved pane 5.5 meters long at the corner – the largest sheet of curved glass yet manufactured in Europe. The main
entrance to the store featured freestanding displays in the form of glass columns beneath a reflective metal ceiling, a dynamic composition of industrial materials whose transparent supports

121, 122. Sinn department Store, Gelsenkirchen, 1928.
Exterior by day and night.
123. Dischhaus, Cologne, 1930. Exterior.
124. Dischhaus, Cologne, 1930. Interior of stair hall.

represented a subversion of architectural conventions. The design was particularly dramatic at night, when the form of the building was accented with neon lamps and the brightly-lit display windows were reflected in the metal soffits. The Sinn store embodied a harmonious union of modern technology and modern commerce, a composition so successful that it was still featured in publications on commercial design in the 1950s.[319] The planning of the Sinn store was as bold as its external form. Paul employed a structural system that cantilevered beyond the perimeter columns of the building, permitting the use of a true curtain wall.

In 1928, Paul won a contest for the design of the Dischhaus, an office building for the Hotel-Disch AG in Cologne. His winning proposal, with its dynamic asymmetry, banded windows, and rounded corner, was closely related to the earlier Sinn store, but the detailing was fundamentally different. In place of painted plaster, Paul clad the façade with a travertine veneer. He enthusiastically embraced the use of a very thin masonry cladding, again a curtain-wall construction. The actual structure of the Dischhaus was a reinforced concrete frame. In accordance with his elegant adaptation of the Functionalist aesthetic, Paul composed the strip windows from individual casements separated by travertine mullions, rather than an ostensibly continuous band of glass.

The Dischhaus was undeniably a modern building, even in the context of the Neue Sachlichkeit. The window frames and horizontal trim on the façades were fabricated from Durana-Metall, an aluminum alloy that provided a technological counterpoint to the travertine cladding. He conceived the shop windows at the corner of the building as freestanding displays, sheltering a passageway whose interior wall was formed by an undulating series of floor-to-ceiling display windows, with curved glass panels set in thin metal frames. The spatial drama of the passage was repeated in the lobby of the Dischhaus, which was dominated by a wide spiral staircase that rose uninterrupted through the eight stories of the building. Paul illuminated the underside of the stair with a continuous row of individual luminaires. The spectacular view upwards through the circular opening in the center of the stair was accented by the spiraling line composed of more than three hundred tiny lamps. The fluid spatial forms, industrial materials, and technological sophistication of the Dischhaus identified it as an exemplary modern building, notwithstanding its elegant travertine veneer and practical detailing. Although the Dischhaus was a shockingly progressive design in the medieval center of Cologne, it is a relatively anonymous building in the context of the twenty-first century city – an ironic testament to the prescience of Paul's vision.

As Paul was developing his design for the Dischhaus, he spent five weeks in the United States. During his visit, he enthusiastically studied commercial construction in New York. »A building period of five months is not unusual for a structure with a floor area between 1,000 and 2,000 square meters and a height of twenty to thirty stories«, he wrote, »an accomplishment explained by exemplary standards of engineering and construction technology.« He particularly admired the American practice of completing all of the building plans and structural calculations, and awarding all of the contracts, before construction work commenced; this was in stark contrast with contemporary practice in Germany.[320] He applied the lessons of New York to the 1928 commission for a new office building for the Kathreiners Malzkaffeefabrik, a prosperous maker of ersatz coffee in Berlin. His project, a twelve-story tower, was the first skyscraper in the German capital, and one of the first tall buildings in Central Europe built in accordance with American practice. Paul enthusiastically incorporated into his own professional activities principles he had observed in the United States. Although the twelve-story Kathreiner-Hochhaus was a small building by American standards, it was technically and aesthetically sophisticated. Paul ensured that the steel frame and floor plates were erected in a typically American five months, an achievement unprecedented in Berlin. He then sheathed the lightweight steel skeleton in an elegant veneer composed of three different types of travertine: a rich, ochre hued, German stone for the ground floor with light and dark Roman travertine for the upper stories and their bands of fenestration.

The Kathreiner-Hochhaus was located on Potsdamer Straße in Berlin, overlooking Carl von Gontard's baroque Königskolonnaden (royal colonnades) of 1780.[321] Paul responded to the proximity of the historic colonnades by aligning the main entrance of his building with Gontard's central pavilions. The six-story wings flanking the entrance to the tower provided a mediating scale between the twelve-story tower and the colonnades. The travertine piers between the ground floor windows of Paul's building echoed the proportions of Gontard's Ionic columns, establishing a vertical counterpoint to the horizontal windows of the tower. He designed the top two stories with true ribbon windows, continuous curtains of glass uninterrupted by the steel structural frame. Herbert Günther, writing in the Werkbund journal *Die Form* in 1932, praised the harmonious relationship of the Königskolonnaden and the Kathreiner-Hochhaus. »The gracious colonnades appear all the more gracious in comparison with the solid multistoried building beside them«, he wrote, »while their very slenderness enhances its monumental effect.«[322] The influence of the Kathreiner-Hochhaus was considerable. The second steel-framed skyscraper in Berlin, Emil Fahrenkamp's Shell-Haus of 1932, was very much indebted to Paul's design, even in the shape of its windows and the color of its thin travertine veneer.

In addition to projects such as the Dischhaus and the Kathreiner-Hochhaus Paul continued to design in the vocabulary of the Neues Bauen. In 1929, he completed the drawings for a second Sinn department store, in the city of Essen. Externally his second Sinn store was ostensibly similar to the first, with strip windows punctuating white plaster façades. Internally, Paul organized the building around a central light court, featuring a glass elevator enclosed in a glass and metal shaft, a vertical counterpart to the strip windows of the exterior. At the same time Paul was also completing less ambitious commercial projects, such as a storefront for the Ullstein Schnittmusterladen on the Kurfürstendamm in Berlin. In every respect, such projects were exemplary modern designs conceived in accordance with the practical requirements of modern mass commerce and the material opportunities afforded by modern industry. Paul faced a greater challenge in devising a similarly pragmatic response to the domestic requirements of contemporary life.

The modern home

In the same year that the Plattenhaus H 1018 was first exhibited in Hellerau, Paul received a commission to design a new house in Soest for the prosperous factory owner Ernst Sternberg. The majority of the drawings that Paul produced for Haus Sternberg have survived, documenting a design process that began with a proposal that shared little with his contemporary Plattenhaus.[323] The building permit application for Haus Sternberg, Paul's first proposal for the house, was filed in 1925. The application drawings depicted the house as a simple rectangular block beneath a tall tiled roof with a wide central dormer. The windows on the second floor were square, and widely spaced. Paul placed the stone embrasure for the front door slightly off center, flanking it with the large rectangular windows of the study on the left side and the smaller kitchen windows on the right, reflecting planning principles ultimately derived from Haus Westend. The façade shown in the building permit drawings was punctuated by a projecting triangular bay, an Expressionist element in a fundamentally Neoclassical composition derived from Paul's elegant and largely symmetrical Haus Auerbach of 1924. A rendered perspective of the first proposal for Haus Sternberg even included a series of three isolated gables crowning an elongated dormer, echoing the characteristic roofline of Haus Auerbach.

A second proposal for Haus Sternberg, conceived in 1926, introduced a horizontal band of thirteen windows in a broad dormer set beneath an exaggerated, crystalline roof form. The sec-

125. Kathreiner-Hochhaus, Berlin, 1929. Exterior.
126. Ullstein Schnittmusterladen, Berlin, 1928.
127. Haus Sternberg, Soest, 1928. Exterior.

ond design also featured a coursed ashlar veneer, consisting of the characteristic green limestone of Soest, in place of the smooth plaster finish implied by the original drawings. Although a classical influence remained, it was tempered by Paul's Expressionist detailing. His second proposal would have resulted in a modern house, albeit a relatively conservative one. But Ernst Sternberg asked Paul to reduce the scale of the project, prompting a third proposal.

Paul's third and final design for Haus Sternberg, submitted as an amendment to the building permit in the summer of 1927, continued the development of the project towards the vocabulary of the Neues Bauen. In 1927, Paul abandoned the steep tile roofs of the earlier designs in favor of a visually flat configuration with broad eaves. He grouped the windows of the upper floor into a horizontal band, and relocated the front door to eliminate the implied symmetry of the original composition. In reworking the plans for Haus Sternberg, Paul successfully transformed the comfortable and convenient middle-class design of Haus Auerbach in accordance with the progressive formal language of the Plattenhaus H 1018, without sacrificing its fundamental virtues. In so doing, he established the principles of the pragmatic Functionalism that would characterize his residential projects in the final years of the Weimar Republic.

Villa Traub and the architecture of modern life

The villa that Paul designed for Edmund Traub, a prominent Prague industrialist, epitomized his conception of an architecture for modern life. The plans derived from his final design for Haus Sternberg, and hence from the long line of residential projects originating with Haus Westend. Paul intended Villa Traub, like Haus Westend, as a statement of principle. With the earlier house, he established his interpretation of the »zweites Biedermeier« as the language of modern design; with the later, he intended to do the same with the Neues Bauen.

Traub hired Paul in 1928 to design a new home for his family on a prestigious site beneath the ramparts of Prague castle.[324] Paul made several trips to Prague as he designed the house. Traub's daughter Mimi Furst (née Traub) remembered him working diligently in the study of her father's house on Kolkovna Street in the Prague district of Staroměstská, preparing drawings for the villa in solitude.[325] Although Paul designed alone, he retained the services of the architect Egon Votický to act as his local representative and to complete the construction documents for the project.

When completed, Villa Traub appeared as an abstract composition of pure geometric forms, a tall prismatic block surmounted by a second, smaller prism. The windows of the upper floors were arranged in horizontal bands in one of the characteristic motifs of the Neues Bauen. The larger windows of the main floor were simple rectangular openings, incised in the walls of the house. In response to the topography of the site, the villa rose four full stories above the entry courtyard. From the northern Prague – where Traub's factory was located – the tall cubic form of the house provided a visual counterpoint to the evocative skyline of the castle. The rear elevation of the house was only three stories tall, and the floor-to-ceiling windows of the principal floor opened onto a spacious sunken garden. A full-size tennis court stood to the west of the house at the same elevation as the garden, surrounded by a tall white pergola. The pergola, composed of simple wooden elements in a freestanding grid, emphasized the abstract geometries of the house.

The simple, abstract form of the villa belied the material with which it was clad: a finely-honed sandstone. The stone façades were exquisitely detailed, with shallow reveals and projecting sills at the fenestration and rusticated horizontal joints providing a subtle articulation of otherwise smooth elevations. The variations in color and texture inherent to the stone provided the only surface ornament. The wooden windows were painted a deep green, a traditional hue that harmonized with the warm tones of the sandstone and imparted a classical grace to the exteriors of the villa. When completed, the house embodied a palpable tension between the influence of the New Building and the tradition of German Classicism manifested in Paul's earliest work as an architect. Its prismatic masses, which Paul described with characteristic modesty as »cigar boxes«, were emphatically modern. Indeed, the form of the villa, a rectangular block with a recessed attic story opening onto a roof terrace, became the characteristic configuration of Functionalist architecture in urban Prague.[326]

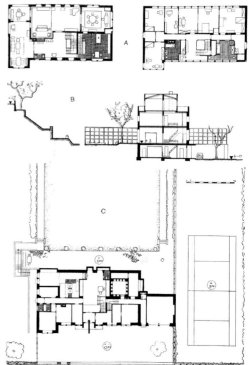

Paul was cautious in his implementation of the prismatic formal language of the New Building. At Haus Sternberg, he had designed conventional roofs with a gradual, five-degree slope, but the roof he designed for Villa Traub was steeper, in response to the climate of central Bohemia, but concealed behind parapets. Consequently, the house suggested geometrical purity and abstraction, notwithstanding the practical concessions to adequate roof drainage.[327] Where a pitched roof was precluded by functional necessity, as in the terraces surrounding the attic story of Villa Traub, Paul was not averse to designing a roof of lower slope. He did not employ architectural features for the sake of a theoretical stylistic purity, but rather for the sake of functional efficiency. Where he elected to employ a pitched roof in Prague, he took full advantage of the spatial opportunities of this form in the sloping ceilings of the bedrooms that it sheltered.

Like the pitched roof of Villa Traub, the sandstone that Paul employed for the façades constituted a response to a functional requirement. It was, rather, a deliberate counterpoint to the smooth neutrality of painted stucco, the ubiquitous finish of the Weißenhofsiedlung and of his own Plattenhaus. When the Traub family moved into the villa, however, the sandstone cladding had not yet been installed. Paul plastered the exterior walls of the house in order to provide a temporary finish, pending the arrival of the finely worked sandstone, and he had the plaster painted white, in accordance with the characteristic architectural finish of the New Building.[328] This temporary finish proved to be predictably unsatisfactory. »It was terrible«, Traub's daughter recalled, »even the rain would stain it.«[329] The sandstone cladding for which Paul had designed the villa immediately eliminated the problems with the plaster façades. This cladding transformed the house, in fact, and illustrated his pragmatic ideal of a Functionalism tempered by the experience of professional practice.

Although Paul was unwilling to compromise proven and efficient design solutions, he was responsive to the possibilities offered by technological developments. The sleek etched glass and polished metal front door that he conceived for Villa Traub, for example, was a purely Modernist composition that he sensibly sheltered from the elements behind a vestibule and a solid outer door.[330] On the other hand, the electrically operated window of the wintergarden, similar to the windows that Mies later employed in the Tugendhat House in Brno,[331] was emphatically innovative.[332] A comparison with the Tugendhat House is particularly apt, in that it illuminates two differing interpretations of Functionalism. In Brno, Mies – working with Paul's former assistant Sergius Ruegenberg – designed a glass wall more than 20 meters long, composed of alternating fixed and electrically movable panes. Two movable panes could be lowered, opening the living areas of the house to the garden. However the garden was a full story below the main floor of the house, so the connection was emotional rather than physical. Moreover, the vertical fall necessitated railings at the operable windows, which Mies continued across the three fixed windows for the sake of consistency. At the Villa Traub, Paul had used the same system to allow the entire wall of the wintergarden to disappear into the floor, converting the comfortable enclosed room into a garden alcove. Mies used the sliding windows primarily for their polemical value, to celebrate industrial

technology and the ideal of a mechanized dwelling. Paul employed the same system two years earlier to solve a longstanding functional challenge: the creation of a wintergarden that could be used as a room in inclement weather, but which retained a direct connection with the landscape. In the bedrooms on the upper floor of the villa, he provided conventional wooden casements with metal shades that could be rolled up into recesses in the exterior wall. This proved an effective means of controlling sunlight and ventilation, providing a practical alternative to metal-framed strip windows that were cold and drafty in the winter, while admitting excessive heat and light in the summer.

Paul planned the interiors of Villa Traub in the same pragmatic manner, adapting proven solutions wherever practicable, and evaluating innovative measures where they could be functionally justified. Topologically, Villa Traub continued the series of domestic designs that Paul had initiated with Haus Westend in 1907. The plan of Villa Traub differed from that of Haus Westend primarily because of its sloping site. Since the front door at Villa Traub was located one level below the main floor of the house, vertical circulation had a greater influence on the planning of the house than in Paul's earlier designs. He responded with a multi-story hall containing a sinuous, cantilevered stair that dramatically linked the three principal floors of the villa. He reduced the open area of the hall in comparison with the two-story halls of English inspiration that he employed in designs such as Haus Westend, to achieve a vertically-proportioned volume through which the flowing stair spiraled. The stair hall was a dramatic and complex volume, a manipulation of space characteristic of the New Building. Although the multi-level planning of the house was not unique in Prague,[333] Mimi Furst recalled that the vertical circulation of the house was an unfamiliar feature in a middle-class residence.[334]

The common rooms of the house reflected conventional notions of comfort and propriety rather than spatial drama. But Paul took advantage of the elevated main floor of the house to recess the radiators in wells beneath the floor-to-ceiling windows of the garden façade, concealing the radiator wells beneath wooden grilles contiguous with the floors. The complex volumes of the principal rooms of the villa permitted efficient winter heating of the cold perimeter walls of the house, without obtrusive radiators. As a technological solution, Paul's design was notably superior to the ducted air system that Mies specified for the Tugendhat House. Although marine engineers had perfected ducted air heating systems by 1907, Mies was unwilling to locate registers at the perimeter of his glazed volume where they were most required. As a consequence, the inefficient heating system of the Tugendhat House had to be rebuilt to function even marginally well, necessitating obtrusive alterations to the original design. In contrast, the proven system that Paul specified for Villa Traub continued to perform satisfactorily after seven decades of use.

The most significant distinctions between Villa Traub and the Tugendhat House, considered as an embodiment of a dogmatic Modernism, may be recognized in the differing attitudes towards architectural craftsmanship maintained by Paul and Mies. Both designers shared an intuitive understanding of the inherent beauty of materials. Paul's use of silver leaf, porphyry, calfskin, and exotic hardwoods in the interiors of Villa Traub, however, was emphatically distinct from the practice of his younger colleague. Although the moldings and furnishings that Paul designed for the villa were generally simple and abstract, they were also inherently artistic, and executed by skilled craftsmen. Even in his Functionalist designs, Paul believed that a machine was a tool like any other. He did not insist that the idiosyncratic brass hardware he designed for each of the major rooms of the house be finished entirely by hand; neither did he seek to give his hinges and door handles the illusory qualities of purely mechanical production. They were works of art, conceived in accordance with the personal convictions regarding the interdependence of the artistic disciplines that informed his leadership of the unified state schools of fine and applied arts. »In this city«, Paul wrote of Prague, »the timeless German building arts are still practiced.«[335]

The Deutsche Werkstätten provided the majority of the furnishings for Villa Traub, and offered similar pieces for sale through its catalogs. By the end of the 1920s, the Deutsche Werkstätten, which had adopted a more progressive aesthetic than the Vereinigte Werkstätten, was producing the majority of Paul's furniture designs. His Modell 275 bedroom, introduced in 1932, was typical of his Modernist interiors. The wardrobe and side table were manufactured using a process similar to that employed for his Expressionist wardrobe, Modell 7843 of 1923. Nine years later, he had eliminated the last vestiges of traditional cabinetry to design an abstract and sculptural wardrobe that combined advanced laminating and molding technologies with an elegant and evocative form. At the same time, Paul was experimenting with the incorporation of metal elements in his designs. Though he was eager to exploit the potential industrial materials by designing furniture that was both light and strong,[336] he was unwilling to design an uncomfortably uncompromising piece of furniture. He preferred to design in wood, reflecting an empathy for traditional materials that was also apparent in his architectural projects. The lavish interiors of Paul's Haus Carl Bergmann in Dresden,[337] completed in 1929, epitomized his masterful and innovative use of natural, or rather traditional, materials such as timber and stone.

While Villa Traub was under construction, Paul designed a similarly impressive modern house in Berlin. The client was Paul Lindemann, though the villa has been known as Haus am Rupenhorn since the Second World War for its location on a hillside overlooking the valley of the river Havel.[338] According to Lindemann's daughter Eva, Paul's design was selected over proposals by several other architects, including Mendelsohn. Though Haus am Rupenhorn was not published during Paul's lifetime, it was among his favorite projects. It is one of the few buildings that he took his family to visit after the war, when the house was being used by the Allies as a reeducation center.[339]

Like Villa Traub, Haus am Rupenhorn was a simple rectangular block with a flat roof. In his design for the house, Paul dispensed with parapets in favor of a gently sloping hipped roof with projecting eaves. Haus am Rupenhorn was built from hard clinker bricks with stone details, including a base of roughly hewn blocks and finely worked window embrasures. The brick was laid in a double-stretcher Flemish bond throughout, without any ornamental details. This severe and utilitarian brickwork was echoed in two houses that Mies completed the following year, Haus Esters and Haus Lange in Krefeld. Consequently Haus am Rupenhorn could be considered Paul's most emphatically modern house, the one that met most closely the ideals of the Functionalist canon. Though Haus am Rupenhorn was remarkably similar to Haus Esters in many aspects of its composition, it was also inherently different.

While Mies utilized metal-framed windows throughout Haus Esters, Paul preferred wooden casements in stone embrasures. Though this design was the more traditional, it was also the more practical. The profile of the stone frame kept rainwater off the window, and the timber frame was more watertight and better insulated than a metal one. But Paul was not opposed to metal frame windows where wood was impractical. He designed an enormous bronze-framed window for the living room of Haus am Rupenhorn, a technical achievement that was comparable to his contemporary department stores and provided a breathtaking view of the Havel. The wintergarden adjacent to the living room featured a glazed corner with windows set in thin bronze frames. Paul located the windows beyond the exterior walls of the house, in a projecting bay. This both enhanced the effect of the glazed corner and permitted the installation of a second set of wooden windows inside the house during the winter, in order to moderate the internal temperature. Once again, such well-conceived details were characteristic of Paul's Functionalist designs.

Internally, Haus am Rupenhorn shared with Villa Traub the fundamental topology of Haus Westend. Paul organized the interior around a two-story stair hall, located behind the street

132. Haus Carl Bergmann, Dresden, 1928. Interior.
133. Haus am Rupenhorn, Berlin, 1929. Exterior.

façade and lit by windows on the upper floor. The stair was marble, with beautifully crafted brass and iron railings. As at Villa Traub, Paul designed idiosyncratic hardware for each of the principal rooms. Many of the interior doors were extravagantly veneered; the floors were marble or hardwood parquet. Every detail of the house was beautifully made in accordance with Paul's ideals of artistry and craftsmanship, from the copper flashing of the terrace on the roof of the dining room to the sculptural iron knockers on the front door. The common rooms were largely simple rectangular volumes, arrayed around the dramatic, two-story stair hall. The bedrooms upstairs were arrayed on the garden side of a double-loaded central corridor as Paul preferred, with bath and service rooms overlooking the entry court. The planning of the house was practical and efficient, again in accordance with his professional experience.

Haus Esters was conceived on completely different principles, notwithstanding its visual similarities with Haus am Rupenhorn. Mies composed his plan on the basis of abstract patterns of interlocking spatial elements, as documented by a well-known photograph of him designing Haus Esters with a thick stub of charcoal, working on a floor plan with the dynamic qualities of a painting by Mondrian. Although this approach resulted in the dramatic spatial relationships inherent in the interiors of the completed house, it also produced awkward and irregularly-shaped rooms with prominent and intrusive corners.

Mies followed Paul's example in developing a simple layout of bedrooms on the upper floor, but composed an austere and institutional plan with a series of identical bedrooms opening off a long, windowless corridor. The large strip windows of the entry façade of the house were contrary to the plan, and illuminated a storage room and a maid's closet (Putzraum) as well as two bathrooms. The structural objectivity of Haus Esters was also questionable, in that the brick garden wall of the upper story of the house did not align with masonry walls below, and instead had to be carried on steel beams above the children's room and the dining room on the ground floor. This complex and expensive solution to a simple problem confounded Ernst Walther, whom Mies had entrusted with supervision of the construction.[340] Although the masonry design of Haus Esters was expressively sculptural, a three-dimensional composition of apparently weightless brick membranes, its underlying structure was neither rational nor objective. Haus Esters was a masterpiece of architectonic sculpture, but an inherently compromised work of architecture. In contrast, Paul's Haus am Rupenhorn was architecturally flawless, if not quite the measure of Haus Esters in sculptural terms.

The dichotomous relationship of Haus am Rupenhorn and Haus Esters is remarkable in that Paul is not likely to have possessed a detailed knowledge of Mies' concurrent design.[341] Haus Esters was not published during the 1920s, even as a project. Moreover, Haus am Rupenhorn was completed in 1929, while Haus Esters was finished in 1930. Rather than an explicit critique of Mies, Haus am Rupenhorn represents the broader trends in Paul's Functionalist architecture, as well as a convincing demonstration of his adaptation of the aesthetic proclivities of his younger colleagues. Yet there is one Functionalist project that Paul did address in his designs for Haus am Rupenhorn: Mendelsohn's own home, which was built on the adjacent lot between 1928 and 1930.[342]

Mendelsohn's house, which was also referred to as Haus am Rupenhorn, lacked the plastic abstraction of Haus Esters. It was a literally Functionalist house, simply planned and simply shaped, clad in the smooth plaster of the Weißenhofsiedlung and painted a pale yellow. The principal rooms of the house were arranged enfilade. On the ground floor, the dining room, hall, living room, and music room faced the Havel without independent corridors, so that only one circulation path connected the principal rooms of the house. This configuration suggested the rational planning of a steamship or a sleeping car, albeit with a similar lack of traditional domestic comfort. Mendelsohn planned the upper floor of his house in accordance with the same principles. In writing about the house, he proudly proclaimed: »The upper floor is a small hotel. Smallest measurements. Everybody independent, every room with bath, telephone and individual arrangements«.[343] Mies designed similarly isolated bedrooms for Haus Lange. In 1929, Mendelsohn and Mies were promoting a reconsideration of established notions of home and family. Their domestic architecture manifested their revolutionary aspirations.

Mendelsohn commemorated his own home in his book Neues Haus – Neue Welt (new house – new world), published in 1932. This lavish document, with a preface by Paul's former assistant Edwin Redslob, celebrated the extravagant, clinical perfection of an environment »fit for a modern Goethe«.[344] Paul, on the other hand, did not intend his Haus am Rupenhorn for the pioneering spirit of a new age of German culture. He designed the house in accordance with contemporary, middle-class standards of comfort and convenience, as well as contemporary building technologies and a progressive aesthetic. Mendelsohn compromised traditional domestic utility for the sake of a polemical modernity. Paul disavowed polemical modernity for the sake of domestic comfort. His Haus am Rupenhorn and Mendelsohn's house provided two differing interpretations of Modernism, both of which, in the summer of 1929, appeared equally valid. Although Paul did not explain his position with publications such as *Neues Haus – Neue Welt*, he remained committed to the cause of artistic reform. His leadership of the Vereinigte Staatsschulen served, in lieu of the manifestoes favored by his younger colleagues, to document this commitment.

134. *Südsee Kitsch*, 1927. Poster for a student party at the Vereinigte Staatsschulen.

Vereinigte Staatsschulen für freie und angewandte Kunst

Paul's conception of Modernism was closely associated with his administration of the Vereinigte Staatsschulen, and resonated in the appointments he made to the faculty of his institution. When Cäsar Klein's tenure as a professor of stage and decorative painting lapsed in October 1925, Paul suggested two artists as potential replacements: Max Pechstein and Bernard Pankok. The two choices reflected the scope of Paul's own professional interest. Pechstein had been the most prominent member of the Expressionist organization Die Brücke, the only one of the group's founders trained as a painter. After the revolution of 1918, he joined both the Novembergruppe and the Arbeitsrat für Kunst, aligning himself with the revolutionary avant-garde of the modern movement. Pankok, nine years older, had worked beside Paul on interiors for the »VII. Internationale Kunstausstellung im Königlichen Glaspalaste München 1897«. His career had paralleled Paul's: he was an architect, painter, graphic artist, and designer; a member of the Werkbund; and head of a school of applied arts.[345] Ultimately, however, neither Pechstein nor Pankok joined Paul's staff. Cäsar Klein retained his position.

Professor Reger, who led the classes in architectural sculpture, was also persuaded to extend his contract, although Paul had suggested Gerhard Marcks as a possible replacement. Marcks left the Bauhaus in 1925 after László Moholy-Nagy initiated his program »Kunst und Technik – eine neue Einheit« (art and technology – a new unity). Afterwards he taught at the school of applied arts in Halle, under the direction of Paul's former assistant Paul Thiersch. Paul's suggestion that Marcks replace Reger attested to his desire to assemble a faculty of preeminent modern designers, including artists whose aesthetic principles differed from his own.

Though Paul did not secure the services of Gerhard Marcks, he did hire one prominent Bauhaus professor, Oskar Schlemmer.[346] Schlemmer had studied under Adolf Hölzel, Paul's friend and former collaborator. He was an early member of the Bauhaus staff, where he developed the innovative plastic and kinetic art of the Bauhaus theatre. In 1922 he premiered his seminal *Triadisches Ballett* (triadic ballet), for which he served as choreographer, designer, craftsman, and dancer. Paul's professional interest in the controversial Schlemmer reflects the progressive position of the Vereinigte Staatsschulen under his direction, justifying Pevsner's conclusion that Paul's school shared with the Bauhaus a position of leadership in German art education.

The Vereinigte Staatsschulen certainly shared the vibrant student life enjoyed at the Bauhaus. Social events were integral to the life of the school. Creativity and free expression were manifested in both the themes and the graphic designs for the regular events that punctuated the school's calendar – a tradition inherited from the former school of applied arts and perpetuated under Paul's administration.

Bruno Paul's philosophy as the head of the Vereinigte Staatsschulen was also reflected in the exhibitions that he sponsored or helped to organize. In 1925 he was a member of the committee that planned the »Ausstellung neuer amerikanischer Baukunst« (exhibition of new American building), presented by the academy in January 1926. This exhibition celebrated American architecture in the form both of contemporary buildings, including Bertram Goodhue's Nebraska State Capitol (completed in 1922) and McKenzie, Voorhees, and Gmelin's Barclay-Vesey Telephone Building (then under construction); and the visionary projects of Hugh Ferriss. The »Ausstellung neuer amerikanischer Baukunst« was the first such exhibition in central Europe.[347] In 1927, Paul and Fritz Höger, architect of the Chilehaus in Hamburg, organized the »Deutsche Ziegelbau-Ausstellung« (German brick-building exhibition) at the school. »The exhibition«, Paul wrote, demonstrated »the youthful strength of a timeless building industry.« It presented new »opportunities and possibilities«, he continued, and emphasized to the school and its students the importance of »technical exhibitions of the fundamental principles of craft on which the applied arts, and ultimately the fine arts depend«.[348] In the same year Paul presented the exhibition »Berliner Werkkunst« (Berlin industrial art). »The space in which I assembled this exhibition of modern German

factory art carries the inscription ›hall of antiquities‹«, he proclaimed. »Here in the old academy, in the age when the hall was built, young artists would draw from plaster casts of ancient works in order to learn the unchanging laws of classical art.« He commended the exhibition of industrial art as a return of the spirit of the workshop to the halls of the academy, a spirit »which for thousands of years was the source of all artistic creation«.[349] His willingness to display products of contemporary manufacture as the successors to the ageless tradition of craftsmanship underscores the inherent modernity of his objectives for the Vereinigte Staatsschulen.

Other exhibitions that Paul organized attest to the breadth of the interests that he shared with his students. He presented »Glas und Metall« in 1928, for which he designed both the display cases and an influential modern bar, composed of panels of opalescent glass supported by a polished metal framework. Notwithstanding his preference for natural materials, Paul's designs for »Glas und Metall« demonstrated his mastery of the vocabulary of the avant-garde. In 1932 he organized »Kunst- und Werkunterricht« (education in art and industry) in the progressive spirit of »Glas und Metall«. He also sponsored exhibitions promoting the study of pure creative form, including »Alte indianische Kunst in Brasilien und Ihre Anwendung« (aboriginal art in Brazil and its relevance) and »Argentinische Kunst« (Argentine art). In addition Paul promoted the »Ausstellung der graphischen Arbeiten von Künstlern aus dem Kreise der Berliner Kunst-Akademie des Zeitraums von 1750–1850« (exhibition of the graphic art of the circle of the Berlin academy in the period 1750–1850) as a commemoration of the emergence of modern European culture and society during these tumultuous years.

The progressive and ecumenical artistic principles inherent in the exhibitions that Paul sponsored were also manifested in his 1926 selections for a new professor of architecture. Mies van der Rohe was one of his two candidates. »Mies is an architect of estimable qualities«, Paul wrote, »and could do much«.[350] This relatively modest praise, recorded in the archives of the Vereinigte Staatsschulen, contradicts Mies' later assertion that Paul had regarded him as a genius.[351] Although Paul evidently respected his former employee, his first choice for the vacant professorship was not Mies, but Heinrich Tessenow, who had studied under Friedrich von Thiersch in Munich and worked in the offices of Martin Dülfer and Paul Schultze-Naumburg before teaching at the Technische Hochschule in Dresden.[352] In 1926, Tessenow was teaching at the Technische Hochschule in Berlin, an association that Paul evidently regarded as a benefit to his school, an opportunity to introduce technical and scientific principles into the curriculum. »Tessenow's appointment to the staff«, he wrote, »would be welcomed in every way.«[353] When Tessenow joined the faculty of the Vereinigte Staatsschulen, Paul gained the services of a talented architect and an experienced professor. By hiring Tessenow, he also facilitated Mies' acceptance of the vacant directorship of the Bauhaus in 1930.

The New World

In 1928, Paul exhibited a dining room at the »International Exhibition of Art in Industry« organized by Macy's department store in New York. This room consisted of furnishings in wood and cane, lacquered pale green with accents in silver leaf. In both colors and materials, it recalled his Gelbes Schlafzimmer (yellow bedroom) of 1925, designed for the Richmodishaus in Cologne. Although the dining room displayed at Macy's was comparable to his contemporary projects for the Deutsche Werkstätten, it was unfamiliar to an American audience. Writing in *Vogue*, Helen Appleton Read cited the Macy's exhibition as the »first appearance in this country of the German interpretation of the modern style«.[354] In actual fact, the Werkbund had organized a 1922 sequel to the 1912 »Touring Exhibition of German Applied Arts« – both of which promoted progressive German design. However, Read interpreted modernity as an international movement »on its way to becoming a world style«, and the Macy's exhibition introduced the German contribution to this movement to a broad American audience.

Read identified Paul as the »well-known architect and leader of the modern movement in Germany«.[355] In praising the German schools of applied arts for teaching a »love of material and craftsmanship engendered by hand-work« essential to an »appreciation of good design and to an understanding of the forms best suited to the materials used«, she demonstrated a refined understanding of the reforms that he had instituted in Berlin.[356] Paul himself proclaimed that the exhibition embodied the development of a new style. »It is the style of modern man«, he wrote, »whose airplanes have conquered the distance between the continents, whose audible and comprehensible voices echo around the globe, and whose thoughts and feelings transcend the confines of

national boundaries.«[357] He positioned himself as a leading figure in the international dissemination of this new style.[358]

Paul himself was awed by what he saw when he visited New York. Writing in the Werkbund periodical *Die Form*, he described a »city of wonders and incomparable beauty«. He recalled stone chasms between mountainous buildings whose fantastic perspectives and bold vertical lines created effects »unparalleled in the history of architecture«.[359] Moreover he was intrigued by the social conditions that he observed in New York, a city in which men of »all social classes and every political shade« seemed to simultaneously exchange their gray felt hats for straw ones on the first warm spring day,[360] and where the daughters of millionaires and factory girls alike could expect to be treated with gentility. Paul marveled at the social conditions achieved under American capitalist democracy, which diminished traditional class distinctions through the upward mobility of the proletariat.[361] Since leaving Munich for Berlin, he had become increasingly centrist in his political inclinations, and in New York, he beheld a model bourgeois society. For Paul, in »the architecture, the institutions, and the very atmosphere of its urban life«, the city »expressed the spirit of the age more strongly than in any other human settlement«.[362]

Paul's admiration for Manhattan prompted him to establish a professional presence in the United States. In the same year as Macy's international exhibition, Paul and Lucian Bernhard financed the incorporation of a new design firm in New York modeled on the practice of the Vereinigte Werkstätten. They intended their partnership to provide an outlet for specifically modern design, and chose the name »Contempora« accordingly. In so doing, they honored Siegfried (Samuel) Bing, whose Paris gallery, L'Art Nouveau, helped transform popular taste at the end of the nineteenth century. Like Bing, Paul and Bernhard hoped to foster the success of a new style. They announced the opening of their business with the »Contempora Exposition of Art and Industry«, displayed at the Art Center at 65 East 56th Street in Manhattan until September 1929. In addition to Paul and Bernhard, the exhibitors included Paul Poiret, Rockwell Kent, Vally Wieselthier, Julius Klinger, and Joseph Sinel. Mendelsohn, who was building his own house adjacent to Paul's Haus am Rupenhorn in 1929, also participated in the exhibition.

Paul's interiors for Contempora were similar to the work he exhibited at Macy's, including a bedroom set with chartreuse green furnishings in wood and cane, with silver accents. As with all of the interiors offered for sale by Contempora, the bedroom was available in several harmonized color schemes in accordance with the firm's commitment to regard each ensemble as a totality, rather than as a collection of individual elements. Matlock Price, writing in *Good Furniture and Decoration*, denounced this policy as evidence of »standardization or regimentation – to neither of which has art ever taken happily«.[363] His ambivalent review serves as an indication of the unprecedented role that Contempora played in the introduction of European Modernism to the United States. Although Paul's interiors for Contempora were true to the typification promoted by the Werkbund that he helped establish, Price found them to be as »devoid of happy accidents as they are of the personal touch«, dehumanized by the presence of an »adroitness and assurance bespeaking long practice and definite skill«.[364] He concluded that the interiors exhibited by

CONTEMPORA
EXPOSITION
OF ART AND
INDUSTRY

BRUNO PAUL
PAUL POIRET
ROCKWELL KENT
LUCIAN BERNHARD
ERICH MENDELSOHN
VALLY WIESELTHIER
JULIUS KLINGER
JOSEPH SINEL

ART CENTER
65 EAST 56 STREET
OPEN UNTIL
SEPT 15

Contempora would inspire Americans to »become modern rather gradually, and not embrace it a whole room at a time«.[365] Paul was, in the eyes of Matlock Price, ahead of his time in America. Price proclaimed Contempora, and particularly the collection of ceramics exhibited in its gallery by Wieselthier, »so far ahead of most of us that we shall never live to catch up with it«.[366]

The worldwide economic crisis that came to a head during the spring of 1929, and which precipitated the collapse of stock values in the United States on 29 October of that year, inevitably doomed Contempora to failure. Nevertheless the experiment had confirmed Paul's position as a proponent of an emerging international Modernism. In 1931, despite a failing economy, the furniture manufacturer Gebrüder Schürmann (Schürmann brothers) of Cologne organized an exhibition of modern interiors. The invited participants were F. A. Breuhaus de Groot, Marcel Breuer, Hans Hartl, Michael Rachlis, Le Corbusier, Ernst Lichtblau, Adolf Loos, Jock D. Peters, Francesco Stapp, and Bruno Paul. Paul and Corbusier had, in fact, worked together before. They were both members of the international jury convened by Thonet-Mundus in 1929 to identify a successor to the legendary Thonet Number 14 bentwood chair.[367] For the 1931 exhibition, Paul contributed a dining room composed of characteristically simple elements, modern in its disavowal of historical models in favor of pure, geometric forms. The chairs were lacquered slate-gray, with sulfur-yellow cushions. The round table was slate-blue and the buffet, which echoed the form of the curving wall against which it was placed, was lacquered slate-blue and yellow with a top of black opalescent glass. Paul's dining room was included in the seminal compendium *Wohnräume der Gegenwart* (contemporary interiors) by Gustav Adolf Platz,[368] confirming the influential position that he maintained, even among his younger colleagues. In fact, the eclectic group of artists that participated in the 1931 exhibition illustrated the diverse and inclusive nature of European Modernism before the founding of CIAM[369] or the canonization of the International Style.

Pragmatic Functionalism

In the first years of the third decade of the twentieth century, Paul had regained a position of pre-eminence among the artistic avant-garde in Central Europe. He had aligned himself with the proponents of the New Objectivity, but was not bound by a dogmatic definition of modernity. Instead he designed modern projects that reflected the ideals of craftsmanship and functional efficiency that he had advocated throughout his career. »Modern«, Edmund Traub's daughter said of Paul's work, »but also elegant: very modern, but not crazy modern«.[370] These were the essential qualities of Paul's design during the formative years of the New Building in Central Europe, when he offered a practical alternative to the experimental projects of his younger colleagues. Although his design philosophy was deeply personal, it was also undeniably popular. He continued to build even after the economic crisis of 1929, just as he had during the inflation. However, the deteriorating political stability of the Weimar Republic would have far more serious consequences for Paul's career than the collapse of the German economy.

7. An anonymous coexistence: 1932–1945

The Wall Street collapse of 1929 and the dissolution of the Weimar Republic following the Nazi electoral victories of 1932 resulted in a crisis in German society comparable to the events of 1918. Though Paul had been successful in adjusting to the circumstances of the first German revolution, he could not support the Nazis or their movement. Censured as politically unreliable, he endured twelve years of hardship, and outright persecution, under the Nazi dictatorship.

Condemnation

In the autumn of 1932, Josef Goebbels' periodical *Angriff* published a front-page article entitled »Der jüdische Akademiedirektor« (the Jewish academy-director), an attack on the administration of the Prussian academy of art and its institutions, including the Vereinigte Staatsschulen. Paul later recalled that the implications of the article struck him like a »thunderbolt from high heaven«.[371] He immediately perceived the danger inherent in Goebbels' accusations in the light of the unrest that was endemic in Germany following the economic failure of 1929. His concern proved eminently justified.

In 1929, Salomon Wininger published his *Große jüdische National-Biographie* (greater Jewish national biography).[372] He intended the national biography as a memorial to the contributions made to German culture by individuals of Jewish descent. Paul was listed in the fourth volume of the book as »Paul, Bruno, Architect, Professor, nephew of Albert Ballin, born on 19 January 1874 in Seifhennersdorf near Zittau«. Yet Wininger was mistaken; Paul was not related to Albert Ballin, the renowned director of the Hamburg–Amerika Linie who had died in 1918. More importantly, he was a baptized Lutheran, as were his parents and grandparents. Although his maternal grandmother bore the common Jewish name Rahel, she too had been baptized as an infant, in the parish church of Seifhennersdorf on 3 June 1810.[373] Maria Paul's parents and grandparents were likewise Christian. Paul himself was a quietly devout Protestant, reading daily from his well-worn Bible until the end of his life.[374] Yet his personal faith, and his childhood in religiously tolerant Saxony, disinclined him to the bigotry of Hitler and his movement.

Paul did have many prominent Jewish clients, including Paul von Mendelssohn-Bartholdy and the Mendelssohn-Bartholdy Bank, the Wertheim family, and Edmund Traub. Yet Traub's daughter did not recall that Paul's religious convictions influenced her father's decision to hire him, and she was personally unaware of his faith.[375] Several of Paul's closest professional colleagues were also Jewish, including Emil Orlik, Lucian Bernhard, and Erich Mendelsohn. »I did not choose my colleagues on the basis of their religious beliefs«, he wrote after the war, »but rather their personal ability and their professional stature.«[376] Nevertheless it was evident that his unprejudiced selection of clients and friends was contrary to the policies of the Nazi party, and provided an easy mark for Goebbels and his fellow propagandists.

As a prominent figure who was not a member of the NSDAP, the official Nazi party, Paul was subject to continuing criticism from the Nazi-controlled press. Articles in the *Völkische Beobachter* were typical, ranging from attacks on the number of private commissions that he undertook as the director of the Vereinigte Staatsschulen and the time these projects kept him away from the school, to condemnation of the »degenerate« modernity of the Dischhaus and the Kathreiner-Hochhaus. Paul recognized that the Nazi campaign of calumny and slander was a form of repression profoundly unlike the Lex Heinze that he had successfully opposed in his youth.[377] The leadership of the Nazi party was committed to removing him from his office, which was a legacy of the discredited Weimar Republic. In the pervasive atmosphere of accusation and mistrust that they engendered, he had little hope of maintaining a prolonged defense. »During his term as president [of the academy], Max Liebermann rejected me as an anti-Semitic nationalist«, Paul recalled; then »a page was turned, and I was labeled a friend of the Jews and a liberal.«[378] »In truth«, he proclaimed, »I was not politically active for either side, because I believed it would have been a betrayal of my official position.«[379]

Although the Nazis were not yet in control of the German government at the end of 1932, they held a plurality in the fractious Reichstag. Hitler had challenged Hindenburg for the presidency, and though he lost in a runoff election, he had emerged as the leading contender for the office of chancellor. Paul, who had remained in Berlin throughout the 1918 revolution, recognized the impending collapse of the republic.[380] Perceiving that his direction of the Vereinigte Staatsschulen was in peril, he elected to step down in the hopes of preserving both the institution that he had

reformed, and his position as an educator. He approached the Prussian minister of culture to ne-
gotiate a compromise that would allow him to continue to teach and practice architecture under
the patronage of the state. He agreed to resign as director of the Vereinigte Staatsschulen in exchange for a lifetime appointment as head of an architectural atelier under the auspices of the
academy.[381] On 1 January 1933, he reluctantly disclaimed his direction of the school that he himself had created.

Following Paul's departure, Hans Poelzig was appointed vice-president of the Prussian academy and assumed the leadership of the Vereinigte Staatsschulen. He was intent on establishing
his own authority over the school at Paul's expense. Poelzig's position was exemplified by his
cancellation of the exhibition »Kirche und Kunst« (church and art) that Paul had organized during
the final year of his direction. »I would find it much better«, Poelzig wrote smugly to Paul in
February 1933, »if we postponed the exhibition church and art until next year, and relocated it to
the academy buildings in Pariser Platz.«[382] But Poelzig himself was subject to racial and political
accusations from supporters of the Nazi regime,[383] and his ascendancy over Paul proved, in
every regard, a hollow and fleeting victory. Hitler was appointed chancellor within a month of
Paul's resignation. On 23 March the Reichstag passed an act abrogating the authority of the constitution and enabling the chancellor to legislate by decree. With the Nazis in power, Poelzig was
summarily dismissed on 10 April.[384]

Max Kutschmann succeeded Poelzig as director of the Vereinigte Staatsschulen. He was a
painter, and a professor at the school, but also one of the founding members of the Nazi party
(under a pseudonym), a fact that Paul was surprised to discover.[385] »In our daily conversations
he had presented himself as a liberal«, Paul later recalled, »and so won my confidence.«[386] His
appointment left little ambiguity regarding the changes envisioned for the school by the government. Under his regime, Paul wrote, »the elite of my professors were dismissed from the state
service«.[387] In 1933 the Vereinigte Staatsschulen became an instrument of the Nazi government,
a tool in their efforts to control every aspect of German culture and society.

In November 1933, Paul was dismissed from his academic atelier under the »Gesetz zur
Wiederherstellung des Berufsbeamtentums« (statute for the restoration of the tenured civil services), legislation passed on 7 April in order to consolidate the power of the Nazi party. Under the
statute, all state employees were subject to immediate dismissal under the authority of state gov-
ernors appointed directly by the NSDAP. Any local official, judge, educator, or public servant employed by the German government could be summarily discharged on the basis of political dis-
loyalty, whether actual or perceived. Together with Konrad Adenauer, Paul Klee, Max Reinhardt,
Erwin Panofsky, and countless others, Paul was expelled from governmental service under the
statute. The records of the Reichskammer der bildenden Künste state that he was dismissed with
a pension on the grounds of his »friendship with the leaders of the corrupt society of the Weimar
Republic, as well as friendship with the Jews«; in addition, the documents state that »his personal
conduct as director of the state schools was not irreproachable«.[388] The political nature of Paul's
dismissal is underscored by the accusation of questionable conduct – namely that he had employed the students and resources of the Vereinigte Staatsschulen in support of his own professional activities. This policy had reflected the curriculum of the school since 1907, when he proclaimed the value of practical experience in the training of artists and craftsmen. More significantly, his political sympathies were alleged to lie not with the National Socialists, but rather with
the »social democrats, the German nationalists, and the center party«, depending on the circumstances.[389] Though Paul was merely politically open-minded, he was classified as an opponent of
the Nazi regime. Following his dismissal he worried that he stood »with one foot in the concentration camps«.[390] Moreover the loss of his atelier was a severe blow. His replacement was, effectively, Poelzig. When Poelzig died in 1936, Peter Behrens was recalled from Vienna to lead his
atelier. Behrens, who had first worked with Paul in Munich forty years earlier, was a member of
the Nazi party and, in contrast with his predecessors, politically acceptable.

Characteristically, Paul did not publicly protest the loss of his atelier. He merely collected his
personal possessions, and relocated his office to the garden of his own house on Budapester
Straße, opposite the Berlin zoo. In the absence of a rebuttal to the accusations published in
Angriff, questions regarding Paul's religious affiliation remained. When the final volume of Wininger's *National-Biographie* was published in Austria in 1935, Paul was listed in an addendum to his
earlier citation. »As a consequence of his Jewish origins«, Wininger wrote, »he was placed in retirement in November 1933.«[391]

Though Paul had been relieved of all official responsibilities, he remained a member of the
Prussian academy of arts until 1937. On 8 July of that year, the academy was reorganized under

a directive issued by Hermann Göring, minister-president of Prussia. Göring's deputy, Bernhard Rust, provided the academy with a list of 59 new members, including Albert Speer, Ernst Sagebiel, and Arno Breker. In order to accommodate the new academicians within the historically limited membership of the institution, Rust consigned a number of existing members to a newly invented inactive status, including Behrens, Tessenow, and Schultze-Naumburg. Nine other members of the old academy were ordered to resign: Bruno Paul, Mies van der Rohe, Emil Rudolf Weiß, Ernst Barlach, Ernst Ludwig Kirchner, Ernst Nolde, Max Pechstein, Rudolf Belling, and Ludwig Gies.[392] After thirty years of government service, Paul was forced to relinquish his public life.

Paul considered leaving Germany, as so many of his fellow artists were doing. He helped his *Simplicissimus* colleague Thomas Theodor Heine flee the country in 1933, and it would have been relatively easy for him to follow.[393] »But to resettle my family overseas at the age of sixty?« he lamented after the war. Instead he maintained the »illusory hope of a swift end to the unbearable Himmler-Goebbels-Hitler-dictatorship«.[394] Although he had expressed his admiration for American society following his visit to New York in 1928, Paul was unwilling to embrace it as his own. Ultimately, he was a patriot; having committed his life to the reform of German culture, he was unwilling to abandon his project unfinished. But his personal belief in national identity was very different from that of the Nazi party. When he submitted a biographical summary to the Reichskammer der bildenden Künste, the government agency responsible for the arts, he listed his country of origin as Prussia. In so doing, he evoked the national distinctions that existed prior to 1918, when national and regional identities still coexisted within the German state. The typist who transcribed Paul's written notes substituted »German empire«, an echo of the nationalism that had engulfed Central Europe.

Paul and the aesthetics of the »Drittes Reich«

Though Paul was found to be personally objectionable by the NSDAP, official attitudes regarding his work were more ambiguous. His Weimar projects were criticized in the *Völkischer Beobachter*, but his earlier buildings embodied the sturdy, German classicism clearly favored by Hitler and his architects. Even projects such as the Dischhaus retained the lessons of the »zweites Biedermeier«, and Paul never fully renounced this tradition. When circumstances required, Paul continued to evoke the severe elegance of his pre-war designs.

In 1930, Paul designed an office building for the headquarters of the Gerling Konzern, an insurance company in Cologne. He conceived the project in spare and graceful classical vocabulary, devoid of historical ornament yet with finely worked ashlar details reminiscent of the Zollernhof of 1910. This vocabulary responded to the inherent conservatism of the insurance industry as well as the preferences of Konrad Adenauer, who as mayor of Cologne favored a restrained classicism for public buildings. The conservatism of Paul's design was not merely aesthetic: its masonry shell was a load-bearing element. Yet the Gerling headquarters also prefigured the ordered composition of subsequent projects such as Sagebiel's Reichsluftfahrtministerium (air ministry) of 1936, suggesting Paul's influence on the official aesthetic of the »Drittes Reich«. However the building was unusual in the context of his work of the 1930s, evidence of the unique circumstances surrounding its commission.

Paul designed his office building as an addition to the Palais von Langen, the original headquarters of the Gerling Konzern. Designed by Hermann Pflaume in 1880, the palais was a private home in the style of a Renaissance palazzo, albeit with the heavy detailing typical of German Historicism at the end of the nineteenth century. Paul maintained the cornice height and pattern of fenestration of the Palais von Langen in the design of his addition, but abandoned the Renaissance ornament of the original building in favor of abstract, geometric detailing. Though he conceived the fossiliferous limestone façades with elegant, classical proportions, the character of the building was more concisely reflected in the main entrance. The entrance stood at the intersection of the new building and the old, with a projecting slab that sheltered a passageway leading to an inner court. Paul located the porter's lodge behind a bronze gate incorporating the name of the firm, similar to the one that he had designed in aluminum alloy for the Dischhaus. The lodge had a rounded corner facing the entry gate, with dramatically curved windows set in bronze frames, and adjoined the main stair hall of the building, with stone and metal detailing reminiscent of the entry hall of Villa Traub. The interiors of the building were equally well-designed, expressing the structural frame that worked in concert with the bearing masonry shell. The refined, contem-

140. Headquarters of the Gerling-Konzern, Cologne, 1930. Exterior.

porary detailing of the Gerling headquarters was characteristic of Paul's projects. It was an elegant modern extension to a historical building, comparable to Erik Gunnar Asplund's addition to the Göteborg law courts of 1934–37. [395]

Though Paul never embraced the monumental historicism of the »Drittes Reich«, his earlier work was favored by ranking members of the NSDAP. Three of the houses that he had designed in Berlin for affluent Jewish families were confiscated by the government in 1934 and presented to prominent Nazi officials. From 1934, Heinrich Himmler lived in Paul's 1913 Haus Herz in Berlin-Dahlem, and in 1938 Speer located his architectural practice in Paul von Mendelssohn-Bartholdy's former town house in Berlin-Wannsee, also designed by Paul in 1913. Hitler himself appropriated Haus Waltrud on the Schwanenwerder island in 1934 as his summer residence; Paul had designed the house in 1913 for Walter and Gertrud Sobernheim. In addition, the Gestapo occupied Paul's own apartment at the former Kunstgewerbeschule on Prinz-Albrecht-Straße, after establishing their headquarters in the buildings of the school. However, none of the new occupants ever consulted the architect concerning the adaptation of his buildings. The Nazi government celebrated the aesthetic that Paul created prior to 1914, while condemning his living person.

A personal complication

Paul's domestic life during the years of his greatest success was relatively unremarkable, as was his long marriage to Maria Graf. He proved a dutiful if distant husband, and prior to the economic crisis of 1929 he provided his wife with a life commensurable with his wealth and fame. His daughter Hilde recalled yearly trips to Venice, where her father was honored wherever he went. She and her mother dressed six or seven times daily in response to an endless series of social engagements, necessitating wardrobe trunks of fashionable clothing brought from Berlin and the efficient attention of devoted servants. Paul himself was fastidious in his appearance; with his tailored suits and monocle he was the very image of a German gentleman. His tastes and demeanor were equally refined. Though an accomplished horseman he never learned to drive a car, relying instead on the services of a dedicated chauffeur.[396]

In the 1930s Paul's domestic situation changed with far-reaching consequence to his professional life. Maria celebrated her sixtieth birthday in 1935. Paul himself was sixty-one, though he had retained a youthful enthusiasm that his wife had not. With the passing years, the two drifted apart and Paul sought sympathetic companionship outside his marriage. Yet he was always discrete, and remained attentive to the needs of his family. But at a carnival party in the early 1930s, Paul met a talented young woman with whom he felt an immediate attachment.[397] Her name was Ursula Schnitt, a native of Berlin born in 1907 and a student at the Vereinigte Staatsschulen. Red-haired Ulla, as Ursula was known to her friends, was an image of the young Maria Graf.[398]

By the end of the decade, Paul and Ulla were living together in his garden studio on Budapester Straße, while Maria remained upstairs in the grand and expensively furnished home. Paul's daughter Hilde served as a liaison between the two women, an uncomfortable role that she fulfilled with good humor, notwithstanding the fact that Ulla was nine years her junior.[399] Hilde eventually married and left the family home, however, and Paul could not maintain his complicated domestic arrangements indefinitely. In 1941, he divorced his wife of forty-two years and married Ulla. The same year she gave birth to Paul's second daughter, Julia, and in 1945 to a third daughter, Susanne. Paul remained distant from his two youngest daughters. »He was so full of enthusiasm for his work«, Susanne recalled, »and we were two crying children. He was a great artist, but not a great father.«[400] Conditions in Germany in 1940s were hardly conducive to a settled family life. »Everything was chaotic, we lived like gypsies«, she recalled.[401]

Farewell to the Vereinigte Werkstätten

Paul designed his final project for the Vereinigte Werkstätten in 1928, the New York dining room. He named the suite of furnishing in honor of his visit to the United States, but there was nothing American about the individual designs. The buffet embodied features characteristic of his work at the end of the 1920s, including simple geometric forms, beautifully worked walnut veneers, and cabinet doors that returned at the corners and hung on prominent, silver-plated hinges. Equally simple, the round table was composed of pure geometric forms without any recollection of the historical styles. The upholstered chairs prefigured the biomorphic forms of the 1950s, although

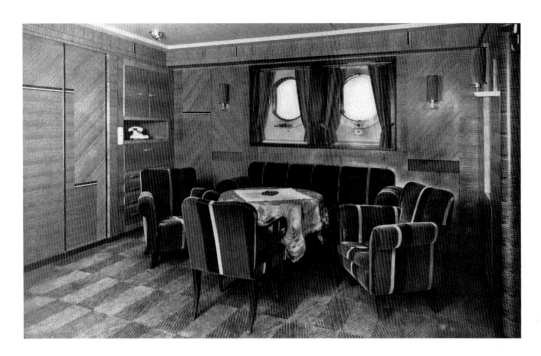

their sculptural arms, the only wooden elements of the New York dining room that were solid rather than veneered, revealed the influence of traditional craftsmanship.

Paul's emphatically modern New York dining room was atypical of the contemporary products of the Vereinigte Werkstätten, which had become increasingly traditional. During the 1920s, Paul Ludwig Troost had risen to prominence with the firm as the favored designer of the Norddeutscher Lloyd shipping line of Bremen. He furnished the liners *München* (1922), *Sierra Ventana* (1922), *Stuttgart* (1924), *Columbus* (1924), and *Europa* (1929) in a sumptuous, historicist style. His designs for the Norddeutscher Lloyd during the lean years of the inflation established his reputation as a leading proponent of a German counterpoint to the French aesthetic, and brought his work to the attention of Hitler and his party. Troost's Dampferstil (steamer style) served as the model for the representative interiors of the Nazi government; as a consequence, the Vereinigte Werkstätten received what Paul sarcastically described as a court appointment from Hitler.[402] The firm would eventually furnish such prominent official buildings as the Alte Reichskanzlei (old imperial chancellery), Hitler's Berghof in the Bavarian Alps, the German embassy in London, and Speer's monumental Neue Reichskanzlei (new imperial chancellery). The close relationship between the Vereinigte Werkstätten and the Nazis precluded the continued employment of the politically unreliable Paul. Yet the interiors that the Werkstätten provided to the government clearly derived from Paul's work for the firm. Many of the fixtures used in Troost's restoration of the Alte Reichskanzlei, for example, were closely related to Paul's fixtures for Haus Hainerberg.[403]

Though ostracized by the Vereinigte Werkstätten, Paul was able to strengthen his relationship with the Deutsche Werkstätten, collaborating with F. A. Breuhaus de Groot and R. A. Schröder on the prestigious interiors for the liner *Bremen* in 1929.[404] In 1931 Paul conceived the bedroom Modell 273 for the Deutsche Werkstätten, a suite of furniture that prefigured the interior design of the 1950s even more emphatically than his earlier New York dining room. The characteristic detail of the nightstands and dressing table included with bedroom 273 consisted of a blue oval plate, supported above a pale-yellow lacquered base by a single, eccentrically located and nickel plated steel tube. The basic elements of the individual pieces were oak, although no trace of grain was visible through their softly colored finishes. Like all of Paul's best work, their expressive forms were not merely aesthetic, but derived from functional requirements. Each of the steel tubes contained a pivot, permitting the oval plates to rotate. Those on the nightstands could be used as book rests, that on the dressing table positioned to suit the convenience of the user. Paul used steel only where wood was structurally unsuitable, creating a rational and harmonious design.

Although Paul's opportunities to complete experimental designs such as his bedroom 273 were compromised by the events of 1933, he continued to receive commissions from Hellerau. He planned few unique furnishings for individual clients during the Nazi dictatorship, but he was able to maintain the development of affordable furnishings for the middle-class home that he had begun with the Typenmöbel of 1908. In 1935, he introduced a line of furniture entitled »Die wachsende Wohnung« (the expanding dwelling), a series of simple, modular elements. The elements

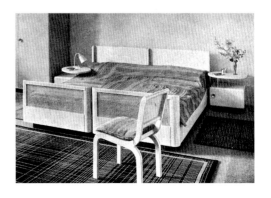

141. First class cabin for the liner *Bremen*, 1929.
142. Salon of the liner *Boissevain*, 1936. Wall painting by Ulla Schnitt.
143. »Die wachsende Wohnung« for the Deutsche Werkstätten, 1934.
144. Bedroom model 273 for the Deutsche Werkstätten, 1932.
145. Coathook assembled from laminated veneers for the Deutsche Werkstätten, 1939.
146. Handmade dining-room suite for the Deutsche Werkstätten, 1937. In the mirror can be seen a reflection of an intarsia mosaic designed by Ulla Schnitt.

of »Die wachsende Wohnung« drew from the original Typenmöbel with cabinets and shelves that could be flexibly combined, as well as matching desks, chairs, and tables. By 1935 Paul had disavowed the stylistic precedent of the Typenmöbel in favor of abstract geometric forms devoid of applied ornament. His new furnishings were available only with a walnut veneer, the natural grain of the wood replacing the delicate intarsia or stenciled patterns of the Typenmöbel. The geometric purity of »Die wachsende Wohnung« was characteristic of the best modern furniture, and imbued the individual pieces with a timeless quality. In fact, the Deutsche Werkstätten would continue manufacturing Paul's standardized furniture well after the end of the war. As late as 1958, VEB Deutsche Werkstätten produced and sold Paul's designs in the German Democratic Republic.

In 1936, Paul prepared designs for the furnishing of the Dutch liner *Boissevain*. Although he had always relished the opportunities afforded by artistic collaboration, Nazi persecution had deprived him of the pool of students and subordinate professors with whom he had previously worked. In their absence he turned to Ulla Schnitt, a talented artist in her own right. Together they designed several pieces for the line of expensive hand-made furniture (handgearbeitete Möbel) marketed by the Deutsche Werkstätten. They also worked together on the first-class vestibule, salon, dining room, and stair hall of the *Boissevain*. The project was Paul's last prominent interior. Most of the furniture that he designed for the ship was manufactured from TEGO-plywood, a material that could be molded into fluid forms under high temperature and pressure. Paul's use of this versatile, lightweight material emphasized his continued interest in technological developments. As he had earlier experimented with curvilinear furnishings assembled from laminated veneers, the plywood sheets he now used allowed a similar technique to replace the costly and time-consuming process of carving complex elements such as chair arms from solid pieces of wood. In 1939, Paul used a comparable process to produce a line of wooden hardware, including door handles and wardrobe hooks, assembled from laminated veneers. His elegant wooden hardware, fabricated from maple, walnut, and cherry, belied the sinister necessity of its purpose: by the end of the 1930s brass and aluminum were being committed to the needs of the military. Paul's wooden hardware was funded by the Nazi government in order to conserve strategic materials. Military necessity ended Paul's collaboration with the Deutsche Werkstätten when the firm's factories were ordered to devote their resources and expertise to the production of aircraft, utilizing the same techniques that he had pioneered in his designs for furnishings assembled from laminated veneers.

»An anonymous coexistence«

Though Paul was precluded from receiving prestigious commissions during the Nazi dictatorship, he continued to work.[405] He opened a private office in the garden studio of his house on Budapester Straße, with Hilde serving as his assistant and head of the tiny office. After she married,

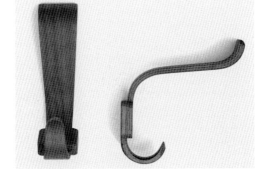

Paul was left to work alone. Yet his earlier fear that he was living with one foot in the concentration camps soon abated, and he was able to live in what he termed »anonymous coexistence« with the German government.[406] By 1943, he had three employees working in his office: two male draftsmen and a female clerk. He listed his clients as the Deutsche Werkstätten in Hellerau and the Gollnow Brückenbau, the Gollnow steelworks, in Stettin,[407] and he also worked for the Argus motorworks and IG Farben, designing industrial buildings and workers' housing.[408]

The Nazis' denunciation of Paul and his work did not exclude him from public acknowledgement. During the early years of the »Drittes Reich«, governmental suppression of civil liberties, subversion of democratic institutions, and military mobilization occurred beneath a veneer of social stability. Initially, German publications on art and design scarcely acknowledged the aesthetic predilections of the new regime. Although Paul had been discredited by the government and dismissed from public service in part because of his projects for Jewish clients, he published a fifteen-page article on Villa Traub in *Innen-Dekoration* in 1935.[409] In 1936, he published an article in the same journal concerning the Expressionist country house he had designed on behalf of a former expatriate for the Schwanenwerder island in Berlin-Nikolassee in 1924.[410] While the Expressionist tendencies in his Haus auf Schwanenwerder were relatively modest, they were sufficient to identify Paul with the embattled proponents of German Modernism in 1936, one year before the government sponsored the infamous exhibition »Entartete Kunst« (degenerate art) in Munich. Yet the journal *Kunst* continued to publish favorable reviews of his work, including a 1937 article »Handgearbeitete Möbel im neuen Hause der Deutschen Werkstätten in Berlin« (handmade furniture in the new showrooms of the Deutsche Werkstätten in Berlin) by Fritz Hellwag. »The decades have not left a mark on his creative abilities«, Hellwag wrote; »his inventiveness appears inexhaustible.«[411] Paul continued to publish his own articles as late as 1942, when his »Gefolgschaftsräume eines Handwerkbetriebs« (workers' rooms for a handwork concern) appeared in *Moderne Bauformen*.[412] But the war soon extinguished his opportunities to publish on German art and architecture.

As the Second World War intensified, Paul relocated his office from Budapester Straße to the Berlin suburb of Zehlendorf. He also attempted to disperse his personal papers, the archives of his office, and his collection of art and antiques. The allied bombing of Berlin resulted in the destruction of Paul's house on Budapester Straße, the majority of his possessions, and much of Charlottenburg. Consequently he had a personal interest in his principal work of the 1940s: the design of prefabricated housing for the settlement of the dispossessed. He was able to pursue this interest through employment by Deutsche Bau AG, a nationalized concern under the direction of Dr. Robert Ley.

Paul's resettlement houses incorporated the technical expertise that he had developed in designing the manufactured Plattenhaus H 1018, but did not reflect the progressive aesthetic of the earlier project. Two decades after conceiving his prismatic, he was now designing simple prefabricated houses with pitched roofs and timber siding for the Deutsches Wohnungshilfswerk der Deutschen Bau AG, inexpensive temporary housing for Germans bombed out of their homes. He was also designing permanent settlements, including projects for Buchholz and Stettin. Paul sketched small timber houses, with steep roofs and wooden shutters. Although superficially evocative of the »Heimatkunst« popularized by the Nazi government, the vernacular style that Schultze-Naumburg had advocated for its supposed Arian purity, there was nothing political or polemical in Paul's designs. In response to the horrors of the war, he proposed housing that was simple, efficient, and familiar. In so doing he recalled the timeless ideals of middle-class German culture that had served him so well in the past.

At the end of the war, Paul was seventy-one years old. His home had been severely damaged during the aerial bombardment of Berlin, and was reduced to rubble during the house-to-house fighting of 1945. His papers and possessions had been lost or destroyed. His two most faithful supporters during the Nazi years, the Deutsche Werkstätten and the Gollnow steelworks of Stettin, lay within the Soviet zone of occupation. With a new wife and a young family, Paul faced the most desperate professional circumstances he had ever endured. He belonged to a generation discredited by a decade and a half of political oppression. He himself had suffered under the Nazi dictatorship while many of his colleagues had emigrated to promote their visions of modern German design abroad. Ironically, the very fact that he had remained in Berlin left him tainted by the shameful legacy of the »Drittes Reich«. In 1945, Paul was faced with the challenge of establishing himself, once again, in a new and skeptical society.

8. Beginnings and endings: 1945–1968

By 1945, Paul had lost much of what he had achieved prior to Hitler's accession. Like most Germans, he and his young family found themselves in desperate circumstances at the end of the war. Ever resilient, however, he sought to resume the career he had been forced to abandon in 1933. He had, after all, been successful in reestablishing himself following earlier crises, but conditions in 1945 were fundamentally different from those of 1918. Paul had chosen not to emigrate in order to avoid the uncertainties of beginning a new life in an unfamiliar country. Ironically, postwar Germany was completely unfamiliar to him: a nation humiliated, partitioned, governed by foreign powers, and consumed with a shame and loathing of its recent history so abject that it accepted the perpetual abolition of the state of Prussia, of which Paul considered himself an honorable citizen. Moreover the practice of architecture was profoundly different following the war. With German cities in ruins, and the generation of young artisans of the Weimar Republic decimated by twelve years of political oppression and six years of warfare, it was impossible to return to the standards of craftsmanship that Paul had promoted throughout his career.

Starting over

At the beginning of 1945 Paul was living in Hellerau, in the factory complex of the Deutsche Werkstätten. After the bombardment of Dresden in February he joined his family in Wiesenburg, a small and ancient town 60 kilometers southwest of Berlin. From the relative safety of the countryside, he observed the nightly glow of the burning capital on the horizon, as the war approached its inevitable conclusion. On 2 May, Wiesenburg itself was taken, without resistance, by a Soviet regiment. Paul watched in dismay as the town and its venerable castle were plundered and laid waste by Russian troops. In addition to looting the town, the invading soldiers confiscated all the produce from its surrounding farms, leaving little food for its inhabitants. »The population went hungry«, Paul later recalled, »as did we«.[413] Conditions in Wiesenburg were so desperate that he developed edema as a consequence of malnutrition, and he was confined to a hospital bed.

Although Paul was incapacitated, he received a commission from the provisional government in Potsdam for the restoration of Schloß Wiesenburg. Initially he worked from the hospital, and was able to secure payment for his services in the form of foodstuffs and basic necessities for Ulla and their young daughters. When his health was restored, he moved with his family into the Schloß. During the year following the end of the war, he became the effective castellan of Wiesenburg, a substitute for the Graf von Plauen who had abandoned his ancestral seat in 1943 to accompany his Swedish wife to her neutral homeland.[414] Paul's daughter Julia remembered her father serving as mayor of the town, though he never held a formally elected office.[415] A distinguished citizen untainted by association with the Nazi party, he was a prominent figure in Wiesenburg in the chaotic aftermath of the German surrender. Nevertheless he did not intend to remain in the village, but planned a return to Berlin and the life he had relinquished in 1933.

Paul completed his work in Wiesenburg during the spring of 1946, and moved with his family to Lehnitz near Oranienburg, the northern terminus of the Berlin Stadtbahn (city railway). There, he rented a small house in a settlement similar to those that he had designed for the dispossessed during the war. From Lehnitz, he pursued the reinstatement of his lost academic atelier with the government in Potsdam. »My applications were received in a cordial manner by the Kulturamt and were neither rejected nor accepted«, Paul recalled. »I had the impression that hidden forces hindered my reemployment.«[416] In fact, members of the provisional government in Potsdam concluded that he had been a member of the NSDAP. »The allusion to my presumed affiliation with the Nazi party was all the more surprising in that the faculty of the reestablished school of art in Berlin, refounded without my participation, included several ordinary party members as well as an important member of the former government«, he remembered. »Of course, all had been successfully rehabilitated.«[417]

The Vereinigte Staatsschulen reopened within weeks following the cessation of hostilities, under the direction of Paul's former professor Karl Hofer. Paul had cited the academicians Hofer and Poelzig as his principal rivals for leadership of the school in 1924. Unsurprisingly, Hofer spurned Paul just as Poelzig had done during his brief tenure as director. However Paul's opportunities were also limited by the fact that he had not been officially rehabilitated, or denazified, by the allies. He returned to Charlottenburg, where his home on Budapester Straße had been utterly destroyed, to apply to the denazification office on the Kurfürstendamm. He explained to the inter-

147. Schloß Wiesenburg, circa 1914. Exterior. The Renaissance castle was begun after the destruction of its medieval predecessor in 1547.
148. Typenhaus-Möbel, wardrobe, 1948. Drawn by the author from a dimensioned sketch by Paul.
149. Gereonsdriesch 9–11, Cologne, 1953. Exterior.
150. Gereonsdriesch 9–11, Cologne, 1953. Detail. Condition in 2001.

viewing officer that he had no party number, as he had never joined the NSDAP. He later recalled the officer's response. »We went to great lengths to confirm your party membership«, he said, »but unfortunately you never belonged to the NSDAP – consequently we cannot rehabilitate you.«[418] Thereafter he was confounded by a party affiliation that he had never maintained, yet could not renounce.

Paul left his family in Lehnitz, while he traveled in search of an opportunity to restore his professional life, and provide the means to support Ulla and their daughters. »As children, we were always alone with our mother«, Susanne, the younger, recalled.[419] Throughout Germany, Paul actively sought to reestablish his distinguished career, persisting without success in his claims for the restoration of his atelier. He had celebrated his seventieth birthday in 1944, and was six years past the official age of retirement by the end of the war. Although he suggested that he be permitted to teach as an emeritus professor, his petitions remained unanswered. As his hopes for an atelier in Berlin faded, he unsuccessfully pursued a professorship at the Technische Hochschule in Dresden. In 1948 he was one of the candidates for the presidency of the new German academy established in the Soviet sector of Berlin. Ironically the political opinions that had excluded him from public service under the Nazi dictatorship proved no more acceptable in Soviet-dominated East Berlin, and Paul was not seriously considered to lead the new academy.

Paul's frequent absences from home and family accompanied a fundamental change in the conditions of his domestic life. While he was married to Maria, he had always designed the interiors of their homes to the smallest detail. The custom-made furnishings that he had created for his own use embodied his latest ideas, and were frequently published. After 1940, on the other hand, his daughter Julia recalled that »mother always decorated the house«.[420] Paul chose the colors for the individual rooms, but Ulla »did the painting, put the nails in the walls, and decorated with her own artwork«.[421] Paul even abandoned the design of his own furnishings, instead assembling a varied collection of historical pieces. Despite designing thousands of pieces of furniture during his prolific career, Paul took to keeping his own clothes in an eighteenth-century Dutch wardrobe, an exemplar of the solid, Biedermeier Classicism that had inspired so much of his own work.

Yet Paul did not completely forsake the design of furniture and interiors. In May 1948, he completed a series of designs for Typenhaus-Möbel: furniture for the standardized home. In design as in name, the Typenhaus-Möbel recalled his Typenmöbel of 1908. The individual pieces were simple and elegant, embodying the solid, domestic virtues of German Neoclassicism. Paul planned the Typenhaus-Möbel around common elements, and standardized dimensions; as with the Typenmöbel, he developed a series of permutations suitable for the furnishing of a modest home. The 1948 designs were plainer than Paul's work of 1908, however, more reliant on mechanically produced elements and less on traditional craftsmanship.

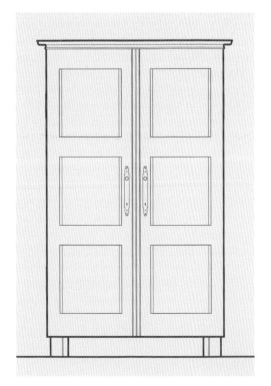

Paul's Typenhaus-Möbel was never manufactured. With the future of the Deutsche Werkstätten uncertain in Soviet-occupied Hellerau, he had unsuccessfully submitted the designs to J. Gollnow & Sohn, the steelmakers for whom he had worked before the war. Although Gollnow sought to find employment for Paul, he was primarily concerned with the reestablishment of his manufacturing capabilities following the partition of Prussia in August 1945, which ceded his headquarters in Stettin to Poland. His firm was not interested in establishing a factory for the production of wooden furniture, but rather in finding the commissions that would enable a rebuilding of its operations.[422] To this end, Gollnow ultimately enlisted Paul's assistance. In 1948 Paul prepared a design submitted by Gollnow & Sohn for the rebuilding of the suspension bridge over the Rhine at Mülheim, Cologne. He was familiar with the site, having entered the competition for the original bridge in 1926. Although his 1948 design was unsuccessful, as his 1926 designs had been, he demonstrated his ability to contribute to Gollnow's principal business.

After 1948, Paul resolved to leave the Soviet zone and resettle in the west. He finally received an opportunity when he was called to the American Zone of Occupation to assist in the rebuilding of the city of Hanau, under the direction of the newly appointed building authorities in Frankfurt. In 1949, he settled in Höxter and was reunited with Ulla and their daughters. Two years later the family moved to Düsseldorf, where Gollnow was rebuilding his headquarters. In Düsseldorf, Paul worked from his home at Kühlwetterstraße 7, and from there supervised the construction of the Gollnow steelworks, a simple, practical series of industrial buildings characterized by financial and material necessity rather than artistic ambition. Such projects reflected the realities of postwar Germany, conditions recounted in Paul's contributions to the article »Die Verwertung der Brandruinen« (putting burnt-out buildings to good use), published in Neue Bauwelt in 1949.[423]

As a consultant to J. Gollnow & Sohn, Paul contributed to the design of the projects undertaken by the firm. Although he had no experience in structural engineering, he was able to fulfil a role comparable to that assumed by Peter Behrens of behalf of AEG five decades previously. Like Behrens, he was charged with providing an aesthetic coherence to industrial design. Since the products manufactured by the Gollnow steelworks were generally architectural in scale, Paul's contributions were significant. In 1952, he assisted in the design of a floating dry-dock for the Howaldtswerke Deutsche Werft AG in Hamburg-Rosshafen.[424] This structure, which was capable of lifting a 16,000-ton ship out of the water for repairs, was a purely functional object. Nevertheless Paul was able to provide it with a simple, uncluttered layout that enhanced the impression of its monumental dimensions. He provided a similar aesthetic to the design of a 665 meter long plate-girder bridge crossing the Nile between the regional capital Sawhaj and the city of Akhmim, ancient Panopolis. As he had done in Hamburg, Paul endowed a work of engineering with an aesthetic clarity. He provided detail only where it was functionally justified, designing elegant masonry piers and abutments to provide a counterpoint to the unornamented steel spans that they supported. These modest gestures were sufficient to distinguish Paul's bridge from a purely engineered aesthetic, and their restraint exemplified the discipline that characterized his work throughout his career. The bridge became an iconic image in Egypt, and between 1953 and 1990 a rendering of its central span served as the official seal and flag of the governorate of Sawhaj. In terms of its popular significance, the Nile bridge was perhaps Paul's most successful project, although it is largely unknown outside of Egypt.

While in Düsseldorf, Paul also completed a design for the redevelopment of the site of his destroyed Cologne office, at Gereonsdriesch 9–11. Though he had to sell the property in order to support himself and his family, his professional services were retained by the Westdeutsche Finanzierungsgesellschaft, a merchant bank. Since he worked from his home without a staff, he no longer needed a Cologne office. The new commission was more important to him than preserving the legacy of his former place of business, and he executed it with characteristic vigor.

As rebuilt, Gereonsdriesch 9–11 was typical of urban architecture in postwar Germany. The masonry veneer, pitched tile roof, and cornice height were all specified by the city of Cologne in order to maintain a semblance of the historical character of the inner city. The expression of the floor plates on the façade, a detail unique in the catalog of Paul's work, probably originated with the engineer Hanns Koerfer, his collaborator on the design.[425] This detail reflected the ornamental use of structural elements characteristic of much German architecture during the period of reconstruction. Other details embodied Paul's individual style. The harmonious proportions of the façade and the practical efficiency of functional elements such as the windowsills and downspouts maintained the pragmatic traditions of Biedermeier Classicism. The stone embrasure at the asymmetrically located entry recalled his work of the 1920s, albeit in a simplified and abstracted form. The austerity of the stonework echoed the severity of the entire design. Only the metal grilles on the windows and at the entrance to the garage incorporated ornamental detail.

In his preliminary designs for Gereonsdriesch 9–11, Paul investigated a series of different patterns for the ornamental metalwork. His sketches included antique designs of diagonal crosses and meanders such as he favored prior to the first world war, nested frames recalling Villa Feinhals, linenfold patterns, Expressionist compositions reminiscent of the railings for Haus Fraenkel, and variations on each. Ultimately, Paul selected a severe arrangement of parallel members, the simplest of all the designs that he had studied. Since he began his professional career in 1897, he had worked towards the unification of the fine and applied arts. By 1953, traditional craftsmanship was increasingly rare in German building. Though his plans for Gereonsdriesch required a high level of technical skill on the part of the builders, little scope remained for the expression of refined handwork. A slight reverse curve in the plan of the window railings, a detail imperceptible at any distance from the façade, was the last vestige of applied art in Paul's design.

Though Paul was successful in facilitating the reconstruction of Gereonsdriesch 9–11, and also of the Richmodishaus, he was frustrated in his efforts to receive commissions for significant new projects in the Rheinland. He formed a partnership with a speculator named Wörle, who promoted extravagant schemes for new development in the war-damaged sectors of Cologne. Paul produced elaborate series of drawings for these ventures that included proposals for the Odeonsgärten in 1954 and the Niederländer Ufer in 1956, each a Trabantenstadt, a self-contained satellite community. He worked without compensation, and apparently funded Wörle's marketing expenses as well. But none of the projects came to fruition, and Paul ultimately squandered his savings in their pursuit. Although his daughter Julia recalled Wörle's relationship with her father with bitterness, Paul himself developed a profound interest in the problems of postwar mass housing. His studies and sketches, which have been preserved at the Germanisches Nationalmuseum in Nuremberg, document his methodical approach to planning, and his rigorous attention to detail.

Throughout his career, Paul had capitalized on his ability to discern and internalize emerging trends in design. For fifty years he had been close to the center of every significant movement in German design and had, ultimately, contributed to their development. Twelve years of Nazi control over German culture had destroyed the national system of artistic education and training that Paul had helped to reform, and had driven many of the leading figures of the avant-garde to pursue their careers on foreign soil. There was no new aesthetic movement in Germany for Paul to reform in 1954, and his work in Cologne reflects his efforts to reconcile disparate elements of his own experience. His designs for the Niederländer Ufer recalled the Kathreiner-Hochhaus, with features including a tower bedecked with the steps and terraces characteristic of his commercial designs of the 1920s. The drawings for the Odeonsgärten included an expansive series of residential blocks in an undulating sequence overlooking the Rhine, a rectilinear variant of the scheme that Alvar Aalto adopted in his 1947 design for the Baker House dormitory at MIT. Paul's proposal was larger than Aalto's building in both horizontal and vertical dimensions and was surmounted, somewhat incongruously, by hipped tile roofs.[426] His drawings, despite their skillful resolution of technical details, lacked the coherence mastered by Aalto who, in his designs for standardized furniture and his reconciliation of classical and functional impulses, was very much a follower in Paul's footsteps.

While Paul was preparing drawings for the Odeonsgärten, he celebrated his eightieth birthday. In honor of the occasion, he received the Bundesverdienstkreuz (federal service cross), the highest civilian award issued by the German government. He was honored at the instigation of Theodor Heuss, the first president of the Federal Republic and a longtime friend. Heuss also intended to appoint Paul as ambassador to Poland, belated compensation for two decades of tribulation.[427] At his advanced age and with no diplomatic experience, however, Paul could not be seriously considered for an ambassadorship. He received some consolation in 1955, when he was at last reappointed to the Berlin academy.

Returning to Berlin

In 1957 Paul returned to Berlin with his family, moving into an existing house at Trabener Straße 76a, overlooking the Halensee in the Berlin suburb of Grunewald. Paul took advantage of this location by swimming in the lake, whenever the weather permitted, until the end of his life.[428] Nevertheless, during what should have marked a return to domestic stability, his family was shattered by Ulla's untimely death. Maria had died in 1947. Paul survived both his wives, and was left with the uncomfortable responsibilities of looking after two teenage daughters. The same year he was remembered in the ideosyncratic East German lifestyle publication *Das Magazin*, which belatedly recounted that his eightieth birthday had been celebrated around the world.[429]

After returning to Berlin, Paul did not establish an architectural office. Instead, he labored night and day in his own room on Trabener Straße, in which he lived and worked. He remained distant from his young daughters. Though he had taught Hilde to work as his assistant, and would inspire the careers of her two sons, he shared little of his professional experience with Julia or Susanne. »He was always preoccupied«, Susanne recalled, always seeking new challenges and new commissions.[430]

Around 1957 Paul was committed to designing an expansion to his Asiatisches Museum in Dahlem, one of the few facilities of the Berlin museums located in the western zones of the city. He completed a series of studies for additions consisting of asymmetrical compositions of simple cubic masses flanking a central pavilion with tall, harmonically proportioned windows suggesting the portico of the original building. A recessed parapet, clad in a darker material than the remainder of the façades, provided an effective termination to the elevations without explicitly invoking historical precedents.[431] All of his projects for the Dahlem museum embodied an abstracted classicism that produced a sensitive and complimentary pendant to the 1921 building. However, his commission for the project was »hindered by collegial objections«.[432] Ultimately Wils Ebert and Fritz Bornemann completed the expansion of the Asiatisches Museum in the 1960s, in a style that proved neither sympathetic nor complimentary.

Paul's last executed architectural commission was completed in 1958, when he facilitated the reconstruction of the Deutsches Goldschmiedehaus, the sixteenth-century town hall of Hanau. The elegant building – with its carved sandstone base, half-timbered upper stories, and steep tile roof punctuated by three tiers of dormers – exemplified the late-medieval building traditions of Western Germany, and had served as a museum since 1902. When the building was destroyed during a 1945 air raid, the city of Hanau lost a cherished monument. Paul had studied the restoration of the Goldschmiedehaus since the late 1940s, when he prepared preliminary drawings for the restoration of the historical center of Hanau. When the city had the funding available to rebuild the old town hall, Paul and Otto Kämpfer received the commission.

In his reconstruction of the Goldschmiedehaus, Paul achieved the balance of artistry and craftsmanship that he had promoted throughout his professional career. The building was exquisitely and painstakingly rebuilt by hand, in the spirit of its original construction. A comparison of historical and post-reconstruction photographs of the Goldschmiedehaus demonstrates that the destroyed building was not simply replicated, but rebuilt with small but significant differences in its details. The relevant details do not pertain to the composition or configuration of the historic building, which were faithfully reproduced, but rather to manifestations of the physical process of its construction. Carpenters, masons, plasterers, painters, and smiths collaborated on the project with Paul, as architect, coordinating their work. Each of these artists and artisans exerted a personal influence on the character of his or her work. The rebuilding of the Goldschmiedehaus was a perfect embodiment of the »timeless German building arts« that Paul cherished. However, he had always embraced the timeless building arts as agents of reform. Their relegation to the discipline of historical reconstruction marked a fundamental change in the practice of architecture that he was unwilling to embrace. After 1958, at the age of eighty-four, Paul ceased his efforts to obtain new architectural commissions.

Ending a career

Even after he ceased working as an architect, Paul retained his interest in German art, culture, and politics. Each day he read through the *Frankfurter Allgemeine Zeitung*. When a new exhibition opened in Berlin, he would invariably attend. Those who met him remember a grand old man: modest, polite, and impeccably dressed.[433] His good nature was uncompromised by the injustices that he had endured after 1933. He remained affable and friendly, particularly in his daily visits to the Café Kempinski on the Kurfürstendamm, where he would sit at a table on the sidewalk and drink coffee in the afternoons.[434]

By 1958, Paul was becoming increasingly aware of his own mortality. Few of the friends he had made during his youth in Munich were still alive. When his *Simplicissimus* colleague Olaf Gulbransson died that September, Paul composed a plaintive message to his friend. »This autumn I wanted to visit you after long years«, he wrote, »now you have gone on ahead of me.« He

concluded, »I don't know if I shall ever see you again, in the vastness of the hereafter«.[435] Thinking of his own life, Paul began to compile his memoirs. He remained disinclined to promote his own personal fame, though he recognized that in his silence over the years the events of his own career had gone uncataloged since the publication of Josef Popp's monograph in 1916. He began, slowly and deliberately, to write about his life. With characteristic modesty, he wrote nothing about his own accomplishments, and he described the years 1874 through 1929 in only a few handwritten pages. The majority of his notes pertained to the Nazi dictatorship and its aftermath, a period that still troubled him fifteen years later. He also planned a list of his fifty most significant architectural projects, a compendium that he intended, more than any written work, to serve as his memorial.[436]

In 1964, Paul celebrated his ninetieth birthday in Berlin. At a birthday celebration, he was scheduled to give a speech. »He was very distant in his old age«, his daughter Susanne recalled. »I wrote his notes for him in large letters on cards, and put them in his pocket«, she remembered. »When he stood up he never looked at them, but still delivered a clear, concise, and heartfelt speech.«[437] He is not merely a patriarch, a subsequent speaker proclaimed, »but a sage. He is critical, sarcastic, tolerant, and susceptible to all the humors; he knows how to bear the comforts and inconveniences of age with charm and self-irony.«[438]

Paul remained active and fit into his nineties, walking and swimming whenever the weather allowed. »He was spiritually healthy at ninety-three«, Susanne remembered, but his physical health had declined after 1965.[438] He died on 17 August 1968, at the age of ninety-four. He was buried in a simple grave in the Waldfriedhof, or forest cemetery, on the Potsdamer Chaussee in Berlin.

Germany noted Paul's death as the passing of a significant national figure. Obituaries appeared in newspapers across the country. The one printed in the *Süddeutsche Zeitung* was typical, and typically insightful. This obituary distilled Paul's significance, and the trajectory of his career, into a single sentence. »He was«, the *Suddeutsche Zeitung* proclaimed, »the very spirit of renewal.«[440] In Germany, Paul received popular acknowledgement as one of the founders of the modern movement. Yet in England and America, where the focus of that movement had shifted following the political events of 1933, his death went largely unrecorded. One of the few English-language obituaries appeared in *The Architectural Review* in April 1969.[441] Paul's name »meant little to the English«, the brief announcement began, the author clearly forgetful of the renown Paul had once enjoyed in the pages of *The Studio*, or of the praise he had received from the Royal Academy at Pevsner's instigation. After the war Paul had remained in Berlin, the former capital of a great empire that had become a lonely island, isolated from the centers of Western culture. Modest and self-deprecating, he was largely forgotten when the histories of his reforms were written by his successors, intent on promoting their own visions of modernity.

Like many great professional lives, Paul's ended quietly. His hope that he might restore himself to the forefront of architectural practice, or architectural education, remained unfulfilled. He died just as a new generation of critics and historians had begun to question the nature and origins of the modern movement, and so was unable to contribute to their dialog.[442] Nevertheless the story of Paul's life is relevant to this continuing discussion. It serves as a reminder of the breadth and complexity of the unwritten histories of twentieth-century design, and exhorts a new generation to accept the cause of renewal.

152. Self portrait, 1953. Paul's last published caricature, drawn in honor of Richard Riemerschmid's eighty-fifth birthday.
153. Bruno Paul, 1954.

Conclusion

To the end of his life, Bruno Paul championed a pragmatic and stylistically indeterminate Modernism. In his youth, he was a leading member of the avant-garde. Following the revolution of 1918, his principles distanced him from a modern movement that began to define itself in terms of a putative historical inevitability.[443] Yet Paul's career exemplifies the extent to which Modernism, even if dogmatically defined in terms of the International Style, developed from diffuse and often contradictory influences. His work of the 1920s illustrates an alternative to the International Style, a modernity that was not dependent on a renunciation of the lessons of history.

Paul embraced a Modernism that derived from his experience, his education, and his professional practice. He was, through the context of his own life and social relationships, acutely aware of the needs, desires, and expectations of the middle classes. Although he condemned »bürgerlich« pride, hypocrisy, and vulgarity, he did not denounce the class of industrialists, investors, and patrons of art to which he himself belonged and which, ultimately, financed the modern movement.[444] Moreover, he was profoundly cognizant, through his experience as a designer, of the nature and properties of materials, and of the practical methods of their employment. He successfully reconciled the roles of artist and artisan, and his work was characteristically elegant and refined, but also sturdy and practical.

As a consequence of his pragmatic approach, a notable number of Paul's buildings and interiors continue to serve the purposes for which they were originally designed.[445] The mere survival of these projects is not as remarkable as the extent to which they have retained, often unaltered, their original hardware, windows, fittings, and services. Paul's Plattenhaus of 1925 demonstrates his successful adaptation of the pragmatic rigor of his design philosophy to an experimental project in the vocabulary of the International Style. Unlike the houses exhibited at the Weißenhofsiedlung two years later, however, his Plattenhaus was both affordable and industrially produced. It also remained essentially unaltered seventy-five years after its construction, in stark contrast with the Werkbund houses in Stuttgart – many of which exhibited fundamental errors in design and construction within two years of their completion; most have been substantially rebuilt as a consequence. Paul remained engaged with the avant-garde, but he maintained a fundamentally different position regarding the objectives of architectural practice. His Plattenhaus H 1018 provided a pragmatic counterpole to the polemical modernity of the Weißenhofsiedlung.

Paul's furniture and interiors exhibit the same practical virtues as his architectural projects. His furniture of the 1920s and 30s provided a counterpoint to the tubular steel designs that have become synonymous with the Modernist interior. Although the iconic image of the chrome and leather chair has endured, original examples demonstrate a fundamental disjunction between idealized form and material and technical reality. Paul's wooden furniture, although less radical in form, has proven to be far more durable and practical.[446] In addition to pieces in museum collections, much of Paul's furniture remains in daily use, including his 1929 interiors for the town hall in Seifhennersdorf. The exemplary qualities of this project typify his work.

Paul's designs were not merely capably executed, they were often as stylistically advanced as contemporary technology would allow. He remained committed to aesthetic experimentation even after he was no longer considered among the leaders of the avant-garde. Paul was an artist, and he believed in the role of the artist as an innovator. However he was also convinced that innovation had to be balanced by practical constraints, such as the topological limitations imposed by established types. Paul accepted material constraints as a manifestation of typology, a foil to his creative expression, but his acceptance of technical limitations did not preclude his exploration of technological development. His projects often embodied innovative material and mechanical solutions. Nevertheless Paul, with the sound and measured judgment of an experienced professional, did not experiment with unproven technologies at his clients' expense. It is a legacy of the academic training that Paul received in lieu of a technical education that he placed far more value on empirical demonstrations than on theoretical ones. Paul's belief that practical experience was the necessary prerequisite of artistic expression served as the basis of both his own prolific practice and the curriculum he developed at the Vereinigte Staatsschulen in Berlin. Through the influence of his work, and the education of his students, Paul disseminated a pragmatic Modernism derived from his own professional practice.

Ultimately, consideration of Paul's pragmatic Modernism is essential to an understanding of the history of twentieth-century design. It demonstrates the scope of the discourse concerning contemporary design in the years prior to the Second World War, but also emphasizes the essential role played by mainstream professionals in the propagation of the aesthetic principles of the avant-garde. At the same time, Paul's practice also raises fundamental questions about the nature of Modernism and the validity of Modernist historiography, and – perhaps even more important – the position that his work should occupy in the Modernist canon.

Modernism, as it is canonically defined, presupposes a conscious break with customary practices deemed irrelevant to contemporary urban society. To what extent the past must be disavowed in order to embrace the present, however, remained an open question. Timeless material and linguistic conventions were never dispelled in modern painting, sculpture, literature, and drama. Instead they endured, if only to provide a counterpoint to new forms of expression. In modern architecture, and in the architectonic disciplines of furniture and interior design, the expectation of a fundamental renewal of material and technique arose during the 1920s, fostered by revolutionary zeal and a fascination with industrial and technological progress. Paul did not shape this expectation, which was promoted by a younger generation of artists intent on abolishing conventional aesthetic principles.[447] He foresaw a different path for modern design, one that respected the hard-won lessons of history.

By the end of the twentieth century, indeed by the final years of Paul's life, the renunciation of history had been revealed as a false hope. Yet this renunciation was not essential to modern design, as his own practice during the 1920s demonstrates. The disavowal of history was only one of many theoretical positions that coexisted within a fractious modern movement. The eventual authority of this disavowal was largely the consequence of the historical accidents that led to the widespread acceptance, during the 1940s, of an ideal nurtured during the disintegration of the second German empire. The mechanism of this acceptance, colored as it was by the self-interest of its proponents, and the cult of avant-gardism that it fostered, consigned Paul to obscurity. Yet his confidence in the timeless building arts, and in the creative role of the artist, have remained fundamentally valid. Paul played a pivotal ideological role in the development of the modern movement. An appreciation of this role, and of the pragmatic Modernism that it engendered, is essential to an understanding of the history of twentieth-century design. Paul's career is indicative of the richness and divarication of the modern movement, and the wealth of its potential that remains unfulfilled and often unexplored. Yet Paul's greatest legacy lies not in his contributions to the ascendancy of Modernism, but in the role he might yet play in redeeming it.

Though Bruno Paul wrote very little about his beliefs, his work as an educator and an architect provides a clear record of his principles. All of the arts derive from the timeless skills of craftsmanship. Practical experience rather than theoretical knowledge forms the basis of artistic training. The fine artist is distinguished from the artisan by both creative ability and technical excellence, neither of which can exist in isolation. The arts exist for the betterment of the human condition, whether manifested in the reform of social institutions or in the refinement of domestic comfort. The social purposes of art can only be achieved by positive means, facilitated by the development of new materials and techniques, and by new forms of expression. These are the ideals that shaped Paul's practice. They are timeless, practical, and principled. They are the essence of a pragmatic Modernism that is still imbued with the significance that Paul intended, exemplifying the reform of artistic education and architectural practice. In the decades that have passed since the height of Bruno Paul's career, the need for reform has never been dispelled.

1. »Herrenzimmer für den Regierungspräsidenten von Bayreuth«, 1904.
2. First- and second-class waiting room for Nuremberg main station, 1905.

Catalog

When Bruno Paul began recording his memoirs, he intended to include an account of his fifty most important buildings.[448] This account, were it ever completed, is now irretrievably lost. The following catalog was conceived in the spirit of this missing document. Some of the projects selected by the author are unlikely to have appeared in Paul's list; the importance of an individual work, after all, can only be assessed in the context of history. The decades passing since Paul ceased working on his memoirs have witnessed the survival and restoration of some works that he might not have included in his list, and the destruction of others that might certainly have.

There have been several notable efforts to compile a catalogue raisonné for Paul, most notably Alfred Ziffer's *Bruno Paul: Deutsche Raumkunst und Architektur zwischen Jugendstil und Moderne* of 1992. However such a project is hindered both by the loss of Paul's office and its records during the Second World War, and by the overwhelming number of projects that he completed in his long and prolific career as a painter, graphic designer, decorative artist, furniture designer, illustrator, industrial designer, and architect.

Vestibule for the »Kunst-Ausstellung Dresden« (Dresden art exhibition), 1899 (pp. 24, 25)

Paul's work for the 1899 »Kunst-Ausstellung Dresden«, executed by the Vereinigte Werkstätten, illustrates the origins of his practice as an applied artist. Paul used opulent and expensive materials in his design, albeit in a painterly manner. He employed mahogany, brass, bookmatched black marble slabs, and yellow opalescent glazing, utilizing each material to create a sumptuous visual experience without acknowledging their differing tectonic capabilities. The free and expressive forms that he employed demonstrated his mastery of the emerging Jugendstil. No element of Paul's vestibule is known to have survived.

Ernst Zimmermann, »Das Kunstgewerbe der ›Deutschen Kunst-Ausstellung‹ zu Dresden«, *Kunst und Handwerk* 49 (1899), 281–294; Carl Meissner, »Deutsche Handwerkskunst von neuer Art auf der Deutschen Kunst-Ausstellung in Dresden«, *Innen-Dekoration* X (August 1899), 117–129; Alfred Ziffer, *Bruno Paul* (1992), 123; Sonja Günther, *Bruno Paul* (1992), 153.

»Jagdzimmer«, 1899 (pp. 25, 26)

Paul's »Jagdzimmer«, designed for the Vereinigte Werkstätten in 1899, received a Grand Prix at the Paris »Exposition Universelle« of 1900. This honor helped to propel him to the forefront of the Kunstgewerbebewegung. The room was subsequently exhibited at the »1. Ausstellung für Kunst im Handwerk« in Munich in 1901 and the »Prima Espozisione Internazionale d'Arte Decorativa Moderna« in Turin in 1902, to widespread acclaim. Unlike Paul's earlier interiors, his design for the »Jagdzimmer« exploited the ornamental and architectonic qualities of a single material, elm wood, in lieu of applied surface ornament. The Jugendstil chairs that Paul designed for the hunter's room, produced by the Vereinigte Werkstätten as Modell 1744, were notably successful. He produced a number of related designs, varia-

tions on their characteristic splayed forms, between 1901 and 1904. The »Jagdzimmer« has not survived.

Max Osborn, »Deutsches Kunst-Gewerbe auf der Welt-Ausstellung«, *Innen-Dekoration* XI (June 1900), 90, 100–101; Sonja Günther, *Interieurs um 1900* (1971), 66–73; Alfred Ziffer, *Bruno Paul* (1992), 124; Sonja Günther, *Bruno Paul* (1992), 153.

»Herrenzimmer für den Regierungspräsidenten von Bayreuth«, 1904 (pp. 25, 26)

In 1904, Paul designed the »Herrenzimmer für den Regierungspräsidenten von Bayreuth« (office for the head of the provincial government of Upper Franconia at Bayreuth). The suite of furniture that Paul conceived on behalf of the Vereinigte Werkstätten included Modell 652 and Modell 2531 armchairs derived from his hunter's room of 1899. In the Bayreuth office, however, these characteristically Jugendstil chairs served as a counterpoint to an interior dominated by straight lines and simple geometries. The office was exhibited at the »Louisiana Purchase International Exhibition« of 1904 in St. Louis, where it received a gold medal. It is no longer extant.

Leo Nachlicht, *Deutsches Kunstgewerbe St Louis 1904* (1904), 12, 51–53; Hermann Muthesius, »Die Wohnungskunst auf der Weltausstellung St. Louis«, *Deutsche Kunst und Dekoration* 15 (December 1904), 209–211; Sonja Günther, *Interieurs um 1900* (1971), 89–95; *Stadt* (1982), 29; Alfred Ziffer, *Bruno Paul* (1992), 124; Sonja Günther, *Bruno Paul* (1992), 153.

First- and second-class waiting room for Nuremberg main station, 1905 (p. 27)

In 1905, Paul designed the interiors of the first- and second-class waiting room of the main railway station in Nuremberg, furnished as a café-restaurant by the Vereinigte Werkstätten. Paul's designs for Nuremberg represented his first prominent commercial project. In response to the budgetary and functional requirements of the program, he designed a series of simple, carved chairs assembled in a variety of configurations from standardized components. While the use of common elements to produce a range of furnishings echoed the manufacture of Thonet's contemporary bentwood chairs, the solid materiality of Paul's design made a far more explicit reference to the ideals of high culture. The translation of cultural identity to objects of mass production was intimated by a 1906 article in *Dekorative Kunst* by Paul Johannes Rée that praised the Nuremberg waiting room as an example of the best achievements of contemporary interior design.[449] Although not identified as such by name, Paul's furnishings for Nuremberg were the first of his Typenmöbel. The waiting room is still extant, although much of the original furniture is lost.

Johannes Rée, »Der Wartesaal im Nürnberger Bahnhof«, *Dekorative Kunst* X (October 1906), 1–10; Joseph Popp, *Bruno Paul* (1916), 12; Alfred Ziffer, *Bruno Paul* (1992), 160; Sonja Günther, *Bruno Paul* (1992), 157.

Festival decoration for the Schwere-Reiter-Kaserne, Munich, 1906 (p. 29)

In 1906, Paul received a commission to decorate the stark façades of the Munich barracks of the heavy cavalry regiment »Prinz Karl von Bayern«, the Schwere-Reiter-Kaserne, for a visit by Kaiser

Wilhelm II. This ephemeral project marked his transformation from a painter to an architect. In composing this façade, Paul adapted elements that he had also employed in his graphic and furniture design, including the motif of an orthogonal grid interrupted by a single lozenge as a focal element. This adaptation underscored the interrelationship of Paul's work in differing fields, and epitomized the ideals of the Kunstgewerbebewegung. His festival decoration marked a watershed in his career, and was likely instrumental to his appointment as the director of the school of applied arts in Berlin. The temporary decorations are no longer extant.

Wilhelm Michel, »Münchener Straßendekoration«, *Kunst und Handwerk* 57 (March 1907), 187; Alfred Ziffer, *Bruno Paul* (1992), 289; Sonja Günther, *Bruno Paul* (1992), 157.

Interiors for the »3. Deutsche Kunstgewerbe-Ausstellung Dresden«, 1906 (pp. 22–28)

Paul exhibited three complete rooms, all furnished by the Vereinigte Werkstätten, at the »3. Deutsche Kunstgewerbe-Ausstellung Dresden« of 1906. The first was a version of the office from Bayreuth, with simplified details and furnishings. He also exhibited a vestibule and reception room for the marble quarries of Kiefersfelden, and a dining room for the Vereinigte Werkstätten. All three rooms demonstrated Paul's development of a rational, rectilinear vocabulary in place of the fluid forms of the Jugendstil. The Dresden exhibition was a significant event in the history of modern design in Germany, prompting the establishment of the Deutscher Werkbund the following year. Paul's three rooms have not survived. However copies of individual furnishings, many of which were serially produced, have been preserved in public and private collections.

Erich Haenel, »Die dritte deutsche Kunstgewerbe-Ausstellung Dresden 1906, III. Teil«, *Dekorative Kunst* IX (September 1906), 393–416; Leopold Gmelin, »Die Gruppe München auf der Kunstgewerbe-Ausstellung Dresden 1906«, *Kunst und Handwerk* 57 (October 1906), 37–50; Wilhelm Michel, »Die Münchener Vereinigten Werkstätten auf der kunstgewerblichen Ausstellung in Dresden«, *Deutsche Kunst und Dekoration* 19 (November 1906), 97–112; *Stadt* (1982), 29; Alfred Ziffer, *Bruno Paul* (1992), 165 to166; Sonja Günther, *Bruno Paul* (1992), 153–154.

First-class cabin for the liner *Kronprinzessin Cecilie*, 1906 (pp. 42, 43)

In 1906 Paul won a competition sponsored by the Norddeutscher Lloyd shipping line of Bremen for the modern design of first-class cabins for the liner *Kronprinzessin Cecilie*. His design was executed by the Vereinigte Werkstätten in a simple and elegant vocabulary similar to his subsequent work for the »3. Deutsche Kunstgewerbe-Ausstellung Dresden«. Paul's cabin, and companion designs by Riemerschmid and Olbrich, marked the introduction of contemporary interiors to the Norddeutscher Lloyd, whose ships had previously been fitted in accordance with the period styles. This experiment proved so successful that Paul was retained to design a smoking room for the postal steamer *Derfflinger* of 1907 and a dining room and salon for the Genoa–New York liner *Prinz Friedrich Wilhelm* of 1908. *Kronprinzessin Cecilie* was interned in Boston

upon the outbreak of the First World War. The liner was refitted as the troopship *Mt. Vernon* when the United States entered the conflict. By the time *Mt. Vernon* was dismantled for scrap in 1940, Paul's cabin was long gone.

Max Osborn, »Moderne Schiffskunst«, *Kunstgewerbeblatt* XVIII (September 1907), 229–234, 235, 237, 240; G. Pauli, »Die Einrichtung eines Schnelldampfers«, *Kunst und Künstler* XI (October 1907), 40–44; Karl Schaefer, »Die moderne Raumkunst im Dienst des Norddeutschen Lloyd«, *Innen-Dekoration* XVIII (October 1907), 293–310; Karl Schaefer, »Das moderne Kunstgewerbe im Dienst des Norddeutschen Lloyd«, *Kunst und Handwerk* 58 (November 1907), 37–44; Karl Schaefer, »Der Norddeutsche Lloyd und die moderne Raumkunst«, *Dekorative Kunst* XI (November 1907), 76–89; Joseph Popp, *Bruno Paul* (1916), 23; Heinrich Wiegand, *Heinrich Wiegand: Ein Lebensbild* (1932), 272–273; *Stadt* (1982), 32; Alfred Ziffer, *Bruno Paul* (1992), 174; Sonja Günther, *Bruno Paul* (1992), 71.

Haus Westend, Berlin, 1907 (pp. 32, 33)

Haus Westend was the first architectural project of Paul's Berlin office. The client, Hans Schuppman, was one of the directors of the Vereinigte Werkstätten. His house was conceived as the embodiment of all of the design services offered by the Werkstätten, as well as its manufacturing capabilities. Paul provided a design of remarkable harmony and coherence, qualities that likewise characterized its furniture and interiors. In so doing, he reduced the formal vocabulary of the late eighteenth century to its essential characteristics: simplicity, consistency, and formal discipline. In forsaking the restless ornament of the turn of the century, Paul abandoned the pursuit of a synthetic modern style. Instead he developed a language of typical and normative forms, derived from a dateless classicism. Thus he created a modern architecture of flexibility, functional efficiency, and proportional elegance, characteristics that would be present in Paul's work throughout his long career. The house is still extant, although its furnishings and most of its original interiors have been lost.

Hermann Post, »Bruno Paul als Architekt«, *Deutsche Kunst und Dekoration* 25 (December 1909): 165–180; Joseph Popp, *Bruno Paul* (1916), 66–76; *Stadt* (1982), 35, 56; Alfred Ziffer, *Bruno Paul* (1992), 289–290; Sonja Günther, *Bruno Paul* (1992), 81–86, 149.

Typenmöbel, 1908 (pp. 38, 39)

Paul's Typenmöbel was the first example of modern, unit furniture conceived to allow an unlimited number of combinations of standardized, machine-made elements. As such, it earned its place in the history of the modern movement. However, the Typenmöbel was designed in a formal vocabulary that was evocative of eighteenth-century German Classicism and was, as a consequence, largely ignored by subsequent historians intent on tracing the history of the Functionalist aesthetic. Nevertheless Paul's Typenmöbel epitomized his ideal of a pragmatic Modernism attuned to the needs and desires of the middle classes. Typenmöbel has been preserved in several museum collections, including those of the Münchener Stadtmuseum and the Kunstgewerbemuseum in Berlin.

3. Reception room for the »3. Deutsche Kunstgewerbe-Ausstellung Dresden«, 1906.
4. Haus Westend, Berlin, 1907. Condition in 2001.
5. Typenmöbel, 1908.
6. Stair hall of the Norddeutscher Lloyd liner *George Washington*, 1910.
7. Villa Feinhals, Cologne, 1909. Interior.
8. Interior for the German national exhibit at the Brussels International Exhibition, 1910.

Hermann Post, »Typenmöbel«, *Dekorative Kunst* 12 (March 1909), 258–264; Joseph Popp, *Bruno Paul* (1916), 32–34; *Stadt* (1982), 30; Alfred Ziffer, *Bruno Paul* (1992), 178–184; Sonja Günther, *Bruno Paul* (1992), 23, 44–44; W. Owen Harrod, »Bruno Paul's Typenmöbel, the German Werkbund, and Pragmatic Modernism: 1908–1918«, *Studies in the Decorative Arts* IX (Spring-Summer 2002), 33–57.

Interiors for the liner *George Washington*, 1908 (pp. 43, 44)

In 1908 the Norddeutscher Lloyd shipping company of Bremen hired Paul to design a series of prestigious interiors for the new passenger liner *George Washington,* the culmination of a trend begun with his cabin for *Kronprinzessin Cecilie.* The commission reflected a significant opportunity for the ideology of recently founded Werkbund. Paul's interiors, assembled by the Vereinigte Werkstätten in Bremen, exhibited an understated elegance derived from disciplined design and meticulous craftsmanship, as well as the judicious use of costly materials. These interiors were published in Europe and America in lavish booklets printed for the Norddeutscher Lloyd to celebrate the new, modern identity of its North Atlantic liners. *George Washington* was interned in New York in 1914. The liner served the United States as a troopship, under the same name, before commencing service with the United States Lines in 1921. Although much of Paul's furniture was lost during the war, his interiors survived throughout the 1920s. The liner was withdrawn from commercial service in 1932, and finally destroyed by fire in 1947.

Robert Breuer, »Der George Washington«, *Innen-Dekoration* 20 (October 1909), 333–343; Norddeutscher Lloyd, *Steamship George Washington* (1910); Joseph Popp, *Bruno Paul* (1916), 24–27; *Stadt* (1982), 33; Alfred Ziffer, *Bruno Paul* (1992), 187–188; Sonja Günther, *Bruno Paul* (1992), 72, 75.

Schloß Börnicke, Berlin, 1909 (p. 33)

Schloß Börnicke, designed for the banker Paul von Mendelssohn-Bartholdy, established Paul's reputation as a favored architect of Berlin's cultural elite. Although significantly larger and more complex than Haus Westend, Schloß Börnicke incorporated many of the same formal conventions as the earlier house, reflecting the coalescence of his personal style. In both houses the elevations exhibited an inherent tension between the order suggested by the formal vocabulary of German Neoclassicism, and an informal and domestic distribution of architectural elements. In Schloß Börnicke Paul successfully combined the functional flexibility of the English free style with a quiet, classical dignity. Schloß Börnicke is still extant, although its original interiors have been lost and Mendelssohn-Bartholdy's collection of art works dispersed.

Joseph Popp, *Bruno Paul* (1916), 83–106; *Stadt* (1982), 58; Alfred Ziffer, *Bruno Paul* (1992), 206, 290 to 291; Sonja Günther, *Bruno Paul* (1992), 152.

Interiors for Villa Feinhals, Cologne, 1909 (p. 40)

The completion of Villa Feinhals was a collaborative effort between Paul, Joseph Maria Olbrich, and Max Läuger. As such, it represented the work of three of the leading lights of the Werkbund – even if this collaboration was necessitated by Olbrich's untimely death. The interiors Paul conceived for Villa Feinhals reflected the harmonious culture embodied in typical forms, and included numerous elements of Typenmöbel. Other furnishings for the house reflected influences more dynamic than the Biedermeier models that had inspired the Typenmöbel, including Georgian interiors. As always, however, Paul internalized and transformed these influences. Contemporary critics noted the references to eighteenth-century precedents, but credited Paul with creating a »modern environment for modern man« characterized by the calm and simple refinement of its design.[450] Villa Feinhals is no longer extant.

Max Creutz, »Das Haus Feinhals in Köln-Marienburg: Joseph M. Olbrich – Bruno Paul – Max Läuger«, *Dekorative Kunst* 15 (November 1911), 57–77; Joseph Popp, *Bruno Paul* (1916), 77–80; Alfred Ziffer, *Bruno Paul* (1992), 194–197; Sonja Günther, *Bruno Paul* (1992), 157.

Interiors for the German national exhibit at the Brussels International Exhibition, 1910

Paul led the design of the Raumkunstabteilung (interior design section), of the German national contribution to the Brussels exhibition. His work for the exhibition was confident, simple, and elegant. The geometric and structural character of Paul's design was particularly bold for 1910.[451] Such was the success of Paul's Brussels interiors that he was retained in a similar role for the 1914 »Panama-Pacific International Exposition« in San Francisco. However, the First World War prevented the realization of Paul's plans. None of Paul's temporary interiors for the Brussels exhibition have been preserved.

Georg Jakob Wolf, »Das Deutsche Kunstgewerbe auf der Brüsseler Weltaustellung«, *Dekorative Kunst* 13 (September 1910), 529–557; Robert Breuer, »Deutschland auf der Brüsseler Weltausstellung«, *Moderne Bauformen* 9 (1910), 301–414; Joseph Popp, *Bruno Paul* (1916), 13–19; Sonja Günther, *Interieurs um 1900* (1971), 117–124; Alfred Ziffer, *Bruno Paul* (1992), 198–199; Sonja Günther, *Bruno Paul* (1992), 154.

Zollernhof, Berlin, 1910 (pp. 34, 35)

In 1910 Paul designed a façade and interiors for the Zollernhof office building planned by the architect Kurt Berndt for 36 Unter den Linden. Paul's façade was immediately evocative of the severe and rational classicism of his contemporary residential work. However the Zollernhof diverged from the precedent of Paul's earlier domestic projects in the sculptural and stereometric embellishment of the façade. By the standards of Wilhelmine Berlin, the sculptural program of the Zollernhof was modest, although it was not an element of Paul's original project. He added the sculpture at the instigation of the Kaiser, who believed that the severity of the initial design was unworthy of Unter den Linden. In a 1913 article in *Deutsche Kunst und Dekoration*, Paul stated modestly of the Zollernhof: »It is instinctive, from nowhere, in the shadow of Messel.«[452] If Paul believed himself overshadowed by Messel, he was nevertheless responsible for introducing a new rationalism to the architecture of central Berlin. The Zollernhof is still extant. The exterior was renovated at the close of the twentieth century, but Paul's interiors have been lost.

Robert Breuer, »Großstadthäuser«, *Deutsche Kunst und Dekoration* 32 (April 1913), 26–27; Joseph Popp, *Bruno Paul* (1916), 121–126; Gustav Adolf Platz, *Die Baukunst der neuesten Zeit* (1930), 318; Alfred Ziffer, *Bruno Paul* (1992), 292; Sonja Günther, *Bruno Paul* (1992), 137, 139, 150.

Haus Hainerberg, Königstein, 1910 (p. 35)
In 1910, Paul's office completed the drawings for a palatial house commissioned by Adolf Gans for Königstein im Taunus, to be named Haus Hainerberg. The project provided a compelling demonstration of the flexibility of Paul's architectural vocabulary. The house itself was conceived as a grand country home, in the manner of an eighteenth-century Schloß. Nevertheless, the distinct clarity and abstraction of individual architectural elements and the tension between order and asymmetry were typical of Paul's work. In addition to the house, the project included the design of a complex of service buildings at the edge of the property, including stables, storage, and accommodations for staff. These service buildings employed the same architectural vocabulary as Haus Hainerberg, without compromising the propriety of either. The complex of buildings that Paul designed in Königstein embodied the ideals of modest wealth and noble labor, an equitable relationship between social classes, and a harmonious German culture. Haus Hainerberg and its service buildings are still extant, the house having been adapted for use as a clinic. Their original interiors have largely been lost.

Joseph Popp, »Bruno Pauls Haus Hainerberg im Taunus«, *Deutsche Kunst und Dekoration* 20 (October 1916), 1–22.; Joseph Popp, *Bruno Paul* (1916), 155–209; Alfred Ziffer, *Bruno Paul* (1992), 207, 295; Sonja Günther, *Bruno Paul* (1992), 87, 92–97, 152.

Haus Braun, Berlin, 1910 (p. 34)
Paul's Haus Braun was a simple, practical building, elegantly proportioned and skillfully detailed. The house combined a cool precision reminiscent of Schinkel with a functional efficiency derived from the vernacular tradition of domestic design. This transformation of the German Classical ideal epitomized Paul's contemporary work. It also embodied an ideal that had been sought since the publication of Hermann Muthesius' seminal *Das Englische Haus* of 1904: the creation of a uniquely German counterpart to the practical and convenient domestic architecture of Great Britain. Paul's success in achieving this ideal was reflected in the work of his students, particularly Ludwig Mies. Haus Braun is still extant, although altered. Its original interiors have been lost.

Ernst Schur, »Bruno Paul«, *Dekorative Kunst* 14 (November 1910), 57–59; Joseph Popp, *Bruno Paul* (1916), 59–62; *Stadt* (1982), 57; Alfred Ziffer, *Bruno Paul* (1992), 291; Sonja Günther, *Bruno Paul* (1992), 81, 88, 149.

Haus Herxheimer, Frankfurt/Main, 1911 (pp. 42, 52)
Although Haus Herxheimer belonged to the tradition of Haus Westend, its programmatic requirements necessitated a different design approach. While Paul's earlier houses were essentially rural or suburban buildings of the villa or Landhaus type, Haus Herxheimer was an emphatically urban build-

ing, built on the outer ring of boulevards encircling Frankfurt's city center. Accordingly Paul designed a soberly monumental house, with the extensive use of ashlar detailing. As a consequence, the vocabulary of Haus Herxheimer falls somewhere between that of Haus Westend and of the Zollernhof. This fact underscores the extent to which Paul was seeking to develop a coherent and flexible architectural style, a modern interpretation of the style that flourished in the years prior to the First World War. Haus Herxheimer is still extant, although altered. Its original interiors have been lost.

Carl Weichardt, »Eine Villa von Bruno Paul in Frankfurt«, *Deutsche Kunst und Dekoration* 29 (November 1911), 135–175; Joseph Popp, *Bruno Paul* (1916), 109–118; *Stadt* (1982), 57; Alfred Ziffer, *Bruno Paul* (1992), 293; Sonja Günther, *Bruno Paul* (1992), 151.

Nellinistift of the Rose-Livingston-Stiftung, Frankfurt/Main, 1912 (p. 36)
In 1912 Paul designed the Nellinistift (Nellini home), for the Rose-Livingston-Stiftung in Frankfurt, a home for elderly women dedicated the following year. Stylistically the building was closely related to Haus Hainerberg, despite profound differences in program. The success with which Paul was able to employ the vocabulary of his private domestic projects to suit institutional requirements provides further indication of the harmonious culture embodied in his contemporary works in the form of an architectural language of universal validity. The Nellinistift has survived, and continues to serve its original function. Although the building was damaged in the Second World War and subsequently altered, many details of the original design have been preserved.

Joseph Popp, »Bruno Pauls Haus der Rose-Livingston-Stiftung in Frankfurt am Main«, *Dekorative Kunst* 18 (1915), 73; Joseph Popp, *Bruno Paul* (1916), 210–234; Gustav Adolf Platz, *Die Baukunst der neuesten Zeit* (1927), 316; *Stadt* (1982), 57; Alfred Ziffer, *Bruno Paul* (1992), 209–210, 296; Sonja Günther, *Bruno Paul* (1992), 151.

Haus Leffmann, Cologne, 1912 (pp. 49, 52)
The elevations of the house that Paul designed for the factory owner Paul Leffmann reflected the tradition of his earlier projects, although the severity of its forms reflected a new development in his work. For Haus Leffmann, Paul designed façades that derived their interest from an internal, geometrical tension between horizontal and vertical elements, rather than from the vocabulary of classically derived forms. This tension was enhanced by the material properties of the house, which was clad in rough Dutch clinkers. The interiors that Paul designed for Haus Leffmann were equally innovative, employing forms and colors that prefigured the emergence of architectural Expressionism. Haus Leffmann is no longer extant.

Max Creutz, »Haus Leffmann in Köln von Architekt Bruno Paul«, *Dekorative Kunst* 24 (January/February 1921), 64–87; Hermann Muthesius, *Die schöne Wohnung: Beispiele neuer deutscher Innenräume, herausgegeben und mit Einleitung versehen von Hermann Muthesius* (1922), 24–25, 96–97, 137–138, 186–187; Hermann Muthesius, *Landhaus und Garten: Beispiele neutzeitlicher*

9. Haus Braun, Berlin, 1910. Exterior. Condition in 2001.
10. Nellinistift of the Rose Livingston Stiftung, Frankfurt am Main, 1912. Detail. Condition in 2001.
11. Gelbes Haus, Cologne, 1914.
12. Residence of the director of the Unterrichtsanstalt of the Kunstgewerbemuseum, Berlin, 1914.
13. Haus der Freundschaft, Constantinople, 1916. Project.
14. Haus Friedwart, Wetzlar, 1917. Detail. Condition in 2001.

Landhäuser nebst Grundrissen/Innenräumen und Gartenanlagen (1925), 95–97, 125, 151, 163; Alfred Ziffer, *Bruno Paul* (1992), 210–211, 297; Sonja Günther, *Bruno Paul* (1992), 103, 151.

Buildings for the Werkbund exhibition, Cologne, 1914 (pp. 49–55)

Paul was a member of the organizing committee that planned the 1914 »Deutsche Werkbund-Ausstellung« in Cologne, and to which he contributed the design of three separate buildings for prominent sites overlooking the Rhine: the Gelbes Haus (yellow house), Bierhalle (beer hall) and Weinhaus (wine restaurant). He conceived his finest interiors for the Gelbes Haus, a model home furnished by Herrmann Gerson of Berlin. The expressive forms and emphatic coloration of the furniture echoed the architectural treatment of the interiors: vestiges of a classical ordering were reduced to patterns of free, attenuated forms. Paul employed a dramatic zigzag motif on the walls of the beer hall, presaging the popularity of this pattern during the 1920s. His interiors for the wine restaurant were equally idiosyncratic. Paul's three projects were copiously illustrated in the 1915 Werkbund yearbook, entitled *Deutsche Form in Kriegsjahr*, which commemorated the exhibition. The Gelbes Haus received more illustrations than any other single project at the exhibition, a number surpassed only by the photographs of the Haupthalle (main hall) and its collection of unrelated individual exhibits. None of the temporary buildings erected for the Werkbund exhibition was preserved. However several of Paul's furnishings are still extant, including Paul's buffet from the Gelbes Haus, which is preserved in the Kunstgewerbemu-seum at Schloß Pillnitz, near Dresden.

Deutscher Werkbund, *Deutsche Form im Kriegsjahr: Jahrbuch des Deutschen Werkbundes 1915* (1915); Georg Jakob Wolf, »Der Deutsche Werkbund und die Deutsche Werkbund-Ausstellung in Köln«, *Dekorative Kunst* 17 (September 1914), 529–555; Fritz Stahl, »Bruno Pauls Gelbes Haus«, *Dekorative Kunst* 18 (October 1914), 1–20; *Stadt* (1982), 59; Alfred Ziffer, *Bruno Paul* (1992), 212–215, 299; Sonja Günther, *Bruno Paul* (1992), 154–155.

Residence of the director of the Unterrichtsanstalt of the Kunstgewerbemuseum, Berlin, 1914 (p. 45)

In 1914, Paul rebuilt his official residence in the buildings of the school of applied arts on Prinz-Albrecht-Straße. The furniture and interiors that he designed for this, his own home, reflected the elegance, refinement, and cultural harmony of his commissioned interiors on the eve of the First World War. Paul's living room embodied the timeless virtues of anthropometric proportions, signified by the conscientious use of the antique orders, by the inclusion of rare and inherently beautiful materials such as mahogany, crystal, and marble, and in the harmonious and muted coloration of painted, stained and dyed surfaces. Such work also epitomized the status Paul had achieved in Berlin society, and related directly to such prestigious projects as his reception room for the Reichskanzlerpalais (palace of the imperial chancellor) of 1909 and his interiors for the residence of the president of the Kammergericht of 1914. Paul's

residence on Prinz-Albrecht-Straße was destroyed during the Second World War.

Joseph Popp, *Bruno Paul* (1916), 247–252; *Stadt* (1982), 17, 56; Alfred Ziffer, *Bruno Paul* (1992), 215 to 218, 296; Sonja Günther, *Bruno Paul* (1992), 150.

Project for the Haus der Freundschaft, Constantinople, 1916 (p. 58)

Paul was one of twelve prominent architects invited to participate in a design competition organized by the Werkbund for the Haus der Freundschaft (house of friendship) in Istanbul, a symbol of the alliance between Germany and the Ottoman empire. The competition was planned so that the twelve entrants would also constitute the jury, and would themselves select a winner. Given this system, which favored compromise, along with the diverse and often idiosyncratic nature of the entries, Paul's design did not fare well in the competition, which was won by German Bestelmeyer. However, a variant of Paul's simple, practical design was subsequently built in Berlin. In 1922 Paul designed a façade for the Kunstmessehaus Dülk (Dülk exhibition center for the arts) which adapted the severe, seven-bay palazzo scheme that he had proposed for the House of Friendship. This façade was the only built legacy of the Werkbund's first great design contest. Paul's design for the house of friendship was never constructed. His Kunstmessehaus Dülk was destroyed in the Second World War.

Theodor Heuss, *Das Haus der Freundschaft in Konstantinopel: ein Wettbewerb deutscher Architekten* (1918); Alfred Ziffer, *Bruno Paul* (1992), 300.

Haus Friedwart, Wetzlar, 1917 (pp. 57, 58)

At Haus Friedwart, as at the Villa Feinhals, Paul completed a project begun by another architect. His interiors for the house represent a point of transition in his career, when the Neoclassical motifs of the preceding decade, the forms characteristic of his search for harmonious culture, were giving way to the freer vocabulary of his projects for the 1914 Werkbund exhibition. This transition was embodied in unfamiliar juxtapositions of color and form in an interior that nevertheless retained the comfort and grace characteristic of Paul's residential projects. Haus Friedwart is unique in that many of its furnishings and interiors have survived in largely their original condition, preserved by the descendents of the original owners. In addition, a series of presentation drawings of the design are preserved in Berlin, illustrating both the development of several rooms and Paul's methods as a designer.

Elfriede Mues, »Haus Dr. L. in Wetzlar: Eingerichtet von Professor Bruno Paul – Berlin«, *Deutsche Kunst und Dekoration* 49 (October/November 1921), 71–84; *Stadt* (1982), 57; Alfred Ziffer, *Bruno Paul* (1992), 221–225, 300; Sonja Günther, *Bruno Paul* (1992), 90, 152.

Asiatisches Museum, Berlin-Dahlem, 1921 (pp. 36, 37)

The Asiatisches Museum in Dahlem was originally planned as an annex of the Völkerkunde-Museum in central Berlin. Paul's project was completed in 1921 after lengthy delays in its construction. It was the last, and grandest, of his architectural expressions of the Zweites Biedermeier, the reinterpretation of the simple, practical aesthetic of German Classicism. A building of modest bearing, despite its considerable dimensions, the museum was distinguished by the quality of its detailing, which reflected Paul's mastery of the practice of architecture. The Asiatisches Museum has survived. Although its interiors have been modified over the years, the general character of Paul's project has survived intact.

Wilhelm von Bode, *Jahrbuch der Königlich Preußischen Kunstsammlungen* (1915), 1–5; *Stadt* (1982), 16, 56; Alfred Ziffer, *Bruno Paul* (1992), 299; Sonja Günther, *Bruno Paul* (1992), 88–89, 149.

Haus Fraenkel, Hamburg-Blankenese, 1921 (pp. 61, 62)

Haus Fraenkel was Paul's first overtly Expressionist building. Its exterior walls were sheathed with a veneer of uncoursed sandstone. They were crowned with an emphatic, outward arching cornice with a smooth plaster surface. The sculptural profile of the cornice, which followed the plan of the projecting semicircular bays on the garden façade of the house, belonged to a vocabulary of fluid, sculptural forms that was arousing considerable interest in 1921. The stair hall of the house recalled Haus Friedwart, with a surreal wooden railing roughly carved with twining vines: heavy, thick forms finished in black lacquer. Details of the interior, such as the chevron pattern of the veneers in the paneled hall, prefigured the exaggerated angularity that characterized the final phase of Expressionism. Nevertheless the interiors of the house were comfortable and convenient, devoid of revolutionary social or political ideology. Although Haus Fraenkel has been demolished, the stair hall has been preserved at the Museum für Kunst und Gewerbe in Hamburg.

Hans Rolffsen, »Ein Landhaus in Blankenese erbaut von Professor Bruno Paul – Berlin«, *Deutsche Kunst und Dekoration* 52 (July 1923), 226–229; Max Osborn, »Meister Bruno Paul«, *Innen-Dekoration* 35 (March 1924), 197–201; *Stadt* (1982), 36; Alfred Ziffer, *Bruno Paul* (1992), 233–234, 302; Sonja Günther, *Bruno Paul* (1992), 91, 151.

Exhibitions for the »Deutsche Gewerbeschau«, Munich, 1922 (pp. 62, 63)

The »Deutsche Gewerbeschau« (German trade exhibition) of 1922 epitomized the Expressionist movements in architecture and the decorative arts. Paul was a member of the committee that organized the exhibition, for which he designed a series of abstract, geometric architectural elements. A published description of the »Gewerbeschau« noted that Paul was the only artist at the exhibition to translate the »angles, points and serrations« of Cubism into compelling three-dimensional forms that worked »without any applied ornament, only form and color«.[453] Yet like all of Paul's best work, his Expressionist designs for the trade exhibition were simple, logically consistent, conscientiously detailed, and flawlessly executed. None of the temporary exhibitions for the »Deutsche Gewerbeschau« were preserved.

Joseph Popp, »Bruno Paul auf der Deutschen Gewerbeschau«, *Dekorative Kunst* 26 (April 1923), 137–140; Georg Jakob Wolf, »Die Deutsche Gewerbeschau in München«, *Dekorative Kunst* 25 (July 1922), 225–247; Alexander Koch, *Das neue Kunsthandwerk in Deutschland und Oesterreich: unter Berücksichtigung der Deutschen Gewerbeschau Muenchen 1922* (1923); Alfred Ziffer, *Bruno Paul* (1992), 234–235; Sonja Günther, *Bruno Paul* (1992), 155.

Haus Neven-Dumont, Cologne, 1923 (p. 64)

The house in Cologne that Paul designed for Dr. Kurt Neven-Dumont exploited the geometric tendencies that had emerged in the interiors of Haus Fraenkel. Paul wrote one of his few published articles on Haus Neven-Dumont, the 1928 essay »Ein Kölner Wohnhaus« (a house in Cologne). He described the prismatic form of the house, noting the triangular bay in the street façade, which provided the residents an unobstructed view of both entrances to the house. He referred to this characteristic feature of the house as its »nose«, providing an accent to its principal elevation. Of the exterior as a whole, Paul argued that »it works only through the proportioning of the built elements and each individual component, and asserts itself in its surroundings as one would expect of a good and distinguished house«, notwithstanding its Expressionist details. The ideals of harmony and propriety remained undiminished in his residential work, and not merely as aesthetic criteria. »Just as the owners and their guests will gather together around the blazing fireplace in winter«, he wrote, »so will the open loggia be the most commonly used room during the summer. There they will sit down to meals or to tea«, he continued, »and spend their evenings in the open air, sheltered from the rains, into October.«[454] This domestic idyll epitomized Paul's objectives as a residential architect: order, comfort, and convenience. Although the original interiors of Haus Neven-Dumont are lost, the building itself has survived.

Bruno Paul, »Ein Kölner Wohnhaus«, *Die Pyramide* 14 (1928), 1–4; *Stadt* (1982), 42; Alfred Ziffer, *Bruno Paul* (1992), 304; Sonja Günther, *Bruno Paul* (1992), 151.

Streetcars T24/B24 for BStBG, 1924 (pp. 66, 67)

In 1923 Paul was selected by the Berliner Straßenbahn-Betriebs-GmbH, or BStBG, to provide the artistic design of a new streetcar for the German capital. More than 1,200 of these vehicles were built between 1924 and 1926, making Paul's design a ubiquitous fixture of Weimar Republic Berlin. Though Paul was not involved in the mechanical or structural design of the streetcars, he exerted considerable influence over both their form and their color. The interiors of the streetcars, which were wholly Paul's work, were notable both for their elegance and their practicality. One of Paul's assistants later recalled him squeezing a piece of modeling clay in his hand to develop the shape of the door handles, producing an organic form that was at once expressive and functional. At least three of Paul's streetcars have been preserved. One is at the Deutsches Straßenbahn-Museum Hannover in Wehmingen; one is iat the National Capital Trolley Museum in Colesville, Maryland; the third, the only one in full working order, remains in Berlin.

Hans D. Reichardt, *Die Straßenbahnen Berlins* (Düsseldorf, 1974), 28–29; Sergius Ruegenberg, »Design-Arbeit an einem Straßenbahnwagen (1924)«,

Bauwelt 72 (8 May 1981), 742; Sonja Günther, *Bruno Paul* (1992), 160.

Haus Auerbach, Berlin-Dahlem, 1924 (pp. 74, 76, 77)

This elegant house represents a transitional phase in Paul's career, between the influences of Expressionism and the Neues Bauen. Nevertheless, in both its composition and its exquisite detailing, Haus Auerbach reflects the best traditions of his residential designs. The house is notable for the extent of its built-in furnishings, including, in several rooms, complex hollow doors assembled from laminated veneers. Haus Auerbach has survived, although the original furnishings have been lost. The house, and many original construction drawings, were preserved by the noted Berlin architect Georg Heinrichs.

Stadt (1982), 38, 56; Alfred Ziffer, *Bruno Paul* (1992), 306; Sonja Günther, *Bruno Paul* (1992), 91, 104–111.

DeWe Plattenhaus H 1018, 1925 (pp. 65, 73, 74)

Paul's Plattenhaus H 1018, or panel-house H 1018, was introduced in 1925 at the exhibition »Wohnung und Siedlung« in Hellerau. The tiny building, with a floor area of only 153 square meters, was a composition of prismatic volumes devoid of conventional architectural ornament. As in all of Paul's residential designs, the street façade was the most rigorously ordered, notwithstanding its asymmetry. He planned his Plattenhaus to be assembled from only one hundred individual elements, predominantly plywood panels: far fewer components than other DeWe houses of similar scale. This simplicity belied the spatial complexity of the design, with rooms of differing ceiling heights fitted together within the cubic volume of the exterior. Internally, Paul's Plattenhaus echoed the topology of his earlier middle-class homes. By eliminating the two-story stair hall and minimizing the floor area devoted to circulation, he was able to retain features of his larger houses that were unusual in a building the size of the Plattenhaus H 1018. DeWe produced large numbers of wooden houses in traditional and vernacular styles, but it apparently only produced one Plattenhaus H 1018 – there was simply no market for such a dwelling during the years of economic uncertainty. Remarkably the original Plattenhaus H 1018 survives in Hellerau, on the street named Auf dem Sand.

Ernst Zimmermann, »Das Plattenhaus der Deutschen Werkstäten A.G. – Hellerau«, *Innen-Dekoration* 36 (November 1925), 402–410; Erich Haenle, »Wohnung und Siedlung Dresden 1925«, *Dekorative Kunst* 29 (March 1926), 133–143; Deutsche Werkstätten A.-G., *De-We Plattenhaus* (1928); Alfred Ziffer, *Bruno Paul* (1992), 305; Sonja Günther, *Bruno Paul* (1992), 155; W. Owen Harrod, »The Deutsche Werkstätten and the Dissemination of Mainstream Modernity«, *Studies in the Decorative Arts* X (Spring-Summer 2003), 33–36.

Haus Sternberg, Soest, 1927 (pp. 76, 77)

In 1927, Paul's Cologne office completed the drawings for a new house in Soest commissioned by the prosperous factory owner Ernst Sternberg. The final design abandoned the steep tile roofs characteristic of Paul's earlier residential projects in favor of a visually flat configuration with broad eaves. He grouped the windows of the upper floor into a horizontal band, and selected a dramatically asymmetrical location for the front door of the house. In the completed building, Paul successfully transformed the comfortable and convenient middle-class design of Haus Auerbach in accordance with the progressive formal language of the Plattenhaus H 1018, without sacrificing its fundamental virtues. In so doing, he established the principles of the pragmatic Functionalism that would characterize his residential projects in the final years of the Weimar Republic. Haus Sternberg has survived. The exterior of the house retains, in large measure, its original appearance. Two other houses by Paul also survive in Soest: Haus Plange of 1927 and Haus Jahn of 1931.

Valentin Fuhrmann, »Wohnhäuser von Bruno Paul unter Mitarbeit von Reg. Baumeister Franz Weber, Leiter des Kölner Ateliers«, *Innen-Dekoration* 40 (January 1929), 41–44; *Stadt* (1982), 42, 58; Thomas Drebusch, *Architektur der frühen Moderne, Bruno Paul in Soest* (1988); Alfred Ziffer, *Bruno Paul* (1992), 283–288, 309; Sonja Günther, *Bruno Paul* (1992), 152.

Sinn department store, Gelsenkirchen, 1927 (pp. 74, 75)

In 1927, Paul prepared a design for the Sinn department store in Gelsenkirchen. He conceiving the elevations of the emphatically modern Sinn store in horizontal bands, with continuous strip windows of green opalescent glass contrasting with the white-painted spandrels. The ground floor featured a single curved pane of glass 5.5 meters long at the corner, then the largest sheet of curved glass ever manufactured in Europe, as well as freestanding displays in the form of glass columns beneath a reflective metal ceiling. The Sinn store in Gelsenkirchen embodied a harmonious union of modern technology and modern commerce, a composition so successful that it was still featured in publications on commercial design in the 1950s. The store has survived, having now been in continuous retail use by Sinn Leffers AG for more than seventy-five years. However it has been so extensively modified that it is difficult to perceive the character of the original design.

Valentin Fuhrmann, »Wohnhäuser von Bruno Paul unter Mitarbeit von Reg. Baumeister Franz Weber, Leiter des Kölner Ateliers«, *Innen-Dekoration* 40 (January 1929), 41; Adolf Schuhmacher, *Ladenbau* (1934); *Stadt* (1982), 44, 57; Alfred Ziffer, *Bruno Paul* (1992), 311; Sonja Günther, *Bruno Paul* (1992), 151.

War memorial, Seifhennersdorf, 1927 (pp. 68, 69)

In 1927, Paul completed the design for a First World War memorial located in the square between the town hall and the parish church of his home town of Seifhennersdorf. The monument was composed of carved blocks of stone listing the 262 citizens of Seifhennersdorf lost in the war, plus relief sculptures depicting scenes of combat, evacuation of the wounded, a soldier's funeral, and the mourning wives and mothers of the fallen. Paul's war memorial demonstrated his acceptance of the aesthetic principles of the younger generation of avant-garde designers, providing a counterpart to Mies' contemporary monument to Karl Liebknecht and Rosa Luxemburg. Paul's memorial, unlike that designed by Mies, was a unified design with inscriptions integral to its composition. The Seifhennersdorf memorial has survived. Although the adjacent church was rebuilt following its destruction by fire in 1935, the memorial itself remains essentially as Paul had conceived it.

Gedenkschrift zur Einweihung des Krieger-Ehrenmals in Seifhennersdorf (1929).

Dischhaus, Cologne, 1928 (p. 75)
In 1928, Paul won a contest for the design of the Dischhaus, an office building for Hotel-Disch AG in Cologne. His winning proposal was closely related to the earlier Sinn store, but the detailing was fundamentally different. In place of painted plaster, Paul clad the façade with a very thin travertine curtain wall punctuated with horizontal bands of windows set in aluminum alloy frames. The fluid spatial forms, industrial materials, and technological sophistication of the Dischhaus identified it as an exemplary modern building, notwithstanding its elegant travertine veneer and practical detailing. The Dischhaus has survived, and was restored between 1982 and 1984. The exterior, lobby, and dramatic central stair are preserved in largely their original condition.

Valentin Fuhrmann, *Das neue Geschäftshaus, Bauten des Ateliers für Architektur Professor Bruno Paul, Reg. Baumstr. Franz Weber Köln am Rhein* (1930); Hermann Seeger, *Bürohäuser der privaten Wirtschaft* (1933), 39, 108–110, 123; *Stadt* (1982), 44; Alfred Ziffer, *Bruno Paul* (1992), 273–282, 312–313; Sonja Günther, *Bruno Paul* (1992), 151.

New York dining room for the Vereinigte Zoo-Werkstätten, 1928 (pp. 83, 89, 90)
The Vereinigte Zoo-Werkstätten was established in 1920 as the Typen-Möbel Gesellschaft MBH Zoo-Werkstätten, specifically to produce and market a new line of Typenmöbel. Although Paul's 1920 Typenmöbel was practical and modern, it found few buyers in the chaotic markets of postwar Germany. The Vereinigte Zoo-Werkstätten instead found its market in the production of more expensive furnishings, and indeed manufactured several of Paul's most significant Weimar interiors, including those exhibited at the 1927 »Monza Biennale« and the New York dining room of 1928. The New York dining room commemorated Paul's visit to the United States in the year of its introduction, and epitomized his efforts to establish an international modern style. A buffet from the New York dining room is preserved at the Bröhan Museum in Berlin.

Bruno E. Werner, »Bruno-Paul-Möbel der Vereinigten Zoo-Werkstätten für Kunst im Handwerk Berlin«, *Dekorative Kunst* 32 (1929), 153–164.

Kathreiner-Hochhaus, Berlin, 1928 (p. 76)
As Paul was developing his design for the Dischhaus, he spent five weeks in the United States studying contemporary developments in American construction. He applied the lessons of these investigations to the design of a new office building for the Kathreiners Malzkaffeefabrik. The resulting project was the first skyscraper in Berlin, and one of the first tall buildings in Central Europe built in accordance with American practices in both structural design and construction administration. The Kathreiner-Hochhaus was technically and aesthetically sophisticated. The steel frame and floor plates were erected in five months, an achievement unprecedented in Germany. Paul then sheathed the light-weight steel skeleton in a travertine veneer. The influence of the Kathreiner-Hochhaus was considerable. The Kathreiner-Hochhaus is still extant, and is now occupied by BVG (Berliner Verkehrs-AG), the corporation that succeeded BStBG in 1929. The building was severely damaged during the Second World War, however, and Paul's original interiors were lost in the subsequent reconstruction.

Herbert Günther, »Alt und Neu«, *Form* 3 (1932). Hermann Seeger, *Bürohäuser der privaten Wirtschaft* (1933), 88–90; *Stadt* (1982), 4, 56–57; Alfred Ziffer, *Bruno Paul* (1992), 313–314; Sonja Günther, *Bruno Paul* (1992), 139–140, 150.

Villa Traub, Prague, 1928 (pp. 77–80)
The villa that Paul designed for Edmund Traub epitomized his conception of an architecture for modern life. When completed, Villa Traub appeared as an abstract composition of pure geometric forms. The simple form of the villa belied the material with which it was clad, a finely-honed sandstone. When completed, the house embodied a palpable tension between the influence of the New Building and the tradition of German Classicism manifested in Paul's earliest work as an architect. It was, according to Traub's daughter, a shockingly modern house when it was completed. Nevertheless it also proved a comfortable and convenient home. Paul considered Villa Traub, and the factory buildings that he designed for its owner, among his fifty most important commissions.[455] Although the interiors were modified after the confiscation of the house by the Nazis, several rooms have subsequently been restored.

Bruno Paul, »Haus Traub bei Prag«, *Innen-Dekoration* 46 (April 1935), 113–118; *Stadt* (1982), 42; Alfred Ziffer, *Bruno Paul* (1992), 315; Sonja Günther, *Bruno Paul* (1992), 93, 128–131, 152; W. Owen Harrod, »Villa Traub in Prague (1928): Bruno Paul and Pragmatic Functionalism«, *Umění* 39 (2001), 137–150.

Haus am Rupenhorn, Berlin-Charlottenburg, 1928 (pp. 80–82)
While Villa Traub was under construction, Paul designed a similarly impressive modern house in Berlin for Paul Lindemann. Haus am Rupenhorn could be considered Paul's most emphatically modern house, the one that met most closely the ideals of the Functionalist canon. It was also, according to his daughter, one of his favorite projects. Internally, Haus am Rupenhorn shared with Villa Traub the fundamental topology of Haus Westend, organized around a two-story stair hall. Every detail of the house was beautifully made in accordance with Paul's ideals of artistry and craftsmanship. The planning of the house was practical and efficient, in accordance with his professional experience. Haus am Rupenhorn has survived, although its original interiors have been altered and its original furnishings lost.

Stadt (1982), 41; Alfred Ziffer, *Bruno Paul* (1992), 316; Sonja Günther, *Bruno Paul* (1992), 93–94, 132–136, 149.

20. »New York« dining room for the Vereinigte Zoo Werkstätten, 1928.
21. Villa Traub, Prague, 1928. Detail, Condition in 2001.
22. Haus Am Rupenhorn, Berlin-Charlottenburg, 1928. Detail. Condition in 2001.
23. Interior for »Contempora«, 1929.
24. First-class cabin for the liner *Bremen*, 1929.
25. Bedroom 273 for the Deutsche Werkstätten, 1931.
26. »Die wachsende Wohnung« for the Deutsche Werkstätten, 1931.

Haus Carl Bergmann, Dresden, 1929 (p. 80)

Paul did not intitiate the design of Carl Bergmann's villa in Dresden-Blasewitz. As with Haus Friedwart, he completed and furnished a building that was already under construction. Nevertheless the interiors that he designed for the house were among the most opulent of his designs. Haus Bergmann has survived as the seat of the Architektenkammer Sachsen, but most of the original interiors and all of Paul's furniture have been lost. The house itself has been extensively altered and restored.

Richardson Wright, ed., *House and Garden's Book of Color Schemes* (1929); Max Osborn, »Neue Villenbauten von Bruno Paul«, *Deutsche Kunst und Dekoration* 66 (1930), 40–66; Alfred Ziffer, *Bruno Paul* (1992), 315, 252–253; Sonja Günther, *Bruno Paul* (1992), 150.

Interiors for Contempora, 1929 (pp. 84, 85)

In 1929, Paul and Lucian Bernhard financed the incorporation of a new design firm in New York modeled on the practice of the Vereinigte Werkstätten. Intending their partnership to provide an outlet for specifically modern design, they chose the name Contempora. Paul's interiors for Contempora, including a bedroom set with chartreuse green furnishings in wood and cane, with silver accents, were typical of his contemporary work. All of the interiors offered for sale by Contempora were available in several harmonized color schemes in accordance with the firm's commitment to regard each ensemble as a totality, rather than as a collection of individual elements. The economic crisis of 1929 doomed Contempora to failure.

Helen Appleton Reed, »Art and Industry – ›Contempora‹«, *Creative Art* (June 1929), 18; Matlock Price, »Contempora«, *Good Furniture and Decoration* (August 1929), 71.

First-class cabin for the liner *Bremen*, 1929 (p. 90)

In 1926 Paul was retained to design a first-class cabin for the Norddeutscher Lloyd liner *Bremen*, the design of whose principal public rooms had been entrusted to Fritz August Breuhaus de Groot. Paul's cabin for *Bremen*, executed by the Deutsche Werkstätten, represented the final triumph of the Kunstgewerbebewegung and its ideals. It was also his last prominent public commission prior to the Nazi accession – the extravagant cost of a prestigious transatlantic liner invariably being offset by government subsidies. *Bremen* was warmly received on both sides of the Atlantic, even such popular American magazines as *National Geographic* praising the new liners as »faster and still more luxurious« than anything built in Great Britain or the United States.[456] *Bremen* was destroyed in Bremerhaven by aerial bombardment in 1941.

Wilhelm Michel, »Ozean-Express ›Bremen‹«, *Deutsche Kunst und Dekoration* 65 (November 1929), 111–114; Fritz August Breuhaus de Groot, *Ozean Express Bremen* (1930).

Headquarters of the Gerling Konzern, Cologne, 1930 (pp. 88, 89)

In 1930, Paul designed an office building for the headquarters of the Gerling Konzern, an insurance company in Cologne. He conceived the project in spare and graceful classical vocabulary, devoid of historical ornament yet with finely worked ashlar details reminiscent of the Zollernhof of 1910. Though he conceived the limestone façades with elegant, classical proportions, the character of the building was more concisely reflected in the details, which included glass, stone, and metal elements of a wholly modern character. In 1936 the Gerling Konzern built a second new building to Paul's design, a mirror image of the first. However his services were not retained in its planning. Both Paul's building and its companion have survived. Portions of the exteriors were restored following the Second World War to reflect their original appearance, although the interiors have been extensively modified.

Hermann Seeger, *Bürohäuser der privaten Wirtschaft* (1933), 37, 58–59, 122; *Das Gerling-Hochhaus in Köln* (1953); *Stadt* (1982), 45, 57; Alfred Ziffer, *Bruno Paul* (1992), 278, 317; Sonja Günther, *Bruno Paul* (1992), 151–152; Hiltrud Kier, *Architektur der 50er Jahre: Bauten des Gerling Konzerns in Köln* (1994).

Dining room for Gebrüder Schürmann, Cologne, 1931 (p. 85)

In 1931, despite a failing worldwide economy, the furniture manufacturer Gebrüder Schürmann of Cologne organized an exhibition of modern interiors. The invited participants were F. A. Breuhaus de Groot, Marcel Breuer, Hans Hartl, Michael Rachlis, Le Corbusier, Ernst Lichtblau, Adolf Loos, Jock D. Peters, Francesco Stapp, and Bruno Paul. Paul contributed a dining room composed of characteristically simple elements, modern in its disavowal of historical models in favor of pure, geometric forms. The eclectic group of artists that participated in the 1931 exhibition illustrated the diverse and inclusive nature of European Modernism before the founding of CIAM, or the canonization of the International Style. Paul's dining room is lost.

Luise Straus-Ernst, »Ein Internationale Raumausstellung im Hause Gebrüder Schürmann in Köln, *Die Kunst* 66 (1931), 61–68; Gustav Adolf Platz, *Wohnräume der Gegenwart* (1933), 346; Alfred Ziffer, *Bruno Paul* (1992), 255.

Bedroom 273 for the Deutsche Werkstätten, 1931 (p. 90)

In 1931 Paul conceived the bedroom Modell 273 for DeWe, a suite of furniture that clearly prefigured the biomorphic design of the 1950s. Like all of his best work, the expressive forms of the elements of bedroom were not merely aesthetic, but functional. Their design permitted adjustment to suit the needs of their users: the cantilevered tops of several of the elements could be rotated about their supports to fulfil a number of differing functions. A set of furniture from bedroom 273 has been preserved in the collection of Kunstgewerbemuseum at Schloß Pillnitz.

Carl Burchard, *Gutes und Böses in der Wohnung in Bild und Gegenbild: Grundlagen für neues Wohnen* (1933), 44; Hans Wichmann, *Aufbruch zum neuen Wohnen: Deutsche Werkstätten und WK-Verband 1898–1970* (1978), 244; Alfred Ziffer, *Bruno Paul* (1992), 257–258.

»Die wachsende Wohnung« for the Deutsche Werkstätten, 1931 (pp. 90, 91)

In 1931, Paul introduced a line of furniture entitled »Die wachsende Wohnung« (the expanding dwelling), consisting of a series of simple, modular elements. The individual elements consisted of abstract geometric forms devoid of applied ornament. The geometric purity of »Die wachsende Wohnung« was characteristic of the best modern furniture, and imbued the individual pieces with a timeless quality as well as a far greater flexibility than had been possible with the earlier Typenmöbel. The Deutsche Werkstätten would continue manufacturing Paul's standardized furniture well after the end of the war. As late as 1958, VEB Deutsche Werkstätten produced and sold Paul's designs in the German Democratic Republic. Elements of »Die wachsende Wohnung« survive in several museum collections, including that of the Kunstgewerbemuseum at Schloß Pillnitz.

W. Owen Harrod, »The Deutsche Werkstätten and the Dissemination of Mainstream Modernity«, *Studies in the Decorative Arts* X (Spring-Summer 2003), 37–38; Alfred Ziffer, *Bruno Paul* (1992), 259 to 260.

Interiors for the liner *Boissevain*, 1936 (p. 91)

In 1936, Paul prepared designs for the furnishing of the Dutch liner *Boissevain*[457] for the Deutsche Werkstätten. The project was Paul's last prominent interior, although *Boissevain*'s sailings between Kapstadt and Shanghai, by way of Batavia, never held the same prestige as the transatlantic service. Most of the elegant furniture that he designed for the ship was manufactured from TEGO-plywood, a material that could be molded into fluid forms under high temperature and pressure. Paul's use of this versatile, lightweight material emphasized his continued interest in technological developments. *Boissevain* was one of the few projects on which Paul collaborated with Ulla Schnitt, who designed tapestries and murals for several of the public rooms. The ship was dismantled for scrap in 1968. None of Paul's interiors are known to have survived.

Alfred Ziffer, *Bruno Paul* (1992), 269; Sonja Günther, *Bruno Paul* (1992), 77–80, 161.

Apartment houses on Luxemburger Straße, Cologne, 1937 (pp. 65, 91)

The apartment buildings for the Cologne suburb of Sülz that Paul designed around 1936 for Heimbau GmbH are representative of a building type to which he took a particular interest in the years prior to the Second World War. He had participated in the planning of the Kolonie Ideal, the Berlin housing development, prior to the First World War. In the 1930s, he designed a number of large complexes, including projects for the IG Farben company in Bitterfeld, and several in Cologne. Paul's apartment buildings, like all of his best work, were simple, elegant, and impeccably detailed. With their shared amenities, shops, and comfortable (if modest) homes, his apartment projects must be considered among the more successful examples of pre-war urban housing in Central Europe. Paul's buildings on Luxemburger Straße are still extant, occupied and in good repair.

Alfred Ziffer, *Bruno Paul* (1992), 278, 317; Sonja Günther, *Bruno Paul* (1992), 318, 320.

Laminated veneer hardware for the Deutsche Werkstätten, 1939 (pp. 65, 91)

Throughout his career, Paul maintained a professional interest in technological development. When the Deutsche Werkstätten perfected a new press for laminating veneers, he responded with a series of designs that exploited the opportunities afforded by this development, including his celebrated Furnier-Schrank (veneer cabinet) of 1923. The use of very thin veneers permitted the creation of panels that were disproportionately strong given the mass of material employed, a legacy of the construction of plywood aircraft components in Germany during World War One. In addition to providing unprecedented aesthetic opportunities, the use of laminated veneers offered an alternative to many traditional uses for metal castings. Paul designed a series of simple, practical fittings, from coat hooks to door handles, using naturally-finished laminated veneers. He was a pioneer in the development of the modern plywood furniture of the 1930s and 1940s.

Alfred Ziffer, *Bruno Paul* (1992), 269.

Office building at Gereonsdriesch 9–11, Cologne, 1953 (pp. 95, 96)

Paul's Cologne former office building and its contents were completely destroyed during the Second World War. As rebuilt, Gereonsdriesch 9–11 was typical of urban architecture in postwar Germany. The masonry veneer, pitched tile roof, and cornice height were all specified by the city of Cologne The harmonious proportions of the façade and the practical efficiency of functional elements such as the windowsills and downspouts maintained the pragmatic traditions of Biedermeier classicism. The stone embrasure at the asymmetrically located entry recalled his work of the 1920s, albeit in a simplified and abstracted form. The austerity of the stonework echoed the severity of the entire design. Only the metal grilles on the windows and at the entrance to the garage incorporated ornamental detail. The rebuilt offices at Gereonsdriesch 9–11 are still extant.

Alfred Ziffer, *Bruno Paul* (1992), 322.

Restoration of the Deutsches Goldschmiedehaus, Hanau, 1958 (p. 97)

Paul's last executed architectural commission was the reconstruction of the the sixteenth-century town hall of Hanau, the Deutsches Goldschmiedehaus. He had studied the restoration of the Goldschmiedehaus, a significant monument in the townscape of Hanau since the late 1940s, when he prepared preliminary drawings for the restoration of the historical center of the city. In his reconstruction, Paul achieved the balance of artistry and craftsmanship that he had promoted throughout his professional career. The building was exquisitely and painstakingly rebuilt by hand, a collaborative effort by carpenters, masons, plasterers, painters, and smiths. The rebuilding was a perfect embodiment of the »timeless German building arts« that he cherished. The Deutsches Goldschmiedehaus, as rebuilt by Paul, is still extant.

Alfred Ziffer, *Bruno Paul* (1992), 323.

27. Interior for the Dutch liner *Boissevain*, 1936.
28. Apartment houses on Luxemburger Straße, Cologne, 1937. Detail. Condition in 2001.

Bibliography

Archival resources

Archiv des Gerling-Konzerns, Cologne
Bayerisches Hauptstaatsarchiv, Munich, Kultus-
ministerium, Personalakte »Bruno Paul«
Germanisches Nationalmuseum, Nuremberg
Teilnachlaß Paul
Getty Research Institute for the History of Arts,
Los Angeles, Hans Poelzig Papers
Hochschularchiv, Hochschule der Künste, Berlin
Kaiser-Wilhelm-Museum, Krefeld
Karasek-Museum, Seifhennersdorf
Karl-Ernst-Osthaus-Archiv, Hagen
Kreisarchiv, Soest
Monacensia Literaturarchiv und Bibliothek,
Munich, Nachlaß Ludwig Thoma
National Archives and Records Administration,
Washington, Reichskulturkammer Files
Newark Museum Library, Newark
Sächsisches Hauptstadtarchiv, Dresden, Unter-
lagen der Deutschen Werkstätten Hellerau
Staatliche Graphische Sammlung, Munich
Staatsarchiv München, Munich, Unterlagen
»Die Elf Scharfrichter«
Vereinigte-Werkstätten-Archiv, Munich
Werkbundarchiv, Berlin

Publications by Bruno Paul

»Über Dekorationsmalerei (Zu den Arbeiten von E.
R. Weiss)«, *Wasmuths Monatshefte für Baukunst*
1 (1914), 27–30.
»Passagierdampfer und ihre Einrichtung«, *Der Ver-
kehr: Jahrbuch des Deutschen Werkbundes 1913*
(Jena, 1914), 55–58, 84–86.
»Kriegsgräber in Osten«, *Wieland* 1 (February 1916),
6–7.
»Künstlerlehrzeit«, *Wieland* 3 (April 1917), 15–17.
»Architektur und Kunstgewerbe nach dem Kriege«,
Wieland 3 (May 1917), 17–18.
»Das Wahlplakat«, *Wieland* 4 (March 1918), 20.
»Rettet Potsdam«, *Wieland* 4, (March 1918), 20.
»Erziehung der Künstler an staatlichen Schulen: Aus
der Programmschrift 1919 Erziehung der Künstler
an staatlichen Schulen von Bruno Paul«, *Innen-
Dekoration* 30 (1919), 344–348.
»Erziehung der Künstler an staatlichen Schulen«,
Deutsche Kunst und Dekoration 45 (December
1919), 193–196.
»Sterbendes Handwerk«, n. p. (n.d.).
»Ein Kölner Wohnhaus«, *Die Pyramide* 14 (1928),
1–4.
»Reisebericht über New York: Vor der Vorstands-
sitzung erstattet von Professor Bruno Paul«, *Die
Form* 3 (August 1928), 247–253.
»Rückblicke und Aussichten: Bruno Paul aus dem
Katalog der Ausstellung Europäischen Kunstge-
werbes in Macy-Hause zu New York«, *Die Pyra-
mide* 14 (1928), 42–46.
»Schwimmende Hotels«, *Die Form* 3 (December
1928), 400–404.
»Die Innen-Einrichtung des Lloyddampfers Bremen«,
Die Pyramide 15 (1929), 81.
»Gibt es noch Mäzene?«, n. p. (n. d.)

»Haus Traub bei Prag«, *Innen-Dekoration* 46 (April
1935), 113–118.
»Auf Schwanenwerder«, *Innen-Dekoration* 47 (Janu-
ary 1936), 3–11.
»Gefolgschaftsräume eines Handwerkbetriebs«,
Moderne Bauformen 41 (1942).
»Die Verwertung der Brandruinen: IV. Die Rechts-
grundlage des Abrisses«, *Neue Bauwelt* 4 (24
January 1949), 61.
»Wiederherstellung des Goldschmiedehauses in
Hanau«, *Der Architekt* 3 (June 1954), 140–141.
»Wandlungen um 1900«, *Architektur und Wohnform*
68 (1960).
»Wandlungen vor und nach dreiunddreißig: Aus
den Memoiren«, *Stadt: Monatshefte für Woh-
nungs- und Städtebau* 29 (1982), 46–55.

Secondary sources

Ahlers-Hestermann, Friedrich, *Bruno Paul: oder
die Wucht des Komischen*, Berlin, Gebr. Mann,
1960.
Ahrens, Helmut, *Ludwig Thoma: Sein Leben, sein
Werk, seine Zeit*, Pfaffenhofen, W. Ludwig, 1983.
Allan, Ann Taylor, *Satire and Society in Wilhelmine
Germany*, Lexington, The University Press of
Kentucky, 1984.
Anderson, Stanford, »Deutscher Werkbund – the
1914 debate: Hermann Muthesius versus Henri
van de Velde«, in: Ben Farmer and Hentie Louw,
eds., *Companion to Contemporary Architectural
Thought*. London and New York, Routledge,
1993.
Anderson, Stanford, »The Legacy of German Neo-
classicism and Biedermeier: Behrens, Tessenow,
Loos, and Mies«, *Assemblage* 15 (1991), 63–87.
Anderson, Stanford, *Peter Behrens and a New
Architecture for the Twentieth Century*, Cam-
bridge/Massachusetts, MIT Press, 2000.
Bach, Richard F., »Styles A-borning: Musings on
Contemporary Industrial Art and Decoration«,
Creative Art (June 1928), 37–40.
Bauer, Helmut, *Schwabing: Kunst und Leben um
1900*, Munich, Münchener Stadtmuseum, 1998.
Baum, Julius, ed., *Farbige Raumkunst/Dritter Band:
120 Entwürfe Moderner Künstler*, Stuttgart, Julius
Hoffmann, 1926.
Benvenuto. »Am Scheideweg: Glossen zu Bruno
Pauls Berufung nach Berlin«, *Dekorative Kunst* 10
(November 1906), 96.
Berlin und die Berliner: Leute. Dinge. Sitten. Winke,
Karlsruhe, J. Bielefelds Verlag, 1905.
Berlin und seine Bauten, Teil IV, Wohnungsbau, Ber-
lin, 1975.
*Berlin und seine Bauten, Teil V, Bauwerke für Kunst,
Erziehung und Wissenschaft*, Berlin, 1983.
*Berlin und seine Bauten, Teil IX, Industriebauten,
Bürohäuser*, Berlin, 1971.
Bode, Wilhelm von, *Jahrbuch der Königlich Preu-
ßischen Kunstsammlungen,* Berlin, 1915.
Bode, Wilhelm von, *Mein Leben*, edited by Thomas
Gähtgens and Barbara Paul, Berlin, 1997.
Boedecker, Ludwig. »Die Unterrichtsanstalt des
königl. Kunstgewerbemuseums in Berlin«,
Kunstgewerbeblatt 17 (1906), 18–19.
Böhm, Werner, Heiner Haschke, Hans Klötzer,
Annerose Müller, and Günther Stolle, *Seifhen-

nersdorf: Gestern und Heute*, Horb am Neckar,
Geiger-Verlag, 1996.
Bredt, E. W., »Bruno Paul«, *Dekorative Kunst* 5
(November 1901), 66–67.
Bredt, E. W., »Bruno Paul – Biedermeier – Empire«,
Dekorative Kunst 8 (March 1905), 217–228.
Bredt, E. W., »Ausstellung der Vereinigung für an-
gewandte Kunst I, München, 1905«, *Dekorative
Kunst* 8 (September 1905), 469–503.
Breuer, Robert, »Der George Washington«. *Innen-
Dekoration* 20 (October 1909), 333–343.
Breuer, Robert, »Deutschland auf der Brüsseler
Weltausstellung«, *Moderne Bauformen* 9 (1910),
301–414.
Breuer, Robert, »Großstadhäuser«, *Deutsche Kunst
und Dekoration* 32 (April 1913), 25–32.
*Bruno Paul 1874–1968: das Werk des Karikaturisten,
Möbelentwerfers, Architekten und Hochschul-
lehrer*, Berlin, Hochschule der Künste, 1982.
Buddensieg, Tilmann, *Industriekultur: Peter Behrens
and the AEG, 1907–1914*, Cambridge/Mass., MIT
Press, 1984.
Buesche, Albert, »Ein Architekt in der Zeit: Zu Bru-
no Pauls fünfundsiebzigstem Geburtstage«, *Der
Tagesspiegel* (19 January 1949).
Burchard, Carl, *Gutes und Böses in der Wohnung
in Bild und Gegenbild: Grundlagen für neues
Wohnen*, Leipzig and Berlin, Verlag Otto Beyer,
1933.
Bund der Kunstgewerbeschulmänner, ed., *Kunst-
gewerbe: ein Bericht über Entwicklung und Tätig-
keit der Handwerker- u. Kunstgewerbeschulen in
Preußen*, Berlin, Verlag Ernst Wasmuth, 1922.
Campbell, Joan, *The German Werkbund: the
Politics of Reform in the Applied Arts*, Princeton,
Princeton University Press, 1977.
Creutz, Max, »Das Kunstgewerbe auf der großen
Berliner Kunstausstellung 1907«, *Berliner Archi-
tekturwelt* 10 (August 1907), 161–177.
Creutz, Max, »Das Haus Feinhals in Köln-Marien-
burg: Joseph M. Olbrich – Bruno Paul – Max
Läuger«, *Dekorative Kunst* 15 (November 1911),
57–77.
Creutz, Max, »Die Heilanstalt Pützchen bei Bonn«,
Dekorative Kunst 16 (January 1913), 135–175.
Creutz, Max, »Ein Wohnhaus in Wiesbaden«, *De-
korative Kunst* 16 (January 1913), 177–192.
Creutz, Max, »Haus Leffmann in Köln von Architekt
Bruno Paul«, *Dekorative Kunst* 24 (January/Febru-
ary 1921), 64–87.
Creutz, Max, »Wohnräume im alten Köln von Bruno
Paul,« *Deutsche Kunst und Dekoration* 50 (June
1922), 151–152.
Deubner, Ludwig, »Bruno Paul: Ein Meister neu-
zeitlicher Wohnungskunst«, *Velhagen und Kla-
sings Monatshefte* 33 (no. 2), 589.
Deutsche Werkstätten A.G., *De-We Plattenhaus,
Dresden-Hellerau*, Verlag der Deutschen Werk-
stätten A.G., Hellerau, 1928.
Deutsche Werkstätten A.G., *Jahrbuch der Deut-
schen Werkstätten 1928*, Dresden-Hellerau,
Verlag der Deutschen Werkstätten A.G., 1928.
Deutsche Werkstätten A.G., *Deutsche Werkstätten
Möbel*, Dresden-Hellerau, Verlag der Deutschen
Werkstätten A.G., 1927.
Deutsche Werkstätten A.G., *Deutsche Werkstätten
Möbel*, Dresden-Hellerau, Verlag der Deutschen
Werkstätten A.G., 1936.

Deutscher Werkbund, *Der Verkehr: Jahrbuch des Deutschen Werkbundes 1914*. Jena, 1914.

Deutscher Werkbund, *Deutsche Form im Kriegsjahr: Jahrbuch des Deutschen Werkbundes 1915*. Jena, 1915.

Deutscher Werkbund, *Kriegergräber im Feld und daheim: Jahrbuch des Deutschen Werkbundes 1916–17*, Jena, 1917.

Descriptive Catalog of the German Arts and Crafts at the Universal Exposition, St. Louis, 1904.

»Die Kunst hat nie ein Mensch allein besessen«, Berlin, Henschel Verlag, 1996.

Drebusch, Thomas, *Architektur der frühen Moderne, Bruno Paul in Soest*, Essen, Staatsarbeit Essen, 1988.

Dritte Deutsche Kunstgewerbe-Ausstellung Dresden: Offizieller Katalog, 1906.

Fankl, Paul T., *New Dimensions: The Decorative Arts of Today in Words and Pictures*, New York, Payson and Clarke, 1928.

Fred, W., *Die Wohnung und ihre Ausstattung*, Bielefeld, Verlag von Velhagen und Klasing, 1903.

Fuchs, Georg, »Angewandte Kunst im Glaspalaste 1898«, *Deutsche Kunst und Dekoration* 3 (October 1898), 21–49.

Fuchs, Georg, »Die Wohn-Räume der deutschen Abteilung«, *Deutsche Kunst und Dekoration* 11 (October 1902), 45–52.

Fuhrmann, Valentin, »Wohnhäuser von Bruno Paul unter Mitarbeit von Reg. Baumeister Franz Weber, Leiter des Kölner Ateliers«, *Innen-Dekoration* 40 (January 1929), 41–44.

Fuhrmann, Valentin, »Ein Landhaus in Westfalen«, *Innen-Dekoration* 42 (April 1931), 146–160.

Fuhrmann, Valentin, *Das neue Geschäftshaus, Bauten des Ateliers für Architektur Professor Bruno Paul, Reg. Baumstr. Franz Weber Köln am Rhein*, Cologne, 1930.

Gay, Peter, *Weimar Culture: the Outsider as Insider*, New York, 1968.

Gedenkschrift zur Einweihung des Krieger-Ehrenmals in Seifhennersdorf, Seifhennersdorf, n. p., September 1929.

Geyer-Raack, Ruth H., »›IRA‹ Internationale Raumausstellung Gebr. Schürmann, Köln«, *Moderne Bauformen* 30 (1931).

Günther, Sonja, *Interieurs um 1900: Berhard Pankok, Bruno Paul und Richard Riemerschmid als Mitarbeiter der Vereinigten Werkstätten für Kunst im Handwerk*, Munich, Wilhelm Fink Verlag, 1971.

Günther, Sonja, *Das Deutsche Heim, Luxusinterieurs und Arbeitermöbel von der Gründerzeit bis zum Dritten Reich*, Gießen, Anabas-Verlag, 1984.

Günther, Sonja, *Design der Macht: Möbel für Repräsentanten des »Dritten Reiches«*, Stuttgart, Deutsche Verlags-Anstalt, 1991.

Günther, Sonja, *Bruno Paul, 1874–1968*, Berlin, Gebr. Mann, 1992.

Habich, Georg, »Bruno Paul als dekorativer Künstler«, *Innen-Dekoration* 12 (December 1901), 199 to 214.

Haenel, Erich, »Neue Interieurs von Bruno Paul«, *Dekorative Kunst* 6 (1903), 425.

Haenel, Erich, »Das Kunstgewerbe auf der Düsseldorfer Ausstellung«, *Dekorative Kunst* 6 (Ocober 1903), 25.

Haenel, Erich, »Die 3. deutsche Kunstgewerbe-Ausstellung Dresden 1906«, *Dekorative Kunst* 9 (September 1906), 481–511.

Haenel, Erich, »Neue Räume der Deutschen Werkstätten Dresden«, *Dekorative Kunst* 23 (September 1920), 325–348.

Haenel, Erich, »Wohnung und Siedlung Dresden 1925«, *Dekorative Kunst* 29 (March 1926), 133 to 143.

Haenel, Erich, »Neue Holzhäuser der Deutschen Werkstätten A.G.«, *Die Kunst* 36 (1935), 3–11.

Harrod, W. Owen, »Villa Traub in Prague (1928): Bruno Paul and Pragmatic Functionalism«, *Uměni* 39 (2001), 137–150.

Harrod, W. Owen, »Bruno Paul's Typenmöbel, the German Werkbund, and Pragmatic Modernism: 1908–1918«, *Studies in the Decorative Arts* IX (Spring/Summer 2002), 33–57.

Harrod, W. Owen, »The Deutsche Werkstätten and the Dissemination of Mainstream Modernity«, *Studies in the Decorative Arts* X (Spring/Summer 2003), 21–41.

Heilmeyer, Alexander, »Die Deutsche Werkbund-Ausstellung in Köln«, *Kunst und Handwerk* 64 (1913/14), 269.

Hellwag, Fritz, »Der Deutsche Werkbund und seine Künstler«, *Kunstgewerbeblatt* 27 (1916), 21.

Hermann, Wolfgang, »Hochhäuser am Kleistpark«, *Kunst und Künstler* 27 (1929), 239.

Heuss, Theodor. *Das Haus der Freundschaft in Konstantinopel: ein Wettbewerb deutscher Architekten*, Munich, F. Bruckmann, 1918.

Heyken, Richard, »Das Richmodis-Haus in Köln«, *Deutsche Kunst und Dekoration* 58 (September 1926), 367–368.

Himmelheber, Georg. *Die Kunst des deutschen Möbels*, Munich, 1973.

Hinkel, Gottfried, »Neue Räume der Vereinigten Werkstätten für Kunst im Handwerk«, *Deutsche Kunst und Dekoration* 33 (December 1913), 231 to 233.

Jelavich, Peter, *Munich and Theatrical Modernism: Politics, Playwriting and Performance,* Cambridge/Mass., Harvard University Press, 1985.

Kaes, Anton, Jay Martin, and Edward Dimendberg, eds., *The Weimar Republic Sourcebook*, Berkeley, University of California Press, 1994.

Kalkschmidt, Eugen, »Die Möbel- und Raumkunst auf der Werkbund-Ausstellung zu Köln am Rhein«, *Moderne Bauformen* 13 (September/October 1914), 401–406.

Kalkschmidt, Eugen, »Bruno Pauls Gelbes Haus«, *Die Kunst* 32 (1915), 1.

Karlinger, Hans, »Aus den Verkaufsstellen der Deutschen Werkstätten in München und Berlin«, *Deutsche Kunst und Dekoration* 47 (January 1921), 207–213.

Kiaulehn, Walther, *Berlin: Schicksal einer Weltstadt*, Munich, Biederstein Verlag, 1958.

Kier, Hiltrud, *Architektur der 50er Jahre: Bauten des Gerling Konzerns in Köln*. Frankfurt am Main, Insel Verlag, 1994.

Klopfer, Paul, »Bruno Paul«, *Moderne Bauformen* 8 (January 1909), 1–15.

Koch, Alexander, »Die Vereinigten Werkstätten für Kunst im Handwerk zu München«, *Deutsche Kunst und Dekoration* 8 (1901), 428.

Koch, Alexander, *Alexander Koch's Handbuch neuzeitlicher Wohnungskultur: Band Herrenzimmer*, Darmstadt, Verlag Alexander Koch, 1920.

Koch, Alexander, *Alexander Koch's Handbuch neuzeitlicher Wohnungskultur: Band Speise-Zimmer und Küchen*. Darmstadt, Verlag Alexander Koch, 1920.

Koch, Alexander, *Alexander Koch's Handbuch neuzeitlicher Wohnungskultur: Band Schlafzimmer*, Darmstadt, Verlag Alexander Koch, 1920.

Koch, Alexander, *Alexander Koch's Handbuch neuzeitlicher Wohnungskultur: Das vornehmbürgerliche Heim*, Darmstadt, Verlag Alexander Koch, 1922.

Koch, Alexander, *Das neue Kunsthandwerk in Deutschland und Oesterreich: unter Berücksichtigung der Deutschen Gewerbeschau Muenchen 1922*, Darmstadt, Verlag Alexander Koch, 1923.

Kutscher, Arthur, ed., *Frank Wedekind, sein Leben und seine Werke*, Munich, Georg Müller, 1927.

L., »Repräsentations-Räume der Vereinigten Werkstätten«, *Innen-Dekoration* 22 (May 1911), 213.

L., »Räume von Bruno Paul«, *Innen-Dekoration* 40 (May 1929), 205–207.

Lang, Lothar, ed., *Bruno Paul*, Berlin, Eulenspiegel Verlag, 1974.

Lemp, Richard. *Ludwig Thoma: Bilder, Dokumente, Materialen zu Leben und Werk*, Munich, Süddeutscher Verlag, 1984.

Lux, August. *Das neue Kunstgewerbe in Deutschland*, Leipzig, 1908.

Makela, Maria Martha, *The Munich Secession: Art and Artists in Turn-of-the-century Munich*, Princeton, Princeton University Press, 1990.

Mebes, Paul, *Um 1800: Architektur und Handwerk im letzten Jahrhundert ihrer traditionellen Entwicklung,* Munich, F. Bruckmann A.G., 1908.

Michel, Wilhelm, »Die Vereinigten Werkstätten München in der Ausstellung des Deutschen Künstlerbundes in München«, *Deutsche Kunst und Dekoration* 14 (September 1904), 649–656.

Michel, Wilhelm, »Die Münchner Vereinigten Werkstätten auf der kunstgewerblichen Ausstellung in Dresden«, *Deutsche Kunst und Dekoration* 19 (November 1906), 97–112.

Michel, Wilhelm, »Ausstellung für Wohnungskunst in München«, *Deutsche Kunst und Dekoration* 19 (January 1907), 368–378.

Michel, Wilhelm, »Bruno Paul als Innenkünstler«, *Innen-Dekoration* 18 (February 1907), 49–54.

Michel, Wilhelm, »Vereinigte Deutsche Werkstätten für Handwerkskunst«, *Dekorative Kunst* 12 (June 1909), 179–183.

Michel, Wilhelm, »Die Ausstellung München 1908: Wohnungskunst und Kunstgewerbe«, *Dekorative Kunst* 12 (October 1909), 9–15.

Michel, Wilhelm, »Ozean-Express ›Bremen‹«, *Deutsche Kunst und Dekoration* 65 (November 1929), 111–114.

Mues, Elfriede, »Haus Dr. L. in Wetzlar: Eingerichtet von Professor Bruno Paul – Berlin«, *Deutsche Kunst und Dekoration* 49 (October/November 1921), 71–84.

München und die Münchener: Leute. Dinge. Sitten. Winke, Karlsruhe, J. Bielefelds Verlag, 1905.

Muthesius, Hermann, *Die schöne Wohnung: Beispiele neuer deutscher Innenräume herausge-*

geben und mit Einleitung versehen von Hermann Muthesius, Munich, F. Bruckmann A.G., 1922.

Muthesius, Hermann, *Landhaus und Garten: Beispiele neuzeitlicher Landhäuser nebst Grundrissen, Innenräumen und Gartenanlagen*, Munich, F. Bruckmann A.G., 1925.

Muthesius, Hermann, »Moderne Schiffskunst«, *Kunstgewerbeblatt* 18 (September 1907), 229–234.

Muthesius, Hermann, »Bruno Pauls Säle in neuen Kammergericht zu Berlin«, *Moderne Bauformen* 13 (1914).

Muthesius, Hermann, »Eine Vierzimmer-Wohnung von Bruno Paul«, *Deutsche Kunst und Dekoration* 45 (October 1919), 107–122.

Muthesius, Hermann, »Ein Landhaus von Bruno Paul: Haus Herz in Dahlem bei Berlin«, *Deutsche Kunst und Dekoration* 46 (September 1920), 293 to 300.

Muthesius, Hermann, »Meister Bruno Paul«, *Innen-Dekoration* 35 (March 1924), 76–83.

Muthesius, Hermann, »Wohnräume für die Firma Hermann Gerson in Berlin von Bruno Paul«, *Dekorative Kunst* 38 (January 1925), 81–90.

Muthesius, Hermann, »Neue Arbeiten von Bruno Paul«, *Innen-Dekoration* 36 (June 1925), 197–201.

Muthesius, Hermann, »Haus Walther Lange von Bruno Paul«, *Deutsche Kunst und Dekoration* 63 (March 1929), 401–412.

Muthesius, Hermann, »Neue Villenbauten von Bruno Paul«, *Deutsche Kunst und Dekoration* 66 (1930), 40–66.

Nachtlicht, Leo, *Deutsches Kunstgewerbe St. Louis 1904*, Berlin, 1904.

Osborn, Max, »Bruno Paul in Berlin«, *Der Kunstwart* 20 (1906), 462.

Osborn, Max, »Meister Bruno Paul«, *Innen-Dekoration* 35 (March 1924), 197–201.

Ottomeyer, Hans, and Margot Brandlhuber, eds., *Wege in die Moderne: Jugendstil in München, 1896 bis 1914*, Munich, Klinkhardt & Biermann, 1997.

Pauli, G., »Die Einrichtung eines Schnelldampfers«, *Kunst und Künstler* 6 (October 1907), 40–44.

Pevsner, Nikolaus, »Post-War Tendencies in German Art Schools«, *Journal of the Royal Society of Arts* 84 (January 17, 1936), 248–256 .

Pevsner, Nikolaus, *Pioneers of the Modern Movement from William Morris to Walter Gropius*. London, Faber & Faber, 1936.

Pevsner, Nikolaus, *Academies of Art Past and Present*, Cambridge, Cambridge University Press, 1940.

Platz, Gustav Adolf, *Die Baukunst der neuesten Zeit*, Berlin, Propyläen Verlag, 1930.

Platz, Gustav Adolf, *Wohnräume der Gegenwart*, Berlin, Propyläen Verlag, 1933.

Poelzig, Hans, *Hans Poelzig: Gesammelte Schriften und Werke*, edited by Julius Posener, Berlin, Gebr. Mann Verlag, 1970.

Popp, Joseph, »Bruno Pauls Haus der Rose-Livingston-Stiftung in Frankfurt am Main«, *Dekorative Kunst* 18 (1915), 73.

Popp, Joseph, *Bruno Paul*, Munich, F. Bruckmann A.G., 1916.

Popp, Joseph, »Bruno Pauls Haus Hainerberg im Taunus«, *Deutsche Kunst und Dekoration* 20 (October 1916), 1–22.

Popp, Joseph, »Bruno Paul auf der Deutschen Gewerbeschau«, *Dekorative Kunst* 26 (April 1923), 137–140.

Posener, Julius, *Berlin auf dem Wege zu einer neuen Architektur: Das Zeitalter Wilhelms II*, Munich, Prestel-Verlag, 1979.

Posener, Julius, *Hans Poelzig: Reflections on his Life and Work*. Cambridge/Massachusetts, MIT Press, 1992.

Post, Hermann, »Typenmöbel«, *Dekorative Kunst* 12 (March 1909), 258–264.

Post, Hermann, »Bruno Paul als Architekt«, *Deutsche Kunst und Dekoration* 25 (December 1909), 165–180.

Price, Matlock, »Contempora«, *Good Furniture and Decoration* (August 1929), 71.

R., »Neue Räume von Bruno Paul«, *Deutsche Kunst und Dekoration* 63 (1928), 81.

R., »Ein Wohnhaus und Wohnräume von Bruno Paul«, *Deutsche Kunst und Dekoration* 67 (February 1931), 330–332.

Rée, Paul Johannes, »Der Wartesaal im Nürnberger Bahnhof«, *Dekorative Kunst* 10 (October 1906), 1–10.

Reed, Helen Appleton, »Art and Industry – ›Contempora‹«, *Creative Art* (June 1929), 18.

Reiners, Heribert, »Ein Landhaus von Bruno Paul: Das Haus Röchling in Duisburg«, *Innen-Dekoration* 31 (1920), 217–224.

Rolffsen, Hans, »Ein Landhaus in Blankenese erbaut von Professor Bruno Paul – Berlin«, *Deutsche Kunst und Dekoration* 52 (July 1923), 226–229.

Rösch, Gertrud Maria, ed., *Simplicissimus, Glanz und Eland der Satire in Deutschland*, Regensburg, Universitätsverlag Regensburg, 1996.

Rother, Wolfgang, *Der Kunsttempel an der Brühlschen Terrasse: Das Akademie- und Ausstellungsgebäude von Constantin Lipsius in Dresden*, Basel, Verlag der Kunst, 1994.

Schäfer, Jost, *Bruno Paul in Soest: Villen der 20er Jahre und ihre Ausstattung*. Bonn, R. Habelt, 1993.

Schaefer, Karl, »Die moderne Baukunst im Dienste des Norddeutschen Lloyd«, *Innen-Dekoration* 18 (October 1907), 293–310.

Schaefer, Karl, »Der Norddeutsche Lloyd und die moderne Raumkunst«, *Dekorative Kunst* 11 (November 1907), 76–89.

Schaefer, Karl, »Kunstschulreform«, *Kunst und Künstler* 22 (April 1924), 190–191.

Shifman, Barry, »Design for Industry: The ›German Applied Arts‹ Exhibition in the United States, 1912 to 1913«, *The Decorative Arts Society Journal* 22 (1998).

Schmidt, Paul Ferdinand, »Die Akademien und ihre Beseitigung«, *Sozialistische Monatshefte* 5 (1928).

Schorisch, Adolf, *Aus unserer schönen Heimat: Dörfer und Sclösser, Berge und Wälder aus Zittaus Umgebung*, Zittau, Druck und Verlag der Zittauer Morgen-Zeitung, 1932.

Schorske, Carl E., *Thinking with History: Explorations in the Passage to Modernism*, Princeton, Princeton University Press, 1998.

Schulze, Franz. *Mies van der Rohe: A Critical Biography*, Chicago, The University of Chicago Press, 1985.

Schuhmacher, Adolf, *Ladenbau*, Stuttgart, Julius Hoffmann Verlag, 1934.

Schur, Ernst, »Bruno Paul auf der Großen Kunstausstellung zu Berlin«, *Dekorative Kunst* 10 (August 1907), 441–457.

Schur, Ernst, »Kleine Kunstnachrichten: Neubau des Café Kerkau«, *Dekorative Kunst* 13 (July 1910), 486–487.

Schur, Ernst, »Bruno Paul«, *Dekorative Kunst* 14 (November 1910), 57–81.

Schwartz, Frederic J., *The Werkbund: design theory and mass culture before the First World War*, New Haven, Yale University Press, 1996.

Seeger, Hermann. *Bürohäuser der privaten Wirtschaft*, Leipzig, Gebhardt, 1933.

Sekler, Eduard, *Josef Hoffmann: The Architectural Work, Monograph and Catalog of Works*, Princeton, Princeton University Press, 1985.

Sembach, Klaus-Jürgen, *Jugendstil, Die Utopie der Versöhnung*, Cologne, 1990.

Servaes, Franz, »Haus Waltrud: Eine Schöpfung von Bruno Paul«, *Deutsche Kunst und Dekoration* 44 (1919), 39.

Simplicissimus. Eine satirische Zeitschrift, München 1896–1944, Munich, Haus der Kunst München, 1978.

Singe, Hans W., »German Pen Drawings«, in: Holme, Charles, ed., *Modern Pen Drawings*, London, The Studio, 1901.

Stahl, Fritz, »Bruno Pauls Schule«, *Berliner Architekturwelt* 12 (January 1910), 367–369.

Stahl, Fritz, »Bruno Pauls Gelbes Haus«, *Dekorative Kunst* 18 (October 1914), 1–20.

Steamship George Washington, Bremen, Norddeutscher Lloyd, 1910.

Stephan, Walter, *Zur Einweihung des Rathauses in Seifhennersdorf,* n. p., 1925.

Thiersch, Heinz, ed., *Wir fingen einfach an. Arbeiten und Aufsätze von Freunden und Schülern um Richard Riemerschmid, zu dessen 85. Gerburtstag gesammelt und herausgegeben,* Munich, Pflaum, 1953.

Voss, Heinrich, *Franz von Stuck 1863–1928: Werkkatalog der Gemälde mit einer Einführung in seinen Symbolismus*, Munich, Prestel-Verlag, 1973.

Waldmann, Emil, »Die Gesellschaftsräume des Lloyddampfers Prinz Friedrich Wilhelm«, *Dekorative Kunst* 12 (November 1908), 57–63.

Waldmann, Emil, *Moderne Schiffsräume der Norddeutschen Lloyd nach Entwürfen von Bruno Paul, Rudolf Alexander Schröder und Franz August Otto Krüger*, *Dekorative Kunst* (special print), Munich, 1908.

Weichardt, Carl, »Eine Villa von Bruno Paul in Frankfurt«, *Deutsche Kunst und Dekoration* 29 (November 1911), 135–175.

Werner, Bruno E., »Bruno-Paul-Möbel der Vereinigten Zoo-Werkstätten für Kunst im Handwerk Berlin«, *Dekorative Kunst* 32 (1929), 153–164.

Westheim, Paul, »Das Kerkau-Café von Bruno Paul«, *Innen-Dekoration* 21 (October 1910), 369–377.

Westheim, Paul, »Vereinigte Werkstätten für Kunst im Handwerk«, *Deutsche Kunst und Dekoration* 28 (May 1911), 95–117.

Wichmann, Hans, *Aufbruch zum Neuen Wohnen: Deutsche Werkstätten und WK-Verband 1898 to 1970*, Basel, Birkhäuser Verlag, 1978.

Wiener, Paul Lester, »Contemporary Idea of Decoration in Steamships: The Decoration of the Express Steamer, Bremen, North German Lloyd, Has Solved Some Rather Difficult Problems in the Decorating and Furnishing of Large Spaces, Such as Great Steamers, Hotels and Club Rooms«, *Arts and Decoration* 32 (November 1929), 82–83, 136.

Wiegand, Heinrich, *Heinrich Wiegand: Ein Lebensbild*, edited by Arnold Petzet, Bremen, Verlag G. A. v. Halem, 1932.

Wiesenburg im Wandel der Zeit: eine Ortschronik, n. p., n. d.

Wingler, Hans Maria, *The Bauhaus: Weimar, Dessau, Berlin, Chicago*, Cambridge/Mass., MIT Press, 1969.

Wininger, Salomon. *Große jüdische National-Biographie*, Cernauti, Orient, 1925–35.

Wolf, Georg Jakob, »Das Deutsche Kunstgewerbe auf der Brüsseler Weltaustellung«, *Dekorative Kunst* 13 (September 1910), 529–557.

Wolf, Georg Jakob, »Die neue Ausstellung der Vereinigten Werkstätten«, *Dekorative Kunst* 15 (January 1912), 181–186.

Wolf, Georg Jakob, »Der Deutsche Werkbund und die Deutsche Werkbund-Ausstellung in Köln«, *Dekorative Kunst* 17 (September 1914), 529–555.

Wolf, Georg Jakob, »Die Deutschen Werkstätten in München«, *Dekorative Kunst* 25 (October 1921), 1–10.

Wolf, Georg Jakob, »Die Deutsche Gewerbeschau in München«, *Dekorative Kunst* 25 (July 1922), 225–247.

Wolff, Fritz, »Bruno Pauls Raumkunst auf der großen Berliner Kunst-Ausstellung 1907«, *Deutsche Kunst und Dekoration* 20 (August 1907), 244–252.

Wright, Richardson, ed., *House and Garden's Book of Color Schemes*, New York, Condé Nast Publications, 1929.

Ziffer, Alfred, »Die Vereinigten Werkstätten für Kunst im Handwerk: Eine Gründung aus privater Initiative«, *Kunst und Antiquitäten* (October 1990), 48 to 49.

Ziffer, Alfred, ed., *Bruno Paul, Deutsche Raumkunst und Architektur zwischen Jugendstil und Moderne*, Munich, Münchener Stadtmuseum, 1992.

Ziffer, Alfred, ed., *Bruno Paul und die Deutschen Werkstätten Hellerau*, Dresden, 1993.

Zimmermann, Ernst, »Das Plattenhaus der Deutschen Werkstätten A.G. – Hellerau«, *Innen-Dekoration* 36 (November 1925), 402–410.

»Zur Rathaus-Einweihung in Seifhennersdorf«, *Oberlausitzer Dorfzeitung* 61 (13 March 1925).

Notes

[1] Ludwig Mies van der Rohe, »Technology in Architecture«, quoted in Philip Johnson, *Mies van der Rohe* (New York, 1954), 203.

[2] Nikolaus Pevsner, *Pioneers of the Modern Movement from William Morris to Walter Gropius* (London, 1936), 200.

[3] Both *House and Garden* and *Vogue* were published by Condé Nast, an early proponent of the popular dissemination of twentieth-century Modernism in architecture and the decorative arts.

[4] Bruno Paul, »Villa Traub bei Prag«, *Innen-Dekoration* 46 (April 1935), 118: »uraltes deutsches Bauhandwerk«.

[5] Between 1896 and 1936, Bruno Paul's work was described, and often illustrated, in more than 250 books, exhibition catalogs and articles in professional journals in Germany alone. This number does not include his more than 400 illustrations for *Simplicissimus* and *Jugend* between 1896 and 1906, his editorial and graphic contributions to *Wieland* during the First World War, or the advertisements and illustrated catalogs distributed by the Vereinigte Werkstätten and the Deutsche Werkstätten. For a partial listing see Alfred Ziffer, ed., *Bruno Paul: Deutsche Raumkunst und Architektur zwischen Jugendstil und Moderne* (Munich, 1992), 385–392.

[6] Hannes Meyer, »bauen«, *bauhaus* 2, vol. 4. »architektur als ›fortführung der bautradition‹ ist baugeschichtlich treiben.«

[7] Personal interview with Paul's daughter Susanne Droste in Göttingen, September 2000.

[8] Personal records of Paul's daughter Julia Graf, Berlin. The baptism was witnessed by a maternal uncle, Christian Jentsch; a female relative, Christiane Jentsch; and the young daughter of a local miller, Ernestine Hohlfeld. As Paul's mother was thirty-seven years old when he was born, it is likely that Ernestine Hohlfeld was his nursemaid.

[9] Friedrich Ahlers-Hestermann, *Bruno Paul, oder die Wucht des Komischen* (Berlin, 1960), n. p. The biographical information contained in the book derived from interviews with Paul.

[10] Johannes Richter published this account in *Dorfspiegel für die Gemeinden Seifhennersdorf, Leutersdorf und Spitzkunnersdorf* 12/1960 and 1/1961. A teacher, Johannes Richter was director of the local newspapers of the villages of Seifhennersdorf, Leutersdorf, Spitzkunnersdorf and Niederoderwitz between 1957 and 1971. He was renowned as a scholar of local history.

[11] Bruno Paul, »Etwas von der Dachpappe«, *Vedag Buch 1935* (Berlin, 1935), 10.

[12] Ahlers-Hestermann.

[13] Sonja Günther, *Interieurs um 1900: Bernhard Pankok, Bruno Paul und Richard Riemerschmid als Mitarbeiter der Vereinigten Werkstätten für Kunst im Handwerk* (Munich, 1971), 29.

[14] Personal interview with Susanne Droste, September 2000.

[15] This was the »mill with 450 looms« that Ahlers-Hestermann attributed to Paul's grandfather. However, Johanne Juliane Auguste Jentsch was not the daughter of C. F Jentsch the mill owner, but of Christian Friedrich Jentsch, an orchardist and local judge. Personal interview with Bruno Paul's daughter Julia Graf in Berlin, March 2001.

[16] Personal interview with Julia Graf, March 2001.

[17] Personal interview with Julia Graf, March 2001.

[18] Bruno Paul, »Etwas von der Dachpappe«, 10.

[19] Reichskammer der bildenden Künste, document dated 22 March 1939. National Archives and Records Administration, Microfilm Document A339-RKK-F121.

[20] See Ahlers-Hestermann. The author contends that Paul had already developed an interest in the arts during his childhood in Seifhennersdorf, but was compelled to pursue a professional career by his father.

[21] Paul recorded his attendance at the Kreuzschule in his Reichskammer der bildenden Künste file as well as his memoirs, preserved at the Germanisches Nationalmuseum at Nuremberg. He referred to the school as the Kreuz-Gymnasium.

[22] Personal interview with Julia Graf, March 2001.

[23] The school was identified by Paul as the Friedrichstädter Lehrerseminar. The Lehrerseminar was associated with the Friedrichstädter Real- und Armenschule which was established in 1785 and which is still extant as 48. Grundschule.

[24] Ahlers-Hestermann recorded that Paul worked in the office of an uncle who was an architect.

[25] *Wer ist wer* (Lübeck, 1907).

[26] *Regulativ für die königliche Kunstgewerbeschule zu Dresden* (Dresden, 1890). The regulations of the Dresden Kunstgewerbeschule would have prohibited Paul's immediate enrollment in the architectural, sculptural or painting courses. Admission to the specialized courses required either the completion of one and one half years of study in an introductory curriculum, or Vorschule, or passage of an entrance exam. The entrance exam was specifically intended for applicants who had practical experience in the discipline in which they intended to study. Since Paul would have had no formal instruction as an artist in 1891, it is unlikely that he would have been able to demonstrate the ability to bypass the Vorschule. Thus his experience at the school of applied arts would by necessity have been of an introductory nature.

[27] Franz Stuck himself was ennobled in 1905.

[28] Stuck attended the Kunstgewerbeschule in Passau between 1875 and 1877 and the Kunstgewerbeschule in Munich between 1878 and 1881. In 1881 he was admitted as a student at the Königliche Akademie der Bildenden Künste in Munich.

[29] »Dresden«, *Meyers Konversations-Lexikon: Ein Nachschlagwerk des allgemeinen Wissens* (Leipzig, 1894). In 1894 Lipsius' Academy was one of five buildings in Dresden illustrated in the *Konversations-Lexikon*, the others being the Albertinum, the royal castle, and Semper's gallery and theatre.

[30] Nikolaus Pevsner, »Post War Tendencies in German Art Schools«, *Journal of the Royal Society of Arts* 84 (January, 1936), 250.

[31] Ahlers-Hestermann recorded that Paul's instructor at the academy was an Italian court painter (*Hofmaler*). This unnamed official painter represented conservatism and convention in the visual arts.

[32] Maria Makela, *The Munich Secession: Art and Artists in turn-of-the-century Munich* (Princeton, 1990), 14.

[33] »Wandlungen vor und nach dreiunddreißig«, Teilnachlaß Paul, Germanisches Nationalmuseum,

Nuremberg. »Als Zufluchsstätte hatte sich in den letzten drei Jahrzehnten vor 1900 ein Zentralpunkt geistig-künstlerischer Spannungen gebildet im traditionsgesegneten altbayerischen München. Geruhsam und mit seiner landschaftlichen Eigenständigkeit eng verbunden geblieben, gewährte es auch Gegensätzlichem nachsichtig Asyl. Hier verblühten die Reste historischen Stilgestaltens. Aber auch das neugeboren Realistisch-Gegenwartsbewußte fand bis zur Abstraktion gleichzeitig Raum und Pflege.«

34 The first published membership roster of the Secession, released in June 1892, is reprinted in Maria Makela, 151–152.

35 The dates of Paul's membership in the Secession have not been preserved. The 1905 publication *München und die Münchener: Leute. Dinge. Sitten. Winke* (Karlsruhe, 1905), a guide to Munich and its inhabitants, cites him as a member.

36 Notably the Société Anonyme des Artistes, Peintres, Sculpteurs, Graveurs, etc. of the Impressionists. Sisley, Pissarro, Degas and Monet, all members of the Société Anonyme, exhibited paintings in the periodic exhibitions of the Munich Secession.

37 William Walton, *Art and Architecture (Official Illustrated Publication of the World's Columbian Exposition of 1893),* vol. 3 (Philadelphia, 1893), 38.

38 *Der sozialistische Student* 1 (no 5, 1897), *Sozialistische Monatsheft* 2 (no 5, 1897). Paul's contributions to these journals were not published until after he left the academy.

39 *Süddeutscher Postillon* 14 (no. 26, 1895).

40 IB 1: »Antrag und Rechenschaftsberichte zu seiner Wiedereinstellung in den Staatsdienst nach 1945«, Teilnachlaß Paul, Germanisches Nationalmuseum, Nuremberg. »Ich war zuerst Mitarbeiter des ›Süddeutschen Postillons‹, sowie des ›Simplizissimus‹ und des ›Sozialistischen Akademikers‹.«

41 The artists Reinhold Max Eichler, Max Feldbauer, Walter Georgi, Angelo Jank, Walter Püttner, Leo Putz, Ferdinand von Reznicek and Walter Schulz were all students of Höcker and regular contributors to *Jugend*.

42 Paul never entered Stuck's atelier; acceptance was notably difficult to achieve. Wassily Kandinsky was famously rejected in his first attempt to study under Stuck, and spent an entire year honing his skills before making a second, successful attempt.

43 Paul's subject is identified by the caption »Redaction« (editorial staff).

44 Heinrich Voss, *Franz von Stuck 1863–1928: Werkkatalog der Gemälde mit einer Einführung in seinen Symbolismus* (Munich, 1973), 265.

45 Other works by Stuck of similar character painted prior to 1896 include *Versuchung (*temptation) of 1891(exhibited in Munich in 1894) and *Medusa* of 1892 (published in 1893), as well as numerous paintings and studies that were not publicly displayed but may have been known to Paul at the academy including *Die Sinnlichkeit (*sensuality) of 1889 and *Das Laster (*vice) of 1894. In a telling coincidence, the Herxheimer family of Frankfurt later purchased the painting *Versuchung*. Paul designed the Haus Herxheimer on Zeppelinallee in Frankfurt in 1910.

46 Stuck's first published works were drawings for the series *Allegorien und Embleme* printed by Gerlach und Schenk in Vienna. He subsequently worked for five years preparing illustrations for the Munich publication *Fliegende Blätter* before winning recognition as a painter.

47 *Jugend* 1 (no. 8, 1896).

48 The typical *Jugend* cover, for example, combined traditional representational art with decorative graphic design and type composition – the work of traditionally discrete artistic disciplines.

49 Friedrich Ahlers-Hestermann, *Bruno Paul oder die Wucht des Komischen* (Berlin, 1960). »Sein Atelier teilte er zunächst mit dem (jung verstorbenen) Bruder von Walter Leistikow, dann mit dem großen Zeichner Rudolf Wilke.«

50 No paintings by Paul are known to have survived from this period.

51 Of the founding members of the Secession, Josef Block, Hugo von Habermann, Ludwig Herterich, Paul Höcker, Leopold von Kalkreuth, Paul William Keller-Reutlingen, Gotthard Kuehl, Hugo König, Arthur Langhammer, Bruno Piglhein, Franz Stuck, Fritz von Uhde and Heinrich Zügel were prominent contributors to *Jugend*. A lesser number of the original Secessionists, the artists Bernhard Buttersack, Ludwig Dill, Otto Hierl-Deronco, Guido von Maffei, Robert Poetzelberger, Fritz Voellmy and Victor Weishaupt, were not regular contributors.

52 Hans W. Singer, »German Pen Drawings« in Charles Holme, ed., *Modern Pen Drawings: European and American* (London, 1901), 156.

53 Paul's contributions to *Jugend* were generally characterized by a linear mode of composition that suggested draftsmanship rather than painting, despite his use of gouache or watercolor in many of his illustrations.

54 *Jugend* 1 (no. 21, 1896). The title relies on the German idiomatic use of the word *Rad*, literally wheel, as a synonym for bicycle. *Die Frau vor dem Rad, hinter dem Rad und auf dem Rad* could be translated as »woman before the wheel, behind the wheel, and on the wheel«, although the humor is lost in the English.

55 *Jugend* 2 (no. 12, 1897). This pair of popular illustrations was also available, separately, in the series of *Kunstblätter* (art prints) published by *Jugend*. They were still being sold in 1909, as numbers 1934 and 1935 in the series. George Hirth, ed., *Dreitausend Kunstblätter der Münchener Jugend* (Munich, 1909), 248.

56 *Jugend* 1 (no. 30, 1896).

57 *Jugend* 1 (no. 46, 1896). This drawing was another in the series of *Kunstblätter*, no. 1940. *Dreitausend Kunstblätter der Münchener Jugend*, 248.

58 *Jugend* 1 (no. 34, 1896).

59 *Jugend* 1 (no. 29, 1896).

60 Thomas Theodor Heine (1867–1948) was the best known and most controversial of the *Simplicissimus* illustrators. He was also a talented painter and an accomplished designer.

61 For a history of *Simplicissimus*, see the catalog *Simplicissimus: Eine satirische Zeitschrift, München 1896–1944* (Munich, 1978).

62 *Simplicissimus* 1 (no. 50, 13 March 1897).

63 *Simplicissimus* 1 (no. 49, 6 March 1897). Vis-à-vis was the first satirical drawing by Paul printed in *Simplicissimus*. His first contribution of any kind was a vignette published in *Simplicissimus* 1 (no. 48, 27 February 1897).

64 The colors of Paul's original illustrations were generally subtler and more refined than those of the printed copies.

65 Bernhard Heinrich Martin Graf von Bülow (1849 to 1929) was the fourth chancellor of the German empire. He was, as Paul implied, no Bismarck.

66 *Simplicissimus* 5 (no. 44, 1900).

67 One of these portraits appeared in *Jugend*, and remained among the most popular of the individual prints published by the magazine. Number 1560 in the series, Lenbach's *Otto von Bismarck* served as the color frontispiece of the *Katalog der farbigen Kunstblätter aus der Münchener »Jugend«* (Munich, 1912).

68 *Simplicissimus* 7 (no. 39, 1902). Paul repainted Wertheim's head, and pasted the new version over the original. Such crude corrections were invisible in the printed versions of his illustrations.

69 »Warum sollen wir seinen Geburtstag nicht feiern? Hat er doch das schöne Weihnachtsgeschäft in die Welt gebracht.« This mild criticism of the Jewish Wertheim family, in the context of Paul's satire of hypocritical behavior across all strata of German society, was by no means anti-Semitic.

70 *Simplicissimus* 3 (no. 6, 1898).

71 »Warum nur diese modernen Künstler immer so übertreiben? So häßliche Menschen giebt's ja garnicht.«

72 See Carl Haenlein, ed., *Adolf Hölzel: Bilder, Pastelle, Zeichnungen, Collagen* (Hanover, 1982) and Wolfgang Venzmer, *Adolf Hölzel. Leben und Werk: Monographie mit Verzeichnis der Ölbilder, Glasfenster und ausgewählter Pastelle* (Stuttgart, 1982).

73 Paul himself left no record of having stayed with Hölzel in Dachau. His visits are recounted in Helmut Ahrens, *Ludwig Thoma: Sein Leben, sein Werk, seine Zeit* (Pfaffenhofen, 1983), 271–272.

74 Hölzel exerted a profound influence over his own students, who included Johannes Itten.

75 The cover illustrated is from *Assessor Karlchen und andere Geschichten: Kleine Bibliothek Langen Band XXXIV* (Munich, 1905). The text illustrations were by Heine.

76 Richard Lemp, *Ludwig Thoma: Bilder, Dokumente, Materialen zu Leben und Werk* (Munich, 1984), 18.

77 Opel produced bicycles before manufacturing its first automobile in 1899.

78 *Simplicissimus* 2 (no. 9, 1897).

79 The »Abstammungsnachweis« for Maria Paul maintained by the Nazi-era Reichskammer der bildenden Künste cites the date 14.12.1899 for her marriage. The »Abstammungsnachweis« for Bruno Paul states that he was married on 8 December 1899.

80 Incidentally, Paul's own parents were apparently not formally married when his eldest brother was born in 1857.

81 Ludwig Thoma, *Der Burenkrieg* (Munich, 1900). *Der Burenkrieg* was, on the whole, more sympathetic to the plight of the Boers than it was inflammatory. The publication prompted a grateful handwritten response from Paul Krüger, the bearded, bible-carrying President of the Transvaal Republic.

82 *Simplicissimus* 4 (no. 31, 1899).

83 »Für fünf Schilling täglich können wir Kerle mieten, die für die Ehre unserer Nation die größten Kriege führen. Kein englischer Gentleman wird sich zu diesem schmutzigen Handwerk hergeben.«

84 This characterization occurs in the drawing *Glückwunsch* (congratulations) in which a party of wounded soldiers from the war in Africa greets the Prince of Wales, who is standing with a champagne flute in one hand and the other on the shoulder of a French courtesan. *Simplicissimus* 5 (no. 6, 1900).

85 *Simplicissimus* 5 (no. 11, 1900).

86 (Die Königin:) »Nur keine Angst, Joe, die dahinten stören uns nicht, die gehören ja zur Verwandschaft!«

87 Paul's drawing *Der Raubmord in Südafrika* could have resulted in prosecution of the artist for *lèse majesté* had not the question of Wilhelm's loyalty to his grandmother been so sensitive an issue to the German government. Wilhelm II truly was Victoria's dutiful grandson. When the queen died in 1901, at the height of the conflict in Africa, Wilhelm spent two weeks living at Osborne House with the British royal family, to the dismay of his government.

88 *Simplicissimus* 5 (no. 2, 1900).

89 Teilnachlaß Paul, Germanisches Nationalmuseum, Nuremberg. 1945 letter addressed to the provincial governor of Brandenburg. »daß ich im ›Simplizis-simus‹ gemeinsam mit Th. Th. Heine stets die ›inter-nationale‹ und ›radikale‹ Politik vertreten habe«.

90 Hans W. Singer, 162.

91 Ludwig Thoma and Th. Th. Heine each invested 2100 Marks.

92 Langen paid the artists on his staff between 200 and 400 Marks for each published drawing. Paul contributed more than 400 drawings over nine years. Considering that Langen also paid yearly bonuses, Paul likely received an average of more than 10,000 Marks per year during each of the years that he worked for *Simplicissimus*, not including the income he received from other artistic endeavors.

93 Georg Habich, »Bruno Paul als dekorativer Künstler«, *Innen-Dekoration* 12 (December 1901), 199.

94 *Simplicissimus* 3 (no. 39, 1898).

95 »Weihevoll schwebt der Weihnachtsengel hernieder, Frieden und Glück zu verkünden den Deutschen. Zu seinem lebhaften Bedauern trifft er sie nicht zu Hause an: die ganze Bevölkerung sitzt wegen Majestätsbeleidigung in Gefängnis.«

96 The original eleven executioners were the writers Otto Falckenberg, Leo Greiner, Marc Henry and Willy Rath, the painters Viktor Frisch, Ernest Neumann and Willy Oertel, the sculptor Wilhelm Hüsgen, the architect Max Langheinrich, the composer Richard Weinhöppel and the lawyer Robert Kothe. Wedekind replaced Willy Rath, who left the ensemble soon after its establishment.

97 As an added precaution, the Elf Scharfrichter represented theemselves as a closed society, which was consequently not subject to official censorship. This was merely a ruse, however, and could not withstand a legal challenge brought by the government.

98 Both Heine and Neumann were frequent contributors of graphic designs to the Elf Scharfrichter.

99 Peter Jelavich, *Munich and Theatrical Modernism: Politics, Playwriting and Performance 1890 to 1914* (Cambridge/Massachusetts, 1985), 168.

100 Jelavich, 181.

101 *Simplicissimus* 9 (no. 36, 1905).

102 »Das Reformkleid ist vor allem hygienisch und erhält den Körper tüchtig für die Mutterpflichten.« »So lange Sie den Fetzen anhaben werden Sie nie in diese Verlegenheit kommen.«

103 Paul's story is recounted in Sonja Günther, *Interiors um 1900: Bernhard Pankok, Bruno Paul und Richard Riemerschmid als Mitarbeiter der Vereinigten Werkstätten für Kunst im Handwerk* (Munich, 1971), 29. Surprisingly this account does not appear in Heine's semi-autobiographical novel *Ich warte auf Wunder* (I wait for miracles) with which it accords perfectly in both content and tone.

104 The Glaspalast was an exhibition hall inspired by Joseph Paxton's Crystal Palace at the 1851 London Exhibition.

105 Hans Eduard von Berlepsch, »Endlich ein Umschwung«, *Deutsche Kunst und Dekoration* 1 (October 1897), 6–12.

106 It was a deliberate counterpoint to the title adopted by the Bayerische Kunstgewerbeverein zu München (Bavarian applied arts association in Munich) for its magazine, *Kunst und Handwerk* (artistry *and* craft), founded in 1850.

107 In actual fact the Ausschuß was a subsidiary of the Vereinigte Werkstätten. Its statutes provided that should the committee be dissolved, its capital would revert to the Werkstätten.

108 Paul's first citation in *Wer ist wer* identified him as »Mitbegr. u. künst. Leiter d. Münchener Vereinigt. Werkstätten f. Kunst im Handwerk«, cofounder and artistic leader of the Vereinigte Werkstätten. This claim has been frequently republished since.

109 See Alfred Ziffer, »Die Vereinigten Werkstätten für Kunst im Handwerk: Eine Gründung aus privater Initiative«, *Kunst und Antiquitäten* (November 1990), 48–49.

110 The photographs of Paul's 1898 living and dining room preserved in the Vereinigte Werkstätten archives illustrate the pieces displayed with the same wall mirror that had been exhibited in a room by Theodor Fischer at the VII. Internationalen Kunst-ausstellung.

111 Peter Schlemihl, *Neue Grobheiten: Simplicis-simus Gedichte von Peter Schlemihl* (Munich, 1903).

112 Endell's *Elvira* Photographic Studio was completed in Munich in 1897.

113 Franz Stuck also received a medal in Paris for his furniture. By 1900, Paul was no longer emulating Stuck. In 1902, the painter proclaimed of the Vereinigte Werkstätten, and, implicitly, Bruno Paul: »I find most of their furniture ugly. Irrespective of the tastelessness and artificiality of the details, as a whole the furnishings have such a shabby, prosaic and philistine effect… The only person I could possibly imaging living in such quarters would be a court clerk.« (quoted by Maria Makela, 182, n. 18)

114 A 1910 letter by Hoffmann's friend Wärndorfer quoted in Eduard Sekler, *Josef Hoffmann: The Architectural Work, Monograph and Catalogue of Works* (Princeton, 1985) proclaimed that »Paul sticks strictly with Peppo [Hoffmann], does simply everything that Hoffmann does.« Hoffmann might, with equal truth, be said to have stuck strictly with Paul.

115 Bruno Paul's Herrenzimmer für den Regierungs-präsidenten von Bayreuth was contemporary with Mackintosh's Willow Tea Rooms in Glasgow (1902 to 1904) and Hoffmann's Purkersdorf Sanatorium (1903).

116 E. W. Bredt, »Bruno Paul – Biedermeier – Empire«, *Dekorative Kunst* 8 (March 1905).

117 For example, see Stanford Anderson, »The Legacy of German Neoclassicism and Biedermeier: Behrens, Tessenow, Loos, and Mies«, *Assemblage 15* (1991). This important article addresses the classical contribution to Modernism primarily in terms of the symbolic content of the architectural vocabulary of the period around 1800.

118 Bredt, 223. »Noch sind es die Salons des späten 18. und frühen 19. Jahrhunderts, und schon sind es die Salons Bruno Pauls, die uns am klarsten den Begriff schlichter, wohnlicher Eleganz vermitteln. Das liegt nicht an der Herrschaft gerader Linien, an der Seltenheit rundlicher, weicher Linien allein. Wenn aus den nur schwarz-weißen Abbildungen Paul'scher Räume und Möbel, also aus der Wirkung der Flä-chen und Linien allein eine Kühle der Denkart und der Stimmung spricht, wie wir sie nur noch in den Räumen exklusiver Kreise der napoleonischen und nachnapoleonischen Zeit empfinden mögen, so wird die Berücksichtigung der Farbe der Hölzer, der Wand- und Möbelbespannungen uns im Vergleich jener alten und dieser neuen Räume recht vorsichtig machen.«

119 An American copy of Paul's 1901 Vereinigte Werkstätten candelabrum Number 58, manufactured by the Anderson Brass Works of Chicago, illustrates the popularity of his designs after St. Louis. In a letter to the author, Denis Gallion of Historical Design Inc. in New York noted that he had seen several of the Anderson candelabra sold at auction (often represented as Paul's work, despite significant differences in detail), implying that they had been produced and sold in relatively large numbers.

120 See Kathryn Bloom Heisinger, *Art Nouveau in Munich* (1988), 21.

121 Hermann Muthesius, »Die Wohnungskunst auf der Weltausstellung in St. Louis«, *Deutsche Kunst und Dekoration* 15 (December 1904), 209.

122 *Simplicissimus* 8 (no. 46, 1904).

123 William Morris, *News from Nowhere, or An Epoch of Rest: Being Some Chapters from a Utopian Romance* (Boston, 1890). Morris' »banded workshops« embodied his vision of ennobled craftsmanship in an ideal future.

124 Ziffer, »Die Vereinigten Werkstätten für Kunst im Handwerk: Eine Gründung aus privater Initiative«, 49. Initially the scope of manufacturing undertaken by the Vereinigte Werkstätten was relatively modest. The first production facility opened by the firm, a workshop opened at Erzgießereistraße 18 in Munich on 1 June 1898, employed eight to ten craftsmen for the production of furniture. However the company rapidly expanded.

125 *Simplicissimus* 3 (no. 28, 1898).

126 Paul's illustration »Wilhelm der Schweigsame« was technically a collage, a form that would emerge as a favorite technique of the Cubists fifteen years later, albeit in a somewhat different form.

127 The station itself is a Historicist building, completed between 1900 and 1906 to the designs of Karl Gustav Zenger.

128 Bentwood chairs were also readily available, either from Gebrüder Thonet or from the innumerable manufacturers of unlicensed copies.

129 In the 1990s, the waiting room, which remained in use as the Bahnhofsrestaurant, contained bentwood chairs that had been purchased to replace Paul's lost originals.

130 Paul Johannes Rée, »Der Wartesaal im Nürnberger Bahnhof«, *Dekorative Kunst* (October 1906), 2. »Dieser Raum gehört meines Erachtens zum besten, was die Raumkunst der neueren Zeit geschaffen hat.«

131 The Herrenzimmer that had been displayed in St. Louis was returned to Germany and installed in the government buildings in Bayreuth after the close of the »International Exhibition«. The Vereinigte Werkstätten produced a copy for the exhibition in Dresden.

132 No evidence has survived to indicate that any of these projects, which were not associated with the names of individual clients, was ever constructed. Paul's collaborator, Franz August Otto Krüger, was director of the Vereinigte Werkstätten and an accomplished designer.

133 Hermann Muthesius, *Das englische Haus* (Berlin, 1904).

134 In 1908, Paul employed the same pattern on a coffee service designed for the Vereinigte Werkstätten.

135 The classical effect of Paul's decorations drew heavily upon the character of the existing building.

136 Teilnachlaß Paul, Germanisches Nationalmuseum, Nuremberg.

137 Wilhelm II included a lengthy discussion of his architectural interests in his memoirs.

138 Nikolaus Pevsner, *Pioneers of the Modern Movement from William Morris to Walter Gropius* (London, 1936), 200.

139 The documents of the institution referred to the school as the Unterrichtsanstalt, Unterrichts-Anstalt, or simply UA.

140 The Martin-Gropius-Bau, renamed in honor of its architect after the Second World War, was built between 1877 and 1881.

141 Only the cellars of the school of applied arts have survived, preserved as a grim reminder of their use by the Gestapo between 1933 and 1945. The school itself relocated to the Charlottenburg district of Berlin in 1924.

142 »Kleine Nachrichten«, *Kunst und Handwerk* 57 (1906/07), 103. »Bruno Paul ist zum Direktor der Kgl. Kunstgewerbeschule in Berlin ernannt worden; damit ist eine Angelegenheit zum Abschluß gekommen, die nach vielen Seiten hin allgemeines Interesse erregte. Der Direktorposten war schon seit etwa zwei Jahren verwaist und die Frage, wer an diese so verantwortungsreiche Stelle berufen werde, bewegte die Gemüter um so mehr, als allerlei Gerüchte über die in Aussicht genommenen Persönlichkeiten im Umlauf waren; die Berufung Bruno Pauls findet überall Anerkennung, wenn auch für München der Verlust eines so hervorragenden Künstlers schmerzlich ist. Möge Paul sich als Leiter der Berliner Schule ebenso bewähren wie als Künstler.«

143 Bode was ennobled during the First World War, adding the aristocratic »von« to his surname.

144 Wilhelm von Bode, *Mein Leben*, Thomas Gähtgens and Barbara Paul, eds. (Berlin, 1997), 330. »Unsere Wahl fiel auf Paul, der die Unarten des Jugendstils schon meist abgestreift hatte und uns bei stärkerem Anschluß an ältere Vorbilder doch am eigenartigsten erschien.«

145 In 1873 the princes Wilhelm and Heinrich, together with their mother the crown princess Viktoria,

attended classes in drawing taught by the architect Kachel.

146 Wilhelm von Bode, *Mein Leben*, 330. »Ich kenne außerdem den *Simplicissimus* nicht und will ihn auch nicht kennenlernen.« It is also possible that the Kaiser, who had a complex relationship with his mother, approved Paul's appointment precisely because of the anti-British reputation he had established as an illustrator in Munich. The Kaiserin Viktoria was the eldest child of Queen Victoria. Wilhelm II was frequently compelled by political necessity to distance himself from his mother, and from his British ancestry.

147 Alfred Kerr, verse cited in U.l.a.v.8/104: »Bruno Paul war ein Verdruß / Auswurf Simplizissimus / Wirkte gestern noch verderblich / Heut Direktor kunstgewerblich / Anton Werner »Landesschändung«! / (Welche Wendung, – welche Wendung!)« Anton von Werner (1843–1915) was a history painter in the grand, nineteenth century model, a favorite artist of the royal family, and director of the school of the Prussian academy. He was a vocal opponent of modern painting.

148 Nikolaus Pevsner, »Post War Tendencies in German Art Schools«, *Journal of the Royal Society of Arts* (January 17, 1936), 249.

149 Bruno Paul, »Zu Beginn des Schuljahrs 1907/08 vollzogene sowie vorgeschlagene Veränderungen im Lehrkörper und in der Organisation der Unterrichtsanstalt«, U.l.a v. 5/125, Universitätsarchiv, Universität der Künste Berlin. »Je weniger Schularbeit, je mehr Werkstatt- oder Büroarbeit geleistet wird, um so brauchbarer werden die Hilfskräfte sein, welche das Gewerbe von der Schule empfängt.«

150 Bruno Paul, »Über kunstgewerblichen Unterricht«, U.l.a v. 5/217, Universitätsarchiv, Universität der Künste Berlin. »Die Schule muß sich zunächst darauf beschränken, die Massenaufnahmen von Mädchen einzustellen und nur wirklich begabte aufzunehmen.«

151 Ibid. »Eine praktische Lehrzeit im gewerblichen Betriebe ist die Vorbedingung jedes gesunden kunstgewerblichen Unterrichts. Die technischen Handgriffe und die Materialien eines Gewerbes müssen dem Schüler geläufig sein, wenn er in die Schule eintritt.«

152 Bruno Paul, »Zu Beginn des Schuljahrs 1907/08 vollzogene sowie vorgeschlagene Veränderungen im Lehrkörper und in der Organisation der Unterrichtsanstalt«.

153 Bruno Paul, »Über kunstgewerblichen Unterricht«. »In den Fachklassen wird das Entwerfen als Hauptlehrfach getrieben. Es soll den Schülern die Möglichkeit geboten werden, Arbeiten in echtem Material, für deren Entwurf und Ausführung künstlerische Gesichtspunkte maßgebend sind, auszuführen bzw. deren Ausführung zu überwachen. Das kann geschehen in Lehrwerkstätten und durch Heranziehen von Schülern zu den privaten Arbeiten der Fachlehrer.«

154 Kaiserstraße was renamed Ebereschenallee after 1918.

155 Goethe's house in Weimar was actually built in 1709, and is inherently more Baroque than Biedermeier. However Goethe himself, who lived in the house for 47 years, substantially altered the building in 1794 to create its present appearance. Goethe's grandson bequeathed the property to the nation in

1885. In 1907, when Paul was completing his designs for the Haus Westend, the house was being restored to its 1794 condition. The restoration was completed and the house opened to the public in 1908, the year Hans Schuppman took possession of his new house in Charlottenburg.

156 His earlier Haus Prym in Bonn may have been designed in collaboration with F. A. O. Krüger.

157 Joseph Popp, *Bruno Paul: mit 391 Abbildungen von Häusern und Wohnungen* (Munich, 1914), 85. »Bruno Pauls Kunst, Architektur und Natur in Eins zu binden, offenbart sich in diesem Um- und Neubau besonders glänzend: wo die uninteressanten und toten Stellen lagen, wurde verbessert, das wirksame Alte überall erhalten und mit dem Neuen organisch verbunden.«

158 The antique tradition was particularly prevalent in the work of Franz Stuck, and in the design of his own villa.

159 Gustav Adolf Platz, *Die Baukunst der neuesten Zeit in 500 Abbildungen* (Berlin, 1927).

160 Adolf Loos' work was characterized by his efforts to meld the tradition of Schinkel with the informality of the English Free Style, culminating in his development of the plan of volumes (Raumplan) as an ordering system. In 1910, however, Loos and Paul were pursuing similar aims – notwithstanding Loos' identification of Paul as one of the »superfluous ones« (»die Überflüssigen«) in his essay of the same name, a critique of the Werkbund.

161 Robert Breuer, »Büro und Geschäftshaus ›Zollernhof‹«, *Deutsche Kunst und Dekoration* 32 (April 1913), 29.

162 When Haus Hainerberg was designed, Paul's office consisted of the architect Franz Weber, and the apprentices Julius Cunow, Martin (Kem) Weber, Bruno Ernst Scherz, and Hans Bohnen. In a letter to Paul, Cunow recalled the »interesting and stimulating« work on the project. Julius Cunow to Bruno Paul, 3 February 1964, Teilnachlaß Paul, Germanisches Nationalmuseum, Nuremberg. Franz Weber married Maria, Paul's younger sister, and would later head Paul's office in Cologne.

163 The Heilanstalt was sold to the sisters of the order of Sacre Cœur in 1920. In 1924 several of Paul's buildings were demolished for the construction of the main building of the school operated by the sisters, the present »Altbau« of the Sankt-Adelheid-Gymnasium. Paul's surviving structures were demolished and rebuilt after the Second World War. He was not, himself, retained for the design of any of the Gymnasium projects.

164 *Beschäftigungs-Nachweise*, 7/43 U.l.g.sp.1, Universitätsarchiv, Universität der Künste Berlin. The few surviving records of Paul's Fachklasse 1a indicate that the catalog of Paul's known works from the period prior to the First World War represents less than half of the total number of commissions he received during this period. Unfortunately the preserved records are extremely limited in the information they contain, offering little more than a list of clients. For example in October 1912, his student Karl Schmidt prepared drawings for Haus Oppenheimer, Haus Röchling, Haus Jaus and Haus Herz, of which only the Haus Röchling in Duisburg and the Haus Herz in Berlin-Dahlem were published. The others are unknown, and may never have been

completed. Another project from this period, identified only as Silberstein, was the subject of large-scale studies and was clearly intended for construction, though the nature and location of the project have not been preserved.

165 Wilhelm von Bode, »Bruno Pauls Pläne zum Asiatischen Museum in Dahlem«, *Jahrbuch der preußischen Kunstsammlungen* 36 (1915). »Für den Stil war der Anschluss an die monumentalen märkischen Gutsbauten des XVIII. Jahrhunderts gewünscht; nicht nur der Tradition halber und mit Rücksicht auf die Nähe von Potsdam, dem stilvollsten Städtebau, der in Preußen erhalten ist, sondern weil auch die Gruppierung der einzelnen Bauten mit den Anlagen der großen Gutsbauten der Zeit verwandt erschien. Für die Ausführung war innen wie außen möglichste Einfachheit gefordert. Diesen Anforderungen ist der Paulsche Plan im vollen Maße gerecht geworden; er hat für die Anlage als Ganzes wie für die einzelnen Bauten in dem gewünschten freien Anschluß an die märkischen Bauten der zweiten Hälfte des XVIII. Jahrhunderts eine geschmackvolle Lösung gefunden und hat dabei für das zunächst zur Ausführung gelegene Asiatische Museum alle Wünsche der einzelnen Abteilungsleiter zu erfüllen gewußt.«

166 »Zur Gründungsgeschichte des Deutschen Werkbundes«, *Die Form* (November 1932), 329. »Diese Veranstaltung ist keine Ausstellung des Kunstgewerbes als Geschäft, sondern eine Ausstellung des Kunstgewerbes als Kunst.«

167 For the history of the Werkbund, see Joan Campbell, *The German Werkbund: the Politics of Reform in the Applied Arts* (Princeton, 1977) and Frederic J. Schwartz, *The Werkbund: Design Theory and Mass Culture before the First World War* (New Haven, 1996).

168 »Zur Gründungsgeschichte des Deutschen Werkbundes«, 329. The twelve original corporate members of the Werkbund were P. Bruckmann & Söhne, Deutsche Werkstätten für Handwerkskunst Dresden, Eugen Diederichs, Gebr. Klingspor, Kunstdruckerei Künstlerbund Karlsruhe, Poeschel & Trepte, Saalecker Werkstätten, Vereinigte Werkstätten für Kunst und Handwerk München, Werkstätten für deutschen Hausrat Theophil Müller Dresden, Wiener Werkstätte, Wilhelm & Co., and Gottlob Wunderlich.

169 Ibid., 330–331.

170 Paul, Behrens, Niemeyer, and Riemerschmid were members of the Munich Sezession, Hoffmann and Olbrich the Vienna Secession, Schultze-Naumburg (and Paul) the Berlin Sezession.

171 L. Deubner, »German Architecture and Decoration (›Der Deutsche Werkbund‹)«, *Studio Yearbook* (1910), 157.

172 Pevsner, *Pioneers*, 38.

173 Vereinigte Werkstätten für Kunst im Handwerk AG, *Typenmöbel für Stadt und Land von Prof. Bruno Paul* (c. 1908), 5. »Es handelt sich nicht darum, den zahllosen Stilmethoden der letzten vierzig Jahre, all dem Renaissance-, Gotik-, Barock-, Empire-, Rokoko-, ägyptischen-hellenischen-assyrischen Stil, Louis-seize und Jugendstil-Spielereien eine neue hinzuzufügen.«

174 Ibid., 7. »Sie sind in einfachen, typischen Formen gehalten, so daß sie sich den verschiedensten Räumen und Menschen gefügig anpassen. Sie prunken

nicht mit überflüssigem Schmuck, dafür werden sie aber auch ihrem Besitzer keine Enttäuschungen bereiten. So solid ihre äußere Form ist, so solid ist auch ihre Arbeit.«

175 In Wilhelmine Germany, class distinctions had a greater objective reality than they do at the beginning of the twenty-first century. The middle classes, »Mittelstand« or »Bürgertum« in German, were by no means homogeneous in religious, political, or social terms. Nevertheless the »Bürgertum« did posses a specific economic definition in the three-class electoral system of Prussia that was equally applicable, in terms of class distinction, throughout the empire.

176 Sonja Günther, *Das Deutsche Heim: Luxusinterieurs und Arbeitermöbel von der Gründerzeit bis zum Dritten Reich* (Berlin, 1984), 86–89.

177 The sales records of the Vereinigte Werkstätten have not been preserved, so it is not possible to determine the quantities of Typenmöbel actually sold. The best evidence is provided by the relative frequency with which Typenmöbel pieces are offered by antique dealers in Germany, which indicates that substantial numbers were sold between 1908 and 1914, when the furniture was in production. Personal interview with Alfred Ziffer in Munich, March 2001.

178 Angela Schönberger, »It's a Joy to Live – Spirits are Rising«, *Berlin 1900–1933: Architecture and Design* (Berlin, 1987), 87–99.

179 Riemerschmid also designed inexpensive furnishings that did not directly reflect the ideal of the Gesamtkunstwerk, as did Peter Behrens in his projects for »Arbeitermöbel«, or workers' furniture. However, these designs were intended for a different clientele than the middle class customers of the Wertheim exhibitions and the Typenmöbel.

180 The illustrations of Typenmöbel published in *Die Kunst* were notable for the variety of incidental objects that they contained, including work attributed to other designers, in addition to Paul's furniture. The clear implication was that the Typenmöbel was not intended to impose a limiting aesthetic sensibility on its owners, but could be comfortably installed in any typical middle-class home.

181 Paul utilized Typenmöbel for the garden furniture at the Villa Feinhals in Cologne, a prominent and prestigious commission.

182 Feinhals retained progressive artists, including Lucian Bernhard and Ernst Deutsch, to advertise his wares. The graphic work that he commissioned was regularly exhibited by the Werkbund.

183 Max Creutz, »Das Haus Feinhals in Cöln-Marienburg«, *Dekorative Kunst* 15 (November 1911), 68.

184 The general composition of the white lacquer Feinhals buffets, and even the specific configuration of the upper doors, appear to be identical to the Typenmöbel buffet. However, the drawers and lower doors were different. In addition the Feinhals kitchen included additional modular elements that appear never to have been included in the Typenmöbel range.

185 Max Creutz, 69. »Er hat hier eine moderne Umgebung fuer den modernen Menschen unserer Zeit geschaffen.«

186 Ernst Schur, »Kleine Kunstnachrichten: Neubau des Café Kerkau«, *Dekorative Kunst* 13 (July 1910), 487. »Notwendigkeit, Zweckbestimmung, Materialschönheit – das waren die Schlagworte.«

187 This connection was acknowledged, somewhat obliquely, in *Um 1800* through the inclusion of illustrations of eighteenth and early nineteenth century American buildings and interiors. The American examples were invariably simplified versions of Georgian designs.

188 Bruno Paul, »Über kunstgewerblichen Unterricht.« »Durch eingehendes Studium vorbildlicher Kunstwerke aus den Blütezeiten des Handwerks soll dem Schüler der Sinn für logische Behandlung und Anwendung seines Materials und für die Schönheit des in künstlerisch hochstehenden Zeiten Geschaffenen geweckt werden.«

189 Paul expressed this ideal harmony in everything he conceived, including the furniture and interiors for which he was best known, fabrics, wallpapers, carpets and metalwork, and even a series of pianos for Rud. Ibach Sohn, the German piano manufacturer founded in 1794. One of Paul's Ibach pianos, Modell C-118, was reintroduced in 1994 to commemorate the bicentenary of the company.

190 Heinrich Wiegand, *Heinrich Wiegand: Ein Lebensbild* (Bremen, 1932), 272. »Daß es nicht um die Kunst allein ging, daß diese vielmehr zugleich das Wetterglas europäischer Kultur bedeutete, haben damals wohl die wenigsten begriffen.«

191 Ibid.

192 Ibid, 273. The commission for *Kronprinzessin Cecilie* prompted the establishement of a branch of the Vereinigte Wekstätten in Bremen, a venture that Paul actively promoted. »Im Anschluß daran erweiterte Wiegand seine Pläne, indem er die Einrichtung seiner Schnelldampfer zum Anlaß nahm, um in Bremen eine Zweigstelle der Münchener Werkstätten für Kunst im Handwerk, an deren Gründung Paul beteiligt gewesen war, ins Leben zu rufen.«

193 The Historicist school of twentieth-century marine design originated in 1877 with Johannes Poppe of Bremen, the favored architect of the Norddeutscher Lloyd. Poppe was the scion of a noted family of Bremen architects who had been active in their native city since 1766. He was born in 1837 and followed the example of his father, grandfather, and great-grandfather before him in becoming an architect. He was educated in Karlsruhe and Berlin, and worked in Paris before returning to Bremen in 1864. Thereafter he received a number of important civic commissions including the Bremen City Waterworks of 1873, the Alte Sparkasse of 1881, and the City Library of 1896. Poppe was responsible for the development of the so-called North German Lloyd Style, a free interpretation of baroque and rococo models that epitomized the turn of the century conception of luxury.

194 *Steamship George Washington* (n. p., 1910). There are, in fact, at least three different versions of this book, all bearing the same title but differing in their content.

195 Ibid.

196 Ibid.

197 For an overview of the exhibition, see Barry Shifman, »Design for Industry: The ›German Applied Arts‹ Exhibition in the United States, 1912–13«, *The Decorative Arts Society Journal* 22 (1998), 19–31. The archives of the Newark Museum contain an excellent collection of material on the exhibition, including correspondence between the Newark Museum director John Cotton Dana and Karl Ernst

Osthaus, catalogs, and newspaper clippings from the seven cities that hosted the exhibition.

198 These works were included in the exhibition catalog as follows:

60 – The fast steamer *George Washington* of the North German Lloyd, Bremen; hall.

61 – The fast steamer *George Washington* of the North German Lloyd, Bremen; saloon.

62 – Schuppmann residence, Berlin; exterior with garden.

63 – Ladies' room in the Feinhals residence, Cologne.

199 Unfortunately this work, identified as a reproduction, number 191, was not illustrated in the exhibition catalog and has since been lost.

200 Meyer Schönbrunn, »Wall Paper, Linoleum and Linkrusta«, *Deutsches Kunstgewerbe, City Art Museum of St. Louis* 7 (1912), 61.

201 *New York Herald* (13 March 1913).

202 Maude I. G. Oliver, »German Art in Chicago«, *Chicago Record* (11 August 1912).

203 *Chicago Post* (10 August 1912).

204 *New York Herald* (13 March 1913).

205 Personal interview with Julia Graf, March 2001.

206 Letter from Bruno Paul to the president of the academy dated 11 July 1937. M1, Bd. 11a, Aktenbestand des Archivs der Preußischen Akademie der Künste.

207 *Jahresbericht 1910/11*, Universitätsarchiv, Universität der Künste, Berlin. »Dem Direktor der Anstalt Professor Bruno Paul wurde unter dem 4. März 1911 der Rote Adlerorden 4. Klasse verliehen.«

208 Paul would relocate his family to Prinz-Albrecht-Straße two years later.

209 7/43 U.l.g.sp.1 *Beschäftigungs-Nachweise*, Universitätsarchiv, Universität der Künste Berlin.

210 *Moderne Bauformen* 9 (1910): plate 20 (Julius Bühler – Berlin, Fachklasse Prof. Bruno Paul, *Herrenzimmer*), plate 26 (Otto Scholz – Berlin, Fachklasse Prof. Bruno Paul, *Trauzimmer*).

211 Julius Baum, ed., *Farbige Raumkunst. Dritter Band: 120 Entwürfe moderner Künstler* (Stuttgart, 1926). Despite the date of its publications, most of the drawings included in this volume were completed prior to the First World War.

212 *Lehrplan für das Schuljahr 1910/11*, Universitätsarchiv, Universität der Künste Berlin. »In den Fachklassen ist es wünschenswert, daß der Lehrer die Schüler so viel wie möglich mit praktischen Aufgaben beschäftigt und womöglich zur Teilnahme an seinen eigenen Arbeiten heranzieht.«

213 Ludwig Hevesi, »Emil Orlik. Ausstellung im Salon Pisko, 13. März 1902«, *Acht Jahre Secession*, 379. »Er ist heute der japanistische Europäer. Aber eben doch ein Europäer.«

214 As the influence of the Munich Sezession declined after 1900, the exhibitions of the Berlin Sezession attracted many of Paul's colleagues from the early days of his career. The 1908 exhibition of the Berlin Sezession, for example, featured paintings by Heine, Pankok and von Stuck.

215 Bruno Paul, »Über Dekorationsmalerei«, *Wasmuths Monatshefte für Baukunst* (1914/15), 27–30. »So verschieden nun auch die eingeschlagenen Wege und die angewandten Mittel sind sowohl bei den Reifen und Führenden wie bei den Jungen und Suchenden, so fördern sie alle das gleiche Ziel: Die Entwicklung einer Dekorationsmalerei, die dem We-

sen und den Bedürfnissen unserer Zeit entsprechen wird.«

216 »Herr Koch ist zu wenig Drucker, nur Schriftzeichner. Einen solchen habe ich schon in der Person des recht tüchtigen Sütterlin ...«

217 Sütterlinschrift was eventually adopted throughout the country, and only fell out of use when it was proscribed by the National Socialist government in 1941.

218 The title »painter« was in part a reflection of the fact that Sütterlin had not attained the status of a professorship. Nevertheless it indicated a status different from that of a »Lehrer«, or teacher, a title that was also used in the catalogs.

219 Ernst Schur, »Kleine Kunstnachrichten: Neubau des Café Kerkau«, *Dekorative Kunst* 13 (July 1910), 486–487.

220 Ernst Schur, »Bruno Paul«. *Dekorative Kunst* 14 (November 1910), 57–81.

221 Max Creutz, »Das Haus Feinhals in Cöln-Marienburg«, *Dekorative Kunst* 15 (November 1911), 57 to 77.

222 The surviving records of the Unterrichtsanstalt only contain records of the hours worked by Paul's students between the years 1911 and 1914.

223 Wright, like Paul, promoted modern design to successful members of the middle classes.

224 I. B. Gorham, »Comfort, Convenience, Color: Examples from the Designs of Kem Weber on the Pacific Coast«, *Creative Art* 7 (October 1930), 249 to 253.

225 Alfred Ziffer, ed., *Bruno Paul: Deutsche Raumkunst und Architektur zwischen Jugendstil und Moderne* (Munich, 1992), 388.

226 Max Creutz, »Haus Leffmann in Köln von Arch. Bruno Paul«, *Dekorative Kunst* 24 (January/February 1921), 77–78.

227 *Das Gelbe Haus* was also the title of a painting exhibited by Orlik at the 1908 exhibition of the Berlin Sezession.

228 This buffet, which was later exhibited at Werkbund exhibitions in Basel, Winterthur and Bern, has survived, and is exhibited at the Kunstgewerbemuseum at Schloß Pillnitz.

229 Max Creutz, »Haus Leffmann in Köln von Arch. Bruno Paul«. *Dekorative Kunst* 24 (January/February 1921), 64–87. The article appeared nine years after the completion of the house.

230 Haus Röchling appeared in *Innen-Dekoration* 21 (July/August 1920), 217–224, and Haus Herz in *Deutsche Kunst und Dekoration* 46 (September 1920), 293–300.

231 A temporary building, by the standards of 1914, was still expected to be solidly built. The final structures from the Werkbund exhibition were not demolished until 1922, by which year they had survived the exhibition itself, years of unsympathetic use by the military, and the flooding of the Rhine.

232 By 1914, the Werkbund had over 1,000 members.

233 The religious overtones of the foundation of the Werkbund, and the evangelical mission of its twelve original members, were the subject of frequent comment. See L. Deubner. »German Architecture and Decoration«, *Studio Yearbook of Decorative Art* (London, 1914), 93.

234 Poelzig was not represented at the 1914 Cologne exhibition, although he had designed a number of

buildings for the »Jahrhundertausstellung« (centennial exhibition) held in Breslau the year before.

235 Obrist, the creator of the seminal wool and silk embroidery *Peitschenhieb* (whiplash) in 1895, provided the sculptural ornament for van de Velde's theatre.

236 Stanford Anderson, »Deutscher Werkbund – the 1914 debate: Hermann Muthesius versus Henri Van de Velde«, Ben Farmer and Hentie Louw, eds., *Companion to Contemporary Architectural Thought.* (London and New York, 1993); Joan Campbell, *The German Werkbund: The Politics of Reform in the Applied Arts* (Princeton, 1978); A. C. Funk, »Karl Ernst Osthaus gegen Hermann Muthesius«, *Der Werkbundstreit 1914 im Spiegel der im Karl Ernst Osthaus Archiv erhaltenen Briefe* (Hagen 1978).

237 The abstract concept of intellectual property was unknown in Germany during the first quarter of the twentieth century. The Vereinigte Werkstätten and the Deutsche Werkstätten frequently produced nearly identical products, and would copy almost anything that their customers' requested.

238 L. Deubner, 94.

239 The death of Peter Kollwitz at Dixmuiden prompted a heartfelt correspondence between his parents and Paul, preserved in the archives of the school.

240 The editorial board of the magazine included Wilhelm von Bode, Lotte von Mendelssohn-Bartholdy (wife of Paul von Mendelssohn-Bartholdy), and Emil Orlik.

241 Bruno Paul, »Künstlerlehrzeit«, *Wieland* 3 (April 1917), 15–17. »Als unterste Stufe einer erfolgversprechenden schulmäßigen Ausbildung ist der Besuch einer Baugewerk-, Fach- oder Handwerksschule notwendig. Von der guten Organisation dieser Schulen als Basis der weiteren künstlerischen Erziehung hängt heute sehr viel, beinahe alles ab. Sie werden gute handwerkliche Hilfskräfte drillen und gleichzeitig den künstlerischen Talenten die notwendige handwerkliche Anfangsausbildung geben müssen. Die Voraussetzung hierzu ist, daß diese Fach- und Handwerkschulen sich ihrer wichtigen Aufgabe voll bewußt werden und der Pflege eines künstlerischen Dilettantismus ganz entsagen. Je einseitiger und gründlicher sie die handwerkliche Fachausbildung ihrer Schüler bestellen, desto mehr werden sie ihre Aufgabe erfüllen.«

242 Wilhelm von Bode related these objectives, and their implications for art education in *Pan*, vol. II (1896). See also Nikolaus Pevsner, »Post-War Tendencies in German Art Schools«, *Journal of the Royal Society of Arts* 84 (1936), 248–256.

243 Bruno Paul, »Architektur und Kunstgewerbe nach dem Kriege«, *Wieland* 3 (May 1917), 17–18. »Sie wird noch mehr als bisher die Stilerinnerungen an frühere Epochen abstreifen und, je mehr die Erkenntnis Allgemeingut wird, daß gute Architektur nicht auf der Wahl der Motive, sondern auf der Gliederung der Baumassen und der Proportionen aller Einzelteile beruht, um so mehr werden wir zu einer Einheitlichkeit der Ausdruckformen kommen. Dann werden Wirrungen schwinden, die das richtige Maß so oft vermissen ließ. Dann werden wir es erleben, daß das Bauen auf unseren öffentlichen Plätzen und Straßen von gegenseitiger Achtung beherrscht wird, und daß ein würdiges Rathaus als Repräsentant der Stadt nicht zwischen einem neu

aufgeschlossenen pomphaften Gesellschaftsge-
bäude und einem prunkhaften Bierpalast zu einer
Armseligkeit herabgedrückt wird, daß man die Fei-
erlichkeit bei den Kirchen und Tempeln läßt, und daß
in jedem Falle ein Bau nichts anderes darstellen will,
als das, wozu er bestimmt und geeignet ist. Dies ist
nichts weiter als ein selbstverständliches Gebot
tüchtiger Sachlichkeit, und daß dieses Gebot durch
eine lange Reihe von öffentlichen, wie privaten Bauten in allen Teilen Deutschlands seine Erfüllung gefunden hat, gibt uns die ruhige Zuversicht, die
deutsche Baukunst werde nach dem Kriege nicht
nur die Sünden des letzten halben Jahrhunderts
wieder gut machen, sondern sich zur Höhe und
Einheitlichkeit früherer Zeiten entwickeln.«

244 The commission also included Paul's subordinate professor, Franz Seeck, the architect German
Bestelmeyer, and the Prussian sculptor Louis Tuail-
lon.

245 Bruno Paul, »Kriegergräber im Osten«, *Wieland*
1 (February 1916), 6–7. »Manche liegen einzeln, ein-
sam. Auf dem kleinen Kreuz von der Hand eines
Kameraden mit Bleistift der Name geschrieben: Hier
ruht ... Darüber der Helm. Ein verwelktes Reis, ein
paar Blumen auf den Hügel gesteckt. Das Ganze
umfriedigt mit Birkenstämmchen, als ein rührend
einfaches Denkmal für Opferwilligkeit bis in den Tod.
Zugleich ein Mal, das sich treue Kameradschaft
errichtete. Dann können hundert Jahre darüber
hingehen, und sollte die Stätte auch niemanden
finden, der sie pflegt, dann werden die Bäume groß
und mächtig geworden, die Mauern bewachsen,
das Grabmal von Efeu umrankt sein. Es wird mit jedem Jahrzehnt schöner, ernster und ausdrucksvol-
ler geworden sein, als ein Denkmal der Treue, die
Deutschlands Männer ihrem Vaterlande hielten.«
This same essay appeared in *Kriegergräber im Felde
und daheim: Jahrbuch des Deutschen Werkbundes
1916–17* (Jena, 1917).

246 The chain is displayed at the municipal museum
in Göttingen, where it is attributed to Paul. Paul did
facilitate the manufacture of the iron chain, but he
entrusted the actual design to one of his professors,
the goldsmith Wilm, as documented in the archives
of the Universität der Künste, Berlin.

247 1:10 was the standard scale for general arrangement drawings, the plan, sections, and elevations
illustrating the configuration of a finished piece of
furniture. The archives of the Vereinigte Werkstätten
and the Deutsche Werkstätten each contain thousands of drawings in this format. Neither firm preserved the actual working drawings from which furniture was actually produced, but sketches in the
Teilnachlaß Paul at the Germanisches Nationalmuseum demonstrate that Paul often composed the details of his work at full scale.

248 Elfriede Mues, »Haus Dr. L. in Wetzlar«, *Deutsche Kunst und Dekoration 49* (October/November
1921), 71–84. »Die obere Diele ist ein Attacke auf die
Stimmung. Rot die Möbel, rot der Teppich, rot die
Vorhänge, der Leuchter, alles in reinstem Zinnober.
Man könnte hier so vieles ausprobieren zu Schreck
und Freude, unter der Farbe die größte Liebe erleben und die bittersten Kämpfe.«

249 The majority of Paul's furnishings for Haus
Friedwart have remained in use since the completion of the house, and have survived in excellent
condition.

250 The twelve architects were Behrens, Bestell-
meyer, Bonatz, Eberhardt, Elsässer, Endell, Fischer,
Gropius, Paul, Poelzig, Riemerschmid, and Taut.
Gropius was serving in the military in 1916, and did
not prepare a design.

251 Paul's colonnade suggested the influence of
Filippo Brunelleschi's Ospedale degli Innocenti in
Florence (1419–27). Paul may have known this building from his academic studies or from his own travels in Italy. However he would also have been familiar with Leo von Klenze's 1835 derivation, the arcade
of the Hauptpost on the Max-Joseph-Platz in Munich. The detailing of Paul's Haus der Freundschaft
reflected both Byzantine and Ottoman influences.
His project was, ultimately, the embodiment of a universal ideal, an architectural vocabulary that was
both eastern and western, Turkish and German.
This ideal, of course, reflected the programmatic objectives established for the Haus der Freundschaft.

252 Theodor Heuss, *Das Haus der Freundschaft in
Konstantinopel: ein Wettbewerb deutscher
Architekten* (Munich 1918), 33. »Er hat es selber aus-
gesprochen, daß er einen Bau gezeichnet, der
ebensogut in München und Berlin, aber auch in
Italien stehen könne.«

253 Arbeitsrat für Kunst may also be translated as
the artist's soviet, in keeping with the revolutionary
objectives of the organization.

254 The invitation, received by Paul 8 April 1919, is
preserved with the documents of the Unterrichtsanstalt. U.I.a v. 7/142, Universitätsarchiv, Universität
der Künste, Berlin.

255 Typen-Möbel Gesellschaft mbH Zoo-Werkstätten was established in December 1919 by Karl
Schultz. In 1921 the firm was registered as the Zoo-
Werkstätten after its location in Charlottenburg, near
the Berlin zoo. An example of letterhead from the
firm dated August 1922 in the archives of the Universität der Künste in Berlin bears the title Typen-
Möbel Gesellschaft mbH Zoo-Werkstätten. In January 1923 the company was renamed Vereinigte Zoo-
Werkstätten GmbH. See Ziffer, *Bruno Paul*, 227.

256 Riemerschmid was director of the school of applied arts in Munich.

257 A series of letters between Paul and Ministe-
rialdirektor Hendschel is preserved in the Bayerisches Hauptstadtarchiv in Munich.

258 The prospect of ennoblement as a reward for
artistic success was one of the attractions that had
drawn so many students, the young Bruno Paul
among them, to the Munich of the *Malerfürsten*.

259 His published projects alone include one completed in 1920, two in 1921, two in 1922, one in
1923, four in 1924 and three in 1925.

260 Theodor Heuss, 33.

261 Paul was known for his characteristically slow
and deliberate manner of speaking. Personal interview with Susanne Droste in Göttingen, October
2000.

262 The decline in political influence of moderate
members of the middle classes was echoed in the
fortunes of the Demokratische Partei (DDP), which
won 75 seats in the Reichstag elections of January
1919, but lost seats in the elections of June 1920,
May 1924, May 1928, September 1930, July 1932
and November 1932. Only a nominal gain of four
seats in December 1924, an election in which
twenty-one deputies were added to the Reichstag,

countered the decline in fortunes of the DDP as
the original Weimar coalition disintegrated into fac-
tionalism, and increasingly antagonistic polarization.
Paul's personal friend and Werkbund colleague
Theodor Heuss twice represented the DDP in the
Reichstag. See Peter Gay, *Weimar Culture: The
Outsider as Insider* (New York, 1968), 147–164 (Ap-
pendix I, »A Short Political History of the Weimar
Republic«).

263 Hans Rolffsen, »Ein Landhaus in Blankenese,
Erbaut von Prof. Bruno Paul«, *Deutsche Kunst und
Dekoration 52* (July 1923), 226–229.

264 The staff of *Gartenschönheit* included Paul's
Munich colleagues Behrens and Endell; Ernst Ludwig von Hessen, the deposed Grand Duke of Hessen and former patron of the artists' colony on the
Mathildenhöhe in Darmstadt; Paul Schultze-Naumburg; and an international catalog of naturalists,
botanists, and landscape architects. The magazine
was published between 1920 and 1940. Paul had
been interested in garden design for some time. As
early as 1908 he was a member of the jury assembled to evaluate the entries submitted to a contest
sponsored by the journal *Die Woche*.

265 The stair hall has been reconstructed in the
Museum für Kunst und Gewerbe in Hamburg. The
railing is sufficiently similar in technique to the railing
installed at Haus Friedwart to suggest the involve-
ment of Emil Orlik in its design, although no record
of his participation has been preserved.

266 The tile stove itself was an anachronistic fitting.
In 1907, Paul's Haus Westend was already provided
with central steam heating. However the simple,
efficient tile stove provided an inexpensive means
of warming a house. Paul designed at least nine
different types of tile stove, all between 1914 and
1924, years when war, political crisis, and inflation
influenced the price and availability of fuel for home
heating.

267 Hans Rolffsen: »Den in das Haus Eintretenden
empfängt ein andere Welt, im Gegensatz zur Groß-
artigkeit der umgebenden Natur die stille Welt einer
kunstsinnigen Häuslichkeit, die Welt erlesensten
Geschmacks.«

268 Joseph Popp, »Bruno Paul auf der Deutschen
Gewerbeschau«, *Dekorative Kunst 26* (April, 1923),
137–138. »Das war auch der Grund, warum das
Räumlich-Konstruktive im wesentlichen nichts Über-
raschendes bot: in der Hauptsache wurden die
konventionellen Kabinen mit expressionistischen
Ornamenten und Figuren ›ausgestattet‹. Das For-
male an sich wurde, soweit es über die Kleinwelt der
Gebrauchs- und Ziergegenstände hinausging, am
besten von jenen gemeistert, die schon früher die
Form um der Form willen gepflegt hatten. Sie
brauchten jetzt nur den Sinn für deren Dynamik in
sich wach werden lassen, um auch in der Form zu
einer noch knapperen und zugleich sprechenderen
Erscheinung zu gelangen. Mit unter den ersten dieser Art steht auch jetzt wieder Bruno Paul. Er war
auch der einzige, der das Eckige, Spitze, Zerrige
der kubistischen Linien und Flächen interessant auf
das Raumbild anwandte: seine Kojengasse und die
Terrasse der Modediele wirken ohne alle Ornamen-
tik durch die Form und einfache Grundfarbe. Die
Improvisation einer vorübergehenden Ausstellung
sowie die Anpassung an den auffallenden, prickeln-
den, geistreich spielerischen und eigenwilligen Inhalt

der Mode rechtfertigen die Grundanlage wie die Durchführung. Dabei war es besonders interessant, wie mit den paar Formen einer schlanken Pyramide und Kästen, mit offenen und geschlossenen Flächen, im Wechsel verschiedener Größen und Beziehungen ein winkeliges Gescheibe entstand, das in der Kojengasse fast bis zur bizarren Laune ging, in der Gartenterasse in den stelzig freien Stützen eine luftig lustige Freilichtstimmung ergab.«

[269] Although the order employed at Haus Friedwart may have originated with the original design, Paul was still committed to correct classical elements in 1916, as evidenced by his designs for the Haus der Freundschaft in Constantinople.

[270] Kurt Neven-Dumont (or Neven du Mont) edited and published the Zeitschrift Leipziger Morgen, and was a partner in the DuMont-Schauberg-Verlag.

[271] Bruno Paul, »Ein Kölner Wohnhaus (Haus Neven-Dumont)«, Die Pyramide (April 1928), 1–4.

[272] The doors were molded from five layers of veneer, each only 1 millimeter thick.

[273] Alfred Ziffer, ed., Bruno Paul: Deutsche Raumkunst und Architektur zwischen Jugendstil und Moderne, 236.

[274] The form of the chairs was not purely sculptural, in that their dimensions and structural properties derived from functional necessity. Nevertheless, Paul was exploring the limits of the armchair as a type that he himself had helped to create.

[275] Deutsche Werkstätten Möbel (Dresden-Hellerau, 1927), 57–59.

[276] Deutsche Werkstätten Möbel (Dresden-Hellerau, 1927), 60–61.

[277] See Hans Georg, »Unser Stand vor dem Abgrund«, Deutsche Handelswacht. Zeitschrift des deutschnationalen Handlungsgehilfen-Verbandes 3 (26 January 1921) and Hilde Walter, »Die Misere des ›neuen Mittelstands‹«, Die Weltbühne 25 (22 January 1929), both quoted in Anton Kaes, ed., The Weimar Republic Sourcebook (Berkeley 1994), 182–183, 187–189.

[278] Alexander Koch, Alexander Koch's Handbuch neuzeitlicher Wohnungskultur: das vornehm-bürgerliche Heim (Darmstadt, 1922). »Als höchstes Ziel ist schließlich zu fordern, daß Persönlichkeit und Wohnung eine Einheit bilden, daß die Wohnung, als erweitertes Kleid und Spiegelbild der Seele, sich in ihrer Gestaltung dem Charakter ihres Besitzers anpaßt.«

[279] Hilde Walter, quoted in Anton Kaes, 189.

[280] The designations refer to the Triebwagen 24 and the Beiwagen 24 respectively: powered and unpowered streetcars built to the 1924 design.

[281] Sergius Ruegenberg, »Design-Arbeit an einem Straßenbahnwagen (1924)«, Bauwelt 72 (8 May 1981), 742.

[282] »Zur Rathaus-Einweihung in Seifhennersdorf«, Oberlausitzer Dorfzeitung 61 (13 March 1925). »In städtebaulicher Hinsicht ist eine Lösung der Vorplatzfrage zu finden, die vor dem Gemeindeamte einen würdigen, abseits der Verkehrsstraße gelegenen Platz schafft und gleichzeitig die Möglichkeit gibt, den schon bestehenden, jetzt in ungünstiger Tiefenlage sich zeigenden Kirchenbau in der Wirkung zu heben. In der Grundrißgestaltung ist außer auf praktische Anordnung der Amtsräume darauf zu achten, daß ein günstiger Zugang zum Gemeindeamt sowohl von der Marrstraße wie von der Rumburger Straße her ermöglicht wird, sowie daß die Wohnungen unabhängig vom Betriebe des Gemeindeamtes aufgesucht werden können. Die Architektur hat Formen zu wählen, die einerseits keine Störungen für den danebenliegenden Kirchenbau bedeuten, andererseits sich dem örtlichen Baucharakter gut einfügen.«

[283] Likely Wilhelm Jost.

[284] Most likely Theo Burlage (1894–1971), architect of the Kaufmanns-Gedächtniskirche St. Bonifatius in Leipzig-Connewitz (1928–30).

[285] Jost was born in 1887 in the Saxon city of Zwickau. He studied architecture at the Technische Hochschulen in Dresden and Stuttgart before joining the office of Paul Schultze-Naumburg, and established his own architectural practice in 1914. He joined the faculty of the Technische Hochschule in Stuttgart during 1919, and was appointed to a professorship in 1923.

[286] Eheschließungszimmer, Ausschußzimmer, Girokasse, Raum des Bürgermeisters, Ratskeller.

[287] Walter Stephan, Zur Einweihung des Rathauses in Seifhennersdorf (1925), 34.

[288] Walter Stephan, 34.

[289] They were also, like all of his furniture, soundly designed. Eighty years after Paul conceived them, the Seifhennersdorf wedding chairs carved by the workshop of Wilhelm Richter in the neighboring village of Großschönau were subject to daily, and not especially sympathetic, use in the lobby of the town hall. The archives of the Deutsche Werkstätten include a drawing of a chair designed by Paul for his wedding chamber in the Seifhennersdorf town hall (Gemeindeamt Seifhennersdorf Trauzimmer-Stuhl). The DeWe chairs were simpler than the ones carved by Wilhelm Richter that were illustrated in the Festschrift printed for the dedication of the town hall and which are still extant. There is no evidence that the DeWe chairs were ever produced.

[290] The parish church of Seifhennersdorf would be rebuilt after a fire in 1935 by the architect Richard Schiffner of Zittau, who placed second in the competition for the new town hall.

[291] Gedenkschrift zur Einweihung des Krieger-Ehrenmals in Seifhennersdorf (September 1929). »Ihr Opfer wird Gemeingut des Volkes, das in den Gefallenen Helden sieht, die sich gemeinsam höheren Interessen geopfert haben.«

[292] Franz Schulze, Mies van der Rohe: A Critical Biography (Chicago, 1985), 124–125.

[293] Mies later claimed that the form of his monument derived from the brick wall against which Liebknecht and Luxemburg were shot in 1919. Such an association was tenuous at best, however, particularly in light of the fact that the two Spartacist leaders were unceremoniously murdered in the streets, not executed by a firing squad.

[294] Bruno Paul, »Erziehung der Künstler an staatlichen Schulen«, Deutsche Kunst und Dekoration (December 1919), 193–196. The article appeared earlier in 1919 as a pamphlet.

[295] Fritz Stahl, »Arthur Kampffs Rücktritt«, Berliner Tageblatt (24 March 1924).

[296] Fritz Stahl, »Wo ist der Kultusminister?«, Berliner Tageblatt (20 March 1924).

[297] Hans Poelzig, speech to the Werkbund in Mitteilungen des Deutschen Werkbundes, 1919, no. 4, 109–124, reprinted and translated in Julius Posener, Hans Poelzig: Reflections on his Life and Work (Cambridge/Massachusetts, 1992), 129–134.

[298] U541/24, Universitätsarchiv, Universität der Künste, Berlin.

[299] Schulbesuch 1924/5, Universitätsarchiv, Universität der Künste, Berlin.

[300] Sachsen-Weimar-Eisenach was absorbed by the Freistaat Thüringen on 1 May 1920.

[301] Hans Maria Wingler, The Bauhaus: Weimar, Dessau, Berlin, Chicago (Cambridge/Massachusetts, 1969).

[302] This letter, dated 5 May 1917 and concerning Wieland, is in the possession of the author.

[303] Walter Gropius »The necessity of commissioned work for the Bauhaus« in Hans Wingler, 51.

[304] In his monograph Walter Gropius, Work and Teamwork (Zurich, 1954), Sigfried Giedion reluctantly acknowledged that Gropius had worked alone on the buildings of the Bauhaus, as well as most of his contemporary projects, notwithstanding his claim that »the idea of teamwork is part of Gropius' very nature as well as of his actions«.

[305] U541/24, Universitätsarchiv, Universität der Künste, Berlin. »Von der anderen Seite gehört klingt der ›Meisterrat‹ etwas nach ›Sängerkrieg auf der Wartburg‹ ›die Meistär‹ oder nach Ähnlichem tata tati tatatä-ta oder staatliches Bauhaus – tätä tätä – und es klingt ein wenig unmodern pathetisch in meinen Ohren. Aber es ist schließlich sachlich belanglos ob ›Meisterrat‹ oder ›Lehrerrat‹.«

[306] Nikolaus Pevsner, »Post War Tendencies in German Art Schools«, Journal of the Royal Society of Arts (January 17, 1936), 251–254.

[307] Ibid.

[308] »Architekt Professor Bruno Paul Berlin Lebenslauf«, Teilnachlaß Paul, Germanisches Nationalmuseum, Nuremberg. »Als ich 1925 meine Werkkunst-Lehrsäle, und die Werkstätten, Brennöfen, Laboratorien aus der zu eng geworden Prinz-Albrecht-Straße in die weiträumige Gebäudesgruppe ›Hochschule für Bildende Künste‹ am Steinplatz übersiedelte, ließ die Bestätigung der geplante Einheit und Gemeinschaft von Erziehung zur freien und angewandten Kunst nicht auf sich warten. Sie vollzog sich von selbst!«

[309] Pevsner, »Post War Tendencies«, 254.

[310] The site of Paul's house was later occupied by the Europa-Center, the West Berlin landmark built between 1963 and 1965.

[311] Ironically the Plattenhaus that survives in Hellerau is sited with the informal garden façade facing the street, and the street façade (behind which Paul characteristically located the kitchen, pantry, toilets, and stair hall) facing the garden. This is contrary to the orientation of the house when originally exhibited in 1925.

[312] The Plattenhaus actually had a moderately-sloped hip roof. From the ground, the slope of the roof was hidden by the projecting eaves of the house.

[313] Paul planned the house around interlocking »L« shaped blocks of rooms, with taller ceilings in the study, living room, and dining room on the lower floor, and in the bedrooms on the upper; and lower ceilings in the kitchen, pantry, and storeroom downstairs and the second storeroom and bathrooms above. His integration of these interlocking volumes was ingenious.

314 Deutsche Werkstätten A.G. *De-We Plattenhaus*. (Dresden-Hellerau, 1928). »Die äußere Form der neuen Häuser ist so geartet ..., daß sie sich in den städtischen Raum einfügt. Und dieser städtische Charakter ist auch im Innern des Hauses ausgeprägt.«

315 Martin Schulze Beerhorst, »Das ›Plattenhaus‹ 1018 von Bruno Paul«, *Bruno Paul und die Deutschen Werkstätten Hellerau*, Alfred Ziffer, ed. (Dresden, 1993), 31.

316 The sales records of the Deutsche Werkstätten have not survived to confirm that only one Plattenhaus 1018 was ever built, but the only known example is the original in Hellerau.

317 Erich Haenel, »Wohnung und Siedlung Dresden 1925«, *Dekorative Kunst* 29 (March 1926), 133–143; Ernst Zimmermann, »Das Plattenhaus der Deutschen Werkstätten A.G. – Hellerau«, *Innen-Dekoration* 36 (November 1925), 402–410; Deutsche Werkstätten A.G. *De-We Plattenhaus* (Dresden-Hellerau, 1928).

318 Richard Heyken, »Das ›Richmodis-Haus‹ in Köln«, *Deutsche Kunst und Dekoration* 58 (September 1926), 367.

319 Adolf Schuhmacher. *Ladenbau* (Stuttgart, 1951), 102. The Sinn store was also illustrated in Schuhmacher's 1934 book of the same name, which was substantially different from the later edition.

320 Bruno Paul, »Reise-Bericht über New York«, *Die Form* 3 (August 1928), 252. »Eine solche Bauzeit von 5 Monaten für ein Haus von 1000 oder 2000 qm Grundfläche und von 20 oder 30 Stockwerken ist nichts Ungewöhnliches und erklärt sich aus den vorbildlichen Methoden sowohl der Projektierung als der Bauarbeiten. Alle Pläne, Berechnungen, Ausschreibungen und Vergebungen liegen bei Beginn des Baues fertig vor.«

321 Gontard built the Königskolonnaden for a bridge on the Alexanderplatz. They were rebuilt in their present location, overlooking Heinrich-von-Kleist-Park in 1910.

322 Herbert Günther, »Alt und Neu«, *Die Form* (February 1932), 57. »Die graziösen Kolonnaden erscheinen noch graziöser, seit das massive Hochhaus neben ihnen zum Vergleiche herausfordert, umgekehrt verstärkt ihre Schlankheit den monumentalen Eindruck des neuen Baues.«

323 Paul's Cologne office, under the direction of Franz Weber, prepared the actual working drawings for Haus Sternberg.

324 Initially Traub hired a local architect to design his new house, but the original architect died before completing a design and Traub selected Paul to replace him.

325 Telephone interview with Mimi Furst in New York, August 2000.

326 This form was popularized by Jaromír Krejcar's constructivist Olympic House of 1926, and repeated in projects such as Václav Velvarský's ČTK Building of 1930; Arnošt Mühlstein and Viktor Fürth's Te-Ta Department Store of 1933; and Oldřich Starý and František Zelenka's House of the Czechoslovak Werkbund of 1938. In addition, several significant Modernist buildings in Prague, including Josef Gočár's Baťa Department Store on Celetná Street and Jaroslav Fragner's post-war reconstruction of the Carolinum, seem to have been explicitly influenced by Paul's design for Villa Traub. See Rosti-

slav Švacha *Od moderni k funkcionalismu: promeny prazske architektury prvni poloviti dvacateho stoleti* (Prague, 1985); English edition Alexandra Buchler, trans., *The Architecture of New Prague, 1895–1945* (Cambridge/Massachusetts, 1995).

327 The upper roof that Paul designed for Villa Traub functioned extraordinarily well in the context of the notoriously permeable flat roofs of the 1920s. It does not leak, and the lack of visible water damage in any of the seventy-year-old woodwork of the house implies that it never has.

328 Telephone interview with Mimi Furst in New York, May 2001.

329 Telephone interview with Mimi Furst, May 2001.

330 The original glass door was removed from the house after the war, when it had ceased to be a private home, in the interest of security. It was subsequently replaced by a facsimile.

331 The sliding windows were manufactured by a Czech firm, and were commercially available.

332 Paul's metal-framed sliding window did not communicate directly between the garden and the interiors of the house, but between the garden and the wintergarden, which functioned as a vestibule. Although the wintergarden was independently heated, it could also be closed off from the remainder of the house in cold weather.

333 Jan Kotěra's own house of 1908, used between 1911 and 1924 for the architectural ateliers of the Prague academy, was built on a sloping site with the garden and the rooms adjoining it a full story below the street, requiring a flight of stairs between the front door and the hall on the level of the garden. See Rostislav Švacha.

334 Telephone interview with Mimi Furst, August 2000.

335 Bruno Paul, »Villa Traub bei Prag«, *Innen-Dekoration* 46 (April 1935), 118, »in dieser Stadt uralten deutschen Bauhandwerks noch lebendig sind«.

336 Alfred Ziffer, *Bruno Paul und die Deutschen Werkstätten Hellerau* (Dresden, 1993), 56. The Modell 275 bedroom was designed to be as light as possible, in order to avoid paying excessive export duties that were levied on the basis of weight.

337 Paul also designed a house in Dresden for Sindel Bergmann, which was completed in 1927.

338 The house was built at Am Rupenhorn 5 in Charlottenburg.

339 Personal interview with Julia Graf in Berlin, March 2001.

340 Letter from Ernst Walther Sr. to Ernst Walther Jr. dated 1 October 1928 in the archives of the Museum of Modern Art, New York, quoted in Wolf Tegethoff, *Mies van der Rohe: The Villas and Country Houses* (New York, 1985), 61.

341 Both Paul and Mies knew Friedrich Deneken, the director of the Kaiser-Wilhelm-Museum in Krefeld who may have influenced the commissions for Haus Esters and Haus Lange, through the Werkbund. However, neither Haus am Rupenhorn nor Haus Esters was a sufficiently important project to provoke much professional discussion during design. The two architects probably possessed only a passing knowledge of the other's residential work.

342 Paul and Mendelsohn were working together for the New York opening of »Contempora« (see below) in 1928 and 1929.

343 Erich Mendelsohn. *Neues Haus – Neue Welt* (Berlin, 1932).

344 Amédée Ozenfant in Erich Mendelsohn, *Neues Haus – Neue Welt*.

345 Pankok led the school of applied arts in Stuttgart from 1913 until 1937.

346 Schlemmer joined the staff of the Vereinigte Staatsschulen in 1932, after the closure of the academy in Breslau, where he had been a professor.

347 The oft-cited 1910 exhibition of Frank Lloyd Wright's work in Berlin appears to be a misconception. However such an event did occur in 1931, at the academy, as a sequel to »Neue amerikanische Baukunst«. See Anthony Alofsin, *Frank Lloyd Wright – the Lost Years, 1910–1922: a Study of Influence* (Chicago, 1993), 33–34.

348 Bruno Paul, »Baukeramische Ausstellung in den Vereinigten Staatsschulen, Schlußbericht«, Universitätsarchiv, Universität der Künste, Berlin. »Alles in allem: die Ausstellung zeigt ein wiedererstandenes uraltes Baugewerbe in kraftvoller Jugendlichkeit. Sie zeigt Wege und Möglichkeiten. Spätere Ausstellungen dieses Gebietes sollen Resultate handwerklicher und künstlerischer Verarbeitung bringen. Für die Vereinigten Staatsschulen war die Gewinnung dieser vom Architekten Fritz Höger unternommenen und geleiteten Ausstellung von Werte. Es ist wichtig, durch Fachausstellungen diejenigen gewerblichen Gebiete, in denen das handwerkliche Fundament der angewandten (wie letzten Endes auch der freien) Künste liegt, der Schule und ihren Schülern näher zu bringen.«

349 Bruno Paul, »Ausprache Dir. Pauls bei der Eröffnung der Werkkunst-Ausstellung 1927«, Universitätsarchiv, Universität der Künste, Berlin. »Der Raum, in dem diese Ausstellung moderner deutscher Werkkunst von mir eingebaut wurde, trägt die Bezeichnung ›Antiker Saal‹. Hier sollten in der Akademie alten Stiles, in jener Zeit, als dieses Haus erbaut wurde, die jungen Anfänger nach antiken Gipsabgüssen zeichnen, um die unveränderlichen Gesetze antiker Kunst in sich aufzunehmen. Man stellte bekanntlich den jungen für Eindrücke empfänglichen Menschen vor eine Welt, die fremd und zeitlich unendlich weit entfernt ist und suchte ihn zu isolieren von den Einflüssen der Welt aus der er kam und für die er arbeiten sollte. Das gehörte noch bis vor einem viertel Jahrhundert zu den Glaubenssätzen der Kunsterziehung. In der Luft der Werkstätten gedieh das Akademische nicht, um so besser in den Schulen. So schaltete man die Werkstatt aus, die Jahrtausende lang die Quelle künstlerischen Schaffens war. Inzwischen hat sich manches geändert. Jetzt ist die Werkstatt in die Akademien eingedrungen und erobert sich Schritt für Schritt die Erziehung der künstlerischen Jugend zurück.«

350 »Auch Mies ist ein Architekt von schätzenswerten Eigenschaften und viel Können.«

351 Dirk Lohan, interview with Mies (typescript: Chicago, 1986) in the Mies van der Rohe Archive, Museum of Modern Art, New York.

352 Tessenow taught at the building school in Lüchow and the school of applied arts in Trier before accepting a position at the Technische Hochschule in Dresden as Dülfer's assistant. From 1913 until 1919 he was a professor at the school of applied arts in

Vienna. In 1920 he taught at the Akademie der bildenden Künste in Dresden.

353 »Tessenow als Ergänzung des Kollegiums wäre in jeder Weise zu begrüßen.«

354 Helen Appleton Read, »Twentieth Century Decoration: A Significant Meeting of Various Modernists«, *Vogue* (July 15, 1928), 75.

355 Ibid.

356 Ibid., 102.

357 Bruno Paul, »Rückblicke und Aussichten. Bruno Paul aus dem Katalog der Austellung Europäischen Kunstgewerbes in Macy-Hause zu New York«, *Die Pyramide* 14 (1928), 44. »An ihrer Stelle wächst ein neuer Stil, der nicht durch Länder oder Erdteile begrenzt sein wird. Es ist der Stil des modernen Menschen, der mit Flugzeugen die Entfernungen der Länder und Kontinente überwindet, dessen allen vernehmbare und verständliche Stimme rund um die Erde tönt und in dessen Fühlen und Denken die Enge der Grenzen von Ländern und Kontinenten ausgeschaltet ist.«

358 By 1928 European designers such as Paul's former student Kem Weber, Paul T. Frankl, Rudolf Schindler, and Richard Neutra had established themselves in the United States. The emigration of prominent European artists to America was relatively uncommon prior to 1932, however; significantly Frankl, Schindler, and Neutra had all been drawn by the singular personality of Frank Lloyd Wright, initially as students rather than authors of modern culture.

359 Bruno Paul, »Reise-Bericht über New York«, 251–252. »Auch daß in einem fieberhaften Tempo unter freudlosen Wolkenkratzerstädten eine Art Menschen entstanden ist, die nur den Begriff ›business‹ kennen, die in einem fieberhaften Tempo unter freudlosen Umständen arbeiten und denen keine Zeit bleibt, die kulturellen Güter edleren Menschentums weiterzuentwickeln. Eine solche ganz irrige und oberflächliche Beurteilung weicht sehr schnell der größten Achtung vor der großen organisatorischen Leistung, die aus der schmalen Insel an der Hudson-River-Mündung eine Stadt voller Wunder und von unschreiblicher Schönheit entstehen ließ. Der Eindruck des Stadtbildes bei der Einfahrt in den Hafen ist mit nichts zu vergleichen. Er wird noch überboten, wenn man in die Schluchten dieses künstlichen Steingebirges eindringt. Die phantastischen Überschneidungen und kühnen Vertikalen der City-Straßen-Buildings gleichen oft, gigantisch vergrößert, italienischen Städtebildern des Quattro Cento. Im Ausmaß der Proportionen werden aber Wirkungen erreicht, die in der Geschichte der Baukunst keine Vergleichsmöglichkeiten haben.«

360 Ibid., 252. »Mein New Yorker Aufenthalt fiel in jenen für das Leben des New Yorkers bedeutsamen Zeitpunkt, an dem der Gentleman aller sozialen Schichten und aller farbigen Schattierungen seinen grauen Filzhut mit dem weißen Strohhut vertauscht.«

361 Ibid. »Das ist wohl eine der auffallendsten Tendenzen dieser von weitgehendem sozialen Gleichheitsgefühl erfüllten kapitalistischen Demokratie: die Ausgleichung der Standesunterschiede durch Hebung des gesellschaftlichen Niveaus der breiten Massen.«

362 Ibid, 253. »So zeigte sich mir New York in seinen Bauten, seinen Einrichtungen und in der gan-

zen Atmosphäre seines Lebens als die Stadt, deren Ausdruck den Stempel unserer Zeit in viel stärkerem Maße trägt als irgendeine andere bestehende menschliche Siedlung.«

363 Matlock Price, »Contempora«, *Good Furniture and Decoration* (August 1929), 71.

364 Ibid.

365 Ibid.

366 Ibid.

367 The jury also included Pierre Jeanneret, Gerrit Rietveld, Adolf Schenk, and Gustav Siegel.

368 Gustav Adolf Platz. *Wohnräume der Gegenwart* (Berlin, 1933), 346.

369 The Congrès Internationaux de l'Architecture Moderne, the organization established by the younger members of the avant-garde, including Gropius and Le Corbusier.

370 Telephone interview with Mimi Furst, August 2000.

371 »Biographische Notizen«, Teilnachlaß Paul, Germanisches Nationalmuseum, Nuremberg.

372 Salomon Wininger, *Große jüdische National-Biographie*, vol. 4 (Cernauti, 1929), 613.

373 The religious affiliation of Paul's parents and grandparents was recorded in his *Abstammungsnachweis*, compiled by the Reichskammer der bildenden Künste, National Archives and Records Administration, Microfilm Document A339-RKK-F121.

374 Personal interview with Julia Graf in Berlin, March 2001.

375 Telephone interview with Mimi Furst in New York, August 2000.

376 Bruno Paul, »Biographische Notizen«, Teilnachlaß Paul, Germanisches Nationalmuseum, Nuremberg. »Meine Mitarbeiter hatte ich nicht nach der Konfession, sondern nach persönlichem Können und der beruflichen Bedeutung gewählt.«

377 National Archives and Records Administration, Microfilm Document A339-RKK-F121. Though Goebbels attacked Paul as a Jew, his accusations were manifestly untrue. The file maintained on Paul by the Reichskammer der bildenden Künste, the official Nazi organization for the arts, identified him in the terminology of the day as an Arian of pure blood, and a full citizen of the German Empire.

378 Letter from Bruno Paul to the president of the academy dated 11 July 1937, M1, Bd. 11a, Aktenbestand des Archivs der Preußischen Akademie der Künste. »Mit diesen, meinen rein persönlichen Einstellungen und Neigungen deckte es sich, daß mich Professor Max Liebermann in den Jahren seiner Präsidentschaft wie auch schon vorher als »antisemitischen Nationalisten« ablehnte. Bei der Machtübernahme kehrte sich das Blatt ins Gegenteil, und ich wurde überraschenderweise als Judenfreund und demokratischer Parteigänger bezeichnet.«

379 Ibid. »Die Wahrheit ist, daß ich mich weder nach der einen noch nach der anderen Seite politisch aktiv betätigt hatte, weil ich glaubte, dieses meiner Beamtenstellung schuldig zu sein.«

380 By the end of 1932, the two parties committed to the dissolution of the republic, the Nazis and the Communists, controlled the majority of votes in the Reichstag.

381 Bruno Paul, »Biographische Notizen«.

382 Letter from Poelzig to Paul dated 2 February 1933 in the Universitätsarchiv, Universität der Künste, Berlin. »Und da würde ich es viel besser finden, wenn wir die Ausstellung Kirche und Kunst im nächsten Jahre machen würden, und dann am Pariser Platz in der Akademie.«

383 On 2 April 1933 a poster appeared in Berlin denouncing proported Marxist-Judaic members of the Prussian academy of arts, including Poelzig and Schlemmer.

384 Unlike Paul, Poelzig was permitted to retain his atelier.

385 Bruno Paul, »Biographische Notizen«.

386 Ibid. »Im täglichen Sprechverkehr hatte er sich politisch maskiert und so mein Vertrauen gewonnen.«

387 Bruno Paul, »Biographische Notizen«.

388 *Abschrift*, dated 30 October 1939. National Archives and Records Administration, Microfilm Document A339-RKK-F121.

389 Ibid.

390 Bruno Paul, »Biographische Notizen«. »Ich stand mit einem Fuß im KZ.«

391 Salomon Wininger, *Große jüdische National-Biographie*, vol. 7 (1935).

392 See Hildegard Brenner, ed., *Ende einer bürgerlichen Kunst-Institution: Die politische Formierung der Preußischen Akademie der Künste ab 1933. Schriftenreihe der Vierteljahreshefte für Zeitgeschichte* 24 (Stuttgart, 1972).

393 Bruno Paul, »Biographische Notizen«. »Dazu mußte durchgesickert sein, daß Th. Th. Heine vom Simplicissimus auf der Flucht vor der SS mit meiner Hilfe nach Prag lanciert werden könnte.«

394 Ibid. »Aber – mit 60 Jahren – mit Famile nach Übersee? Auch beherrschte mich wie ein Alb die trügerische Illusion eines baldigen Endes dieser Himmler-Goebbels-Hitler-Machthaberschaft. Also abwarten!«

395 The present appearance of Paul's Gerling headquarters is the result of later modifications. In 1937 the Gerling Konzern built a pendant to Paul's building on the opposite flank of the Palais von Langen. The architect of record for the second addition was Georg Satink, a former student of Paul's who assumed responsibility for his projects in Cologne following the death of Franz Weber in 1935. The Palais von Langen, from which Paul's design was derived, was severely damaged during the Second World War. It was demolished in 1949, and replaced with a new building by Kurt Groote, formerly a government architect in Düsseldorf. Groote's façade derived explicitly from the tradition of Sagebiel, with simplified classical detailing and sculptural ornament. In addition to eliminating the dimensional and proportional basis of Paul's design, Groote replaced his dramatic corner entrances with static compositions based on classical elements. In 1950 the architects Helmut Hentrich and Hans Heuser, collaborators in the planning of Albert Speer's Nord–Süd-Achse in Berlin, designed an office tower for the Gerling Konzern. They also developed a plan to unify the various elements of the headquarters complex, including a sculptural program devised in conjunction with Arno Breker, the sculptor whose admission to the Prussian academy in 1937 had coincided with Paul's expulsion. Though not all of the sculpture that Hentrich and Heuser proposed for Paul's buildings was added, his simple and elegant architectural metalwork was replaced with more elaborate elements.

396 Personal interview with Julia Graf, March 2001.

397 Personal interview with Julia Graf, March 2001.

398 Personal interview with Julia Graf, March 2001.

399 Personal interview with Julia Graf, March 2001.

400 Personal interview with Susanne Droste in Göttingen, October 2000.

401 Personal interview with Susanne Droste, October 2000.

402 Bruno Paul, »Biographische Notizen«.

403 Sonja Günther, Design der Macht: Möbel für Repräsentanten des »Dritten Reiches« (Stuttgart, 1991), 20–28.

404 According to the journal The Seven Seas, published by the Norddeutscher Lloyd for its English-speaking passengers, Paul also designed interiors for the liners Columbus, Berlin, and Europa, ships dominated by Troost's »Dampferstil«. These interiors by Paul, presumably individual cabins, are not well documented and were apparently never published. The Seven Sees 3 (July 1929), 12.

405 See Alfred Ziffer, Bruno Paul: Deutsche Raumkunst und Architektur zwischen Jugendstil und Moderne (Munich, 1992).

406 Bruno Paul, »Biographische Notizen«.

407 Document dated 13 March 1943, National Archives and Records Administration, Microfilm Document A339-RKK-F121.

408 Bruno Paul, »Biographische Notizen«.

409 Bruno Paul, »Haus Traub bei Prag«, Innen-Dekoration 46 (April 1935), 113–128.

410 Bruno Paul, »Auf Schwanenwerder«, Innen-Dekoration 47 (January 1936), 3–11.

411 Fritz Hellwag, »Handgearbeitete Möbel. Im neuen Hause der Deutschen Werkstätten in Berlin«, Kunst 76 (August 1937), 254.

412 Bruno Paul, »Gefolgschaftsräume eines Handwerkbetriebs«, Moderne Bauformen 41 (1942).

413 Bruno Paul, »Biographische Notizen«, Teilnachlaß Paul, Germanisches Nationalmuseum, Nuremberg.

414 Wiesenburg im Wandel der Zeit: Eine Ortschronik (Wiesenburg, n. d.), 34. Heinrich Enzio Graf von Plauen (1889–1973) left Germany for Sweden in 1943, after fulfilling his military obligations as an officer of the reserves. His Swedish wife Henrietta and their two children had fled the country in 1939, upon the commencement of hostilities.

415 Personal interview with Julia Graf in Berlin, March 2001.

416 Bruno Paul, »Biographische Notizen«. »Dementsprechende Bewerbungen wurden vom Kulturamt sehr wohlwollend aufgenommen, zwar nicht abgelehnt, aber auch nicht realisiert. Ich hatte den Eindruck, daß außenstehende Kräfte meine Wiedereinschaltung verhinderten.«

417 Ibid. »Der Hinweis auf meine mutmaßliche Zugehörigkeit zur Nazipartei überraschte mich um so mehr, als in der ohne mich neugegründeten Kunsthochschule unter ehemaligen Durchschnittsparteimitgliedern auch ein bedeutender Nazifunktionär zu finden war. Alle natürlich erfolgreich ›entnazifiziert‹.«

418 Ibid. »Wir haben uns große Mühe gegeben, aus den Akten festzustellen, daß Sie Parteimitglied waren. Leider waren Sie aber nicht Nazi, deshalb können wir Sie auch nicht entnazifizieren.«

419 Personal interview with Susanne Droste in Göttingen, September 2000.

420 Personal interview with Julia Graf, March 2001.

421 Personal interview with Julia Graf, March 2001.

422 Alfred Ziffer, Bruno Paul: Deutsche Raumkunst und Architektur zwischen Jugendstil und Moderne (Munich, 1992), 270. Gollnow did produce housewares, including a series of radios designed by Paul in 1949. His simple, cylindrical radio, available with either a woven cane casing or one with dramatic black and white vertical stripes, is among his last known furnishings.

423 Walter Frost and Bruno Paul, »Die Verwertung der Brandruinen«, Neue Bauwelt 4 (24 January 1949), 60–61. The article references the Arbeitsgemeinschaft Professor Bruno Paul in Berlin-Gatow, another unsuccessful venture.

424 The drydock was originally designed Schwimmdock 5.

425 Bruno Paul, »Biographische Notizen«.

426 This detail may have been required by the city of Cologne, as was the tile roof of Gereonsdriesch 9–11.

427 Personal interview with Julia Graf, March 2001.

428 Personal interview with Julia Graf, March 2001.

429 Herbert Sandberg, »Der freche Zeichenstift; Bruno Paul«, Das Magazin 4 (November 1957), 46–48.

430 Personal interview with Susanne Droste, September 2000.

431 This was the same motif that Paul employed in his Typenmöbel of 1908. The Dahlem museum appears to have been the first time that he employed this design in an architectural project.

432 Bruno Paul, »Biographische Notizen«. »Bisher durch Querschüsse collegialer Concurrenz verhindert.«

433 Personal interview with Georg Heinrichs in Berlin, September 2000. Heinrichs purchased and restored Paul's Villa Auerbach.

434 Personal interview with Julia Graf, March 2001.

435 Teilnachlaß Paul, Germanisches Nationalmuseum, Nuremberg. »Lieber Olaf, diesen Herbst wollte ich Dich nach langen Jahren am Schererhof aufsuchen, nun bist Du mir doch vorausgeeilt. Wegen diesem einen Jahr hättest Du noch warten können. Denn mit dem Wiedersehen wird es nun doch etwas unsicher, wegen der großen jenseitigen Entfernung. Für immer Dein Bruno Paul.«

436 The list of fifty projects was either never finished, or was dispersed following Paul's death. Only one page has been preserved, at the Germanisches Nationalmuseum in Nuremberg.

437 Personal interview with Susanne Droste, September 2000.

438 Albert Buesche. »Bruno Paul – dem 90jährigen«, Die Kunst und das schöne Heim 63 (November 1964), 62–63. »Ein Patriarch ist Paul eigentlich nicht geworden, sondern ein kritischer, sarkastischer, toleranter, zu allen Humoren aufgelegter Weiser, der die Unbequemlichkeiten und Bequemlichkeiten des Alters mit Charme und Selbstironie zu tragen weiß.«

439 Personal interview with Susanne Droste, September 2000.

440 Süddeutsche Zeitung, 19 August 1968. »Er war ein Erneuerer aus dem Geist.«

441 »Bruno Paul: 1874–1968«, The Architectural Review 145 (April 1969), 306.

442 At the end of his life, Paul was interviewed by Sonja Günther in conjunction with her dissertation on the early history of the Vereinigte Werkstätten. In the year of his death Stanford Anderson completed his dissertation on Peter Behrens at Columbia.

443 Ludwig Mies van der Rohe, »Technology in Architecture« quoted in Philip Johnson, Mies van der Rohe (New York, 1954), 203.

444 Despite early hopes that Modernism would facilitate the construction of the »Cathedral of Socialism«, the modern movement gained worldwide prominence under the patronage of the commercial middle classes. Although this was an advance over the religious or aristocratic patronage of earlier artistic movements, it hardly constituted a triumph of proletarian aspirations.

445 In 2001 the Gerling headquarters in Cologne, the Sinn department store in Gelsenkirchen, and the Rose Livingston home in Frankfurt continued to serve their original functions. Many of Paul's domestic projects, including Villa Auerbach in Berlin, Haus Friedwart in Wetzlar, and Haus Sternberg in Soest, were still private homes. Other buildings had changed ownership or use, but survived essentially intact. Haus Westend and Haus am Rupenhorn in Berlin, Haus Herxheimer in Frankfurt, and Haus Hainerberg in Königstein fell into this category.

446 Paul himself designed metal furniture, on those infrequent occasions when he believed the use of this material to be justified. A 1937 teacart for the Deutsche Werkstätten was a typical example. Fabricated from glass and steel tubing, it was both light and strong. Paul's hand was particularly evident in the detailing. He utilized tubing of rectangular section for the frame, and smaller tubing of circular section for the cross members that carried the glass shelves. The cross members passed through circular holes drilled in the flat sides of the frame tubes, a simple, elegant solution that created a stiff joint without the need for complex and costly handwork. Paul's teacart, unlike much metallic furniture of the 1920s and 30s, reflected practical understanding of both the potential and the limitations of plated steel tubing as a material for use in mass production.

447 Hannes Meyer. »bauen«, Bauhaus, Zeitschrift für Gestaltung 2 (Dessau, 1928), 153. Meyer, who assumed the direction of the Bauhaus in 1928, wrote »bauen ist kein aesthetischer prozeß. elementar gestaltet wird das neue wohnhaus nicht nur eine wohnmaschinerie, sondern ein biologischer apparat für seelische und körperliche bedürfnisse.« (Building is not an aesthetic process. In its elemental form the new dwelling house will be not only a machine for living, but a biological apparatus serving mental and physical needs.) The pseudo-scientific determinism that Meyer espoused became the credo of the radical Modernists.

448 Bruno Paul, »Biographische Notizen«, Teilnachlaß Paul, Germanisches Nationalmuseum, Nuremberg. »In der beiliegenden Liste sind 50 meiner größten Bauten verzeichnet.«

449 Paul Johannes Rée, »Der Wartesaal im Nürnberger Bahnhof«, Dekorative Kunst (October 1906), 2. »Dieser Raum gehört meines Erachtens zum besten, was die Raumkunst der neueren Zeit geschaffen hat.«

450 Max Creutz, 69. »Er hat hier eine moderne Umgebung fuer den modernen Menschen unserer Zeit geschaffen.«

[451] Hoffmann's Palais Stoclet, which shares this vocabulary, was not completed until 1911, the year following the Brussels exhibitition.

[452] Robert Breuer, »Büro und Geschäftshaus ›Zollernhof‹«, *Deutsche Kunst und Dekoration* 32 (April 1913), 29.

[453] Joseph Popp, »Bruno Paul auf der Deutschen Gewerbeschau«, *Dekorative Kunst* 26 (April, 1923), 137–138.

[454] Bruno Paul, »Ein Kölner Wohnhaus (Haus Neven-Dumont)«, *Die Pyramide* (April 1928), 1–4.

[455] Unfortunately these projects are among the only ones recorded in the fragments of his original list.

[456] Lincoln Eyre, »Renascent Germany«, *The National Geographic Magazine* 54 (December 1928), 702. Eyre praised the German merchant marine for its new ships »built along the most modern lines and equipped with the most efficient machinery«.

[457] *Boissevain* was built by the Blohm & Voss shipyards of Hamburg. The construction was facilitated by the Nazi government, in that the work was paid for with shipments of tobacco, to be distributed on the German market.

Index

Illustration credits

Agricola 18.17

Arts & Decoration 84.136

Assessor Karlchen 20.21

*Aus unserer schönen Heimat: Dörfer und Schlös-
ser, Berge und Wälder aus Zittaus Umgebung*
68.113, 68.114

Bildarchiv Foto Marburg 26.35

Bruno Paul 32.45, 32.46, 32.47, 33.48, 33.49,
34.51, 35.52, 35.53, 36.55, 37.58, 39.61, 40.65,
42.67, 43.69, 44.73, 45.75, 103.7, 103.8, 105.12

Bürohäuser der privaten Wirtschaft 88.140

*Das Haus der Freundschaft in Konstantinopel: ein
Wettbewerb deutscher Architekten* 58.98,
105.13

*Das neue Kunsthandwerk in Deutschland und
Oesterreich: unter Berücksichtigung der Deutschen Gewerbeschau Muenchen* 1922 57.96

Dekorative Kunst 24.32, 26.36, 27.38, 28.40,
36.56, 39.62, 52.85, 63.104, 63.105, 63.106,
65.109, 101.2

Der Burenkrieg 20.22

*Der Verkehr: Jahrbuch des Deutschen Werkbun-
des 1914* 43.71, 103.6

*Deutsche Form im Kriegsjahr: Jahrbuch des Deut-
schen Werkbundes 1915* 50.79, 50.80, 50.81,
51.82, 51.83, 53.87, 53.88, 105.11

Deutsche Kunst und Dekoration 48.76, 57.95,
61.101, 61.102

Deutsche Werkstätten catalogs 59.99, 90.142,
90.143, 90.144, 91.146, 109.25, 109.26, 110.27

Deutsches Historisches Museum, Berlin 18.16

Deutsches Kunstgewerbe St. Louis 1904 101.1

DeWe Plattenhaus 65.111, 73.118, 73.119, 73.120,
107.17

Die Baukunst der neuesten Zeit 42.68

Die schöne Wohnung 49.77, 49.78

Farbige Raumkunst 41.66

Furst, Mimi 108.21

Gartenschönheit 62.103

Good Furniture and Decoration 84.137, 109.23

Graf, Julia 11.3, 12.5, 99.153

Harrod, W. Owen 23.28, 37.57, 57.97, 71.117,
75.123, 75.124, 81.133, 82.134, 87.139, 91.145,
94.148, 95.149, 95.150, 97.151, 102.4, 104.9,
104.10, 105.14, 106.15, 106.16, 107.18, 107.19,
108.22, 110.28

Heinrich Wiegand: Ein Lebensbild 43.70

House and Garden's Book of Color Schemes
80.132

Innen-Dekoration 52.86, 65.110, 77.127, 78.128,
78.129, 79.130, 79.131

Jugend 16.10, 16.11, 16.12, 17.13, 17.14

*Kriegergräber, Beiträge zu der Frage: Wie sollen
wir unsere Kriegergräber würdig erhalten* 56.93

Kunstbibliothek, Berlin 13.6, 14.8, 28.41, 30.43,
60.100, 94.147

Kunst und Handwerk 24.31, 29.42, 31.44, 44.72,
102.3

Ladenbau 74.121, 74.122, 77.126

Landhaus und Garten 52.84.

Menz, Martin 66.112

Münchener Stadtmuseum 15.9, 22.26, 23.27

Neue Grobheiten 25.33, 25.34

Ozean-Express Bremen 90.141, 109.24

Postcard images 10.1, 10.2, 12.4, 14.7, 28.39,
34.50, 36.54, 69.115, 70.116, 76.125

Pyramide 64.107, 64.108

Rheinisches Bildarchiv, Köln 40.63, 40.64

Simplicissimus 18.15, 19.18, 19.19, 19.20, 21.24,
23.29, 23.30, 27.37

Staatsarchiv München 22.25

*Typenmoebel fuer Stadt und Land von Prof. Bruno
Paul* 38.59, 38.60, 102.5

Über Land und Meer 21.23

Universität der Künste, Berlin 57.94

Velhagen und Klasings Monatshefte 45.74

Vereinigte Zoo Werkstätten catalog 108.20

Vogue 84.135

Wieland 54.89, 54.90, 55.91, 56.92

Wir fingen einfach an 98.152

Wohnräume der Gegenwart 85.138